Polish

D0980839

phrasebooks

and

Piotr Czajkowski

Polish phrasebook
2nd edition – March 2007

Published by
Lonely Planet Publications Pty Ltd ABN 36 005 607 983
90 Maribyrnong St, Footscray, Victoria 3011, Australia

Lonely Planet Offices
Australia Locked Bag 1, Footscray, Victoria 3011
USA 150 Linden St, Oakland CA 94607
UK 72-82 Rosebery Ave, London, EC1R 4RW

Cover illustration
Skrzypek in love by Yukiyoshi Kamimura

ISBN 978 1 74104 141 5

text © Lonely Planet Publications Pty Ltd 2007
cover illustration © Lonely Planet Publications Pty Ltd 2007

10 9 8 7 6 5 4 3

Printed by C&C Offset Printing Co Ltd, China

Editor Francesca Coles would like to acknowledge the following people for their contributions to this phrasebook:

Piotr Czajkowski for conscientiously and skilfully applying himself to the task of translating and transliterating and providing cultural material.

Piotr works in Lonely Planet's Melbourne office as a senior GIS analyst. He hails from Gliwice and Kraków and went to university in Wrocław before migrating to Australian shores where he furthered his education at the University of Melbourne and Swinburne University of Technology. He's well adapted to life in Australia but still pines for Polish *piwo* pee·vo (beer). Piotr would like the world at large to know that, contrary to popular opinion, Polish is not difficult to pronounce. It has, in fact, one more vowel than English.

Piotr would like to thank his wife Gosia for her help and support during the project. He'd also like to thank his daughter Aleksandra for her help with the hip expressions only a teenager could know and little Karolinka (for being so patient).

The editor would also like to thank James Howard, English teacher and long-time resident of Kraków, for contributing his insights into Polish language and culture.

Many thanks to Yukiyoshi Kamimura and Wendy Wright for the inside illustrations.

Lonely Planet Language Products

Publishing Manager: Chris Rennie
Commissioning Editor: Karin Vidstrup Monk
Editor: Francesca Coles
Assisting Editors: Vanessa Battersby, Branislava Vladisavljevic & Adrienne Costanzo
Managing Editor: Annelies Mertens
Project Manager: Adam McCrow

Layout Designers: Steven Cann & David Kemp
Senior Layout Designer: Sally Darmody
Layout Manager: Kate McDonald
Series Designer: Yukiyoshi Kamimura
Cartographer: Wayne Murphy
Production Manager: Jenny Bilos

make the most of this phrasebook ...

Anyone can speak another language! It's all about confidence. Don't worry if you can't remember your school language lessons or if you've never learnt a language before. Even if you learn the very basics (on the inside covers of this book), your travel experience will be the better for it. You have nothing to lose and everything to gain when the locals hear you making an effort.

finding things in this book

For easy navigation, this book is in sections. The Tools chapters are the ones you'll thumb through time and again. The Practical section covers basic travel situations like catching transport and finding a bed. The Social section gives you conversational phrases, pick-up lines, the ability to express opinions – so you can get to know people. Food has a section all of its own: gourmets and vegetarians are covered and local dishes feature. Safe Travel equips you with health and police phrases, just in case. Remember the colours of each section and you'll find everything easily; or use the comprehensive Index. Otherwise, check the two-way traveller's Dictionary for the word you need.

being understood

Throughout this book you'll see coloured phrases on each page. They're phonetic guides to help you pronounce the language. Start with them to get a feel for how the language sounds. The pronunciation chapter in Tools will explain more, but you can be confident that if you read the coloured phrase, you'll be understood. As you become familiar with the spoken language, move on to using the actual text in the language which will help you perfect your pronunciation.

communication tips

Body language, ways of doing things, sense of humour – all have a role to play in every culture. 'Local talk' boxes show you common ways of saying things, or everyday language to drop into conversation. 'Listen for ...' boxes supply the phrases you may hear. They start with the script (so a local can find the phrase they want and point it out to you) and then lead in to the phonetic guide and the English translation.

polish

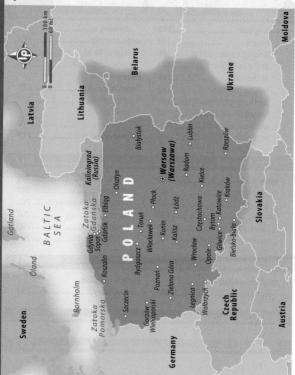

- official language
- generally understood
  (areas are approximate only)
- minority language

Poland
EUROPE

For more details, see the **introduction**.

Ask most English speakers what they know about Polish and they will most likely dismiss it as an unpronounceable language. Who could pronounce an apparently vowel-less word like *szczyt* (meaning 'peak'), for example? To be put off by this unfairly gained reputation, however, would be to miss out on a rich and rewarding language. The mother tongue of illustrious personalities such as Copernicus, Chopin, Joseph Conrad, Marie Curie and Pope John Paul II has a fascinating and turbulent past and symbolises the resilience of the Polish people in the face of domination and adversity.

The story of Polish begins with the arrival of the Polish tribes who occupied the basins of the Oder and Vistula rivers in the 6th century AD. These tribes spoke a range of West Slavic dialects, which over time evolved into Polish. The closest living relatives of Polish are Czech and Slovak, which also belong to the wider West Slavic family of languages.

Polish reached the apex of its influence during the era of the Polish Lithuanian Commonwealth, which was formed in 1569 and lasted until 1795. The Commonwealth covered a swath of territory from what are now Poland and Lithuania, through to Belarus, Ukraine and Latvia and part of Western Russia. Polish became a lingua franca throughout much of Central and Eastern Europe at this time due to the Commonwealth's political, cultural, scientific and military might.

When Poland was wiped off the map of Europe from 1795 to 1918 after three

at a glance ...

language name:
Polish

name in language:
język polski jen·zik pol·skee

language family: Slavic

key country: Poland

approximate number of speakers: 45 million

close relatives:
Czech, Slovak

donations to English:
horde, mazurka, vodka

introduction

9

successive partitions in the second half of the 18th century (when it was carved up between Russia, Austria and Prussia), the language suffered attempts at both Germanisation and Russification. Later, after WWII, Poland became a satellite state of the Soviet Union and it came under the renewed influence of Russian. Polish showed impressive resistance in the face of this oppression. The language not only survived but enriched itself by borrowing many words from both Russian and German. The works of Poland's greatest literary figures who wrote in exile – the Romantic poet Adam Mickiewicz, and, during Communist rule, the Nobel Prize winner Czesław Miłosz – are testament to this fact.

Today Poland is linguistically one of the most homogeneous countries in Europe – over 95% of the population speaks Polish as their first language. There are significant Polish-speaking minorities in the western border areas of Ukraine, Belarus and in southern Lithuania, with smaller populations in other neighbouring countries.

Getting acquainted with Polish is easy. It's not difficult to pronounce and the coloured pronunciation guides in this book are designed to help you say any Polish word with ease. This book gives you all the practical phrases you need to get by, as well as all the fun, spontaneous phrases that will lead to a better understanding of Poland and its people. Local knowledge, new relationships and a sense of satisfaction are on the tip of your tongue. So don't just stand there – say something!

abbreviations used in this book

a	adjective	loc	locative
acc	accusative	m	masculine
adv	adverb	m pers pl	masculine personal plural
dat	dative		
f	feminine	n	neuter
gen	genitive	nom	nominative
general pl	general plural	perf	perfective
imp	imperfective	pl	plural
inf	informal	pol	polite
inst	instrumental	sg	singular
lit	literal	v	verb
	translation	voc	vocative

introduction

wymowa

Although written Polish may seem a bit intimidating, with its apparent excess of consonants, pronouncing Polish isn't hard at all. Many of the sounds also exist in English and each Polish letter is generally pronounced the same way wherever it occurs. If you listen carefully to native speakers and follow the coloured pronunciation guides in this phrasebook, you'll easily get your message across.

vowel sounds

Polish vowels and diphthongs (vowel combinations) are quite similar to those found in English. Vowels are generally pronounced short, giving them a 'clipped' quality.

symbol	english equivalent	polish example	transliteration
a	cut	*tak*	tak
ai	aisle	*tutaj*	too·tai
e	get	*bez*	bes
ee	feet	*wino*	vee·no
ey	they	*kolejka*	ko·ley·ka
i	bit	*czy*	chi
o	not	*woda*	vo·da
oo	put	*zakupy, mój*	za·koo·pi, mooy
ow	cow	*migdał*	meeg·dow
oy	toy	*ojciec*	oy·chets

pronunciation

11

nasal vowel sounds

One distinctive feature of Polish (which it shares with French) is nasal vowels. Nasal vowel sounds are pronounced as though you're trying to force the air out of your nose rather than your mouth. It's easier than it sounds! English also has something similar to nasal vowels – when you say 'sing' in English the 'i' is nasalised by the 'ng'. Nasal vowels are indicated in written Polish by the little hooks under the *ą* and *ę*. Depending upon the letters that follow these vowels, they're pronounced with either an m or an n sound following the vowel.

symbol	english equivalent	polish example	transliteration
em	like the 'e' in 'get' plus nasal conso-	*wstęp*	fstemp
en	nant sound	*mięso*	myen·so
om	like the 'o' in 'not' plus nasal conso-	*kąpiel*	kom·pyel
on	nant sound	*wąsy*	von·si

consonant sounds

Most Polish consonant sounds are also found in English, with the exception of the kh sound (which is pronounced as in the Scottish word 'loch') and the rolled r sound. Consonants are sometimes grouped together without vowels between them where in English you'd expect one, as in the word *pszczoła* pshcho·wa (bee). With a bit of practice these 'consonant clusters' will roll off your tongue with ease. The apostrophe is used in transliterations (as in the word *kwiecień* kfye·chen') to show that the consonant before it is produced with a soft y sound.

In our pronunciation guides you'll notice some syllables made up of the single consonants f, v, s and z. These represent the prepositions w and z ('in/on' and 'with'). When pronouncing them, just run them into the word that follows them.

symbol	english equivalent	polish example	transliteration
b	bend	*babka*	*bap*·ka
ch	child	*cień, czas, ćma*	chen', chas, chma
d	drum	*drobne*	*drob*·ne
f	friend	*fala*	*fa*·la
g	grass	*garnek*	*gar*·nek
j	jar	*dzieci*	*je*·chee
k	kiss	*kac*	kats
kh	loch	*chata, hałas*	*kha*·ta, *kha*·was
l	lever	*lato*	*la*·to
m	milk	*malarz*	*ma*·lash
n	noon	*nagle*	*na*·gle
p	prone	*palec*	*pa*·lets
r	rolled, as in Spanish *arriba*	*róg*	roog
s	scatter	*samolot*	*sa*·mo·lot
sh	shallow	*siedem, śnieg, szlak*	*shye*·dem, shnyek, shlak
t	tank	*targ*	tark
v	violet	*widok*	*vee*·dok
w	welcome	*złoto*	*zwo*·to
y	yield	*zajęty*	za·*yen*·ti
z	zoom	*zachód*	*za*·khoot
zh	leisure	*zima, żart, rzeźba*	*zhee*·ma, zhart, *zhezh*·ba
'	like a soft y	*kwiecień*	*kfye*·chen'

word stress

Stress almost always falls on the second-last syllable. In our pronunciation guides, the stressed syllable is italicised.

reading & writing

The relationship between pronunciation and spelling in Polish is consistent. This means that a letter or a cluster of letters is always pronounced the same way. The Polish alphabet is presented in the table below. It has 32 letters – all the letters of the English alphabet except 'q', 'v' and 'x' (which only appear in some foreign words and names), plus nine letters with diacritical marks (marks above or below the letters). For spelling purposes (eg when you need to spell your name to book into a hotel) the pronunciation of each letter is provided.

polish alphabet					
A a a	Ą ą on	B b be	C c tse	Ć ć chye	D d de
E e e	Ę ę en	F f ef	G g gye	H h kha	I i ee
J j yot	K k ka	L l el	Ł ł ew	M m em	N n en
Ń ń en'	O o o	Ó ó oo	P p pe	R r er	S s es
Ś ś esh	T t te	U u oo	W w voo	Y y* i	Z z zet
Ż ż zhyet	Ż ż zhet	*note that the letter y is not a consonant but a vowel pronounced i			

In addition to the individual letters of the alphabet above, Polish spelling combines pairs of letters to form a single sound. These are ch (pronounced kh), cz (ch), dz (dz or j), dź and dż (both roughly pronounced j), rz (zh or sh) and sz (sh). Also, when the letter i follows s, z and c these letters are 'softened' to sh, zh and ch respectively.

contents

The list below shows which grammatical structures you can use to say what you want. Look under each function – listed in alphabetical order – for information on how to build your own sentences. For example, to tell the taxi driver where your hotel is, look for **giving instructions** and you'll be directed to information on **case** and **demonstratives**. A **glossary** of grammatical terms is included at the end of this chapter to help you. Abbreviations like nom and acc in the literal translations for each example refer to the case of the noun or pronoun – this is explained in the **glossary** and in **case**.

adjectives & adverbs

Adjectives usually come before the noun, and change their gender, number and case endings to agree with the nouns they describe. In the **dictionaries** and word lists in this phrasebook, adjectives are given in the masculine form and nominative case (see **case** and **gender**).

The most common endings in the nominative case for singular nouns are -y -i for the masculine, -a -a for the feminine and -e -e for the neuter gender.

This is a beautiful forest!
To jest piękny las!   to yest *pyenk*·ni las
(lit: this is beautiful-m-nom forest-m-nom)

This is a beautiful river!
To jest piękna rzeka!   to yest *pyenk*·na *zhe*·ka
(lit: this is beautiful-f-nom river-f-nom)

In the plural, Polish distinguishes only between masculine personal adjectives (those describing men only or mixed groups of men and women) which end in -i -ee or -y -i, and a general class of adjectives (encompassing women, children, animals, objects and abstract nouns). The general class takes an -e -e or -ie -ye ending in the plural.

good lads   *dobrzy chłopci*   *dob*·zhi *khwop*·tsi
(lit: good-m pers pl lad-m pers pl)

good girls   *dobre dziewczyny*   *dob*·re jev·*chi*·ni
(lit: good-general pl girl-general pl)

Adverbs are generally formed by removing the final letter of an adjective and replacing it with -o -o or -ie -ye. Their position in the sentence is fairly flexible but they mostly come before the verb.

He played beautifully.
On pięknie grał.   on *pyenk*·nye grow
(lit: he beautifully played)

articles

Polish doesn't have an equivalent for 'a' and 'the' – *dom* dom can mean both 'a house' or 'the house' depending on context.

be

describing people/things • making statements

The verb *być* bich (be) takes the forms shown in the table below in the present tense.

być – present tense			
I	am	*jestem*	*yes*·tem
you sg	are	*jesteś*	*yes*·tesh
he/she/it	is	*jest*	yest
we	are	*jesteśmy*	*yes*·tesh·mi
you pl	are	*jesteście*	*yes*·tesh·chye
they	are	*są*	som

I'm here for a holiday.

    Jestem tutaj na wakacjach.   *yes*·tem *too*·tai na va·*kats*·yakh
    (lit: I-am here for holidays)

In the past tense, the forms of *być* change to match both the gender and the number of the subject as shown below.

być – past tense			
I m/f	was	*byłem/am*	*bi*·wem/wam
you m/f sg	were	*byłeś/aś*	*bi*·wesh/wash
he/she/it	were	*był/była/było*	biw/*bi*·wa/*bi*·wo
we m/f	were	*byliśmy/ byłyśmy*	*bi*·*leesh*·mi/ *bi*·*wish*·mi
you m/f pl	were	*byliście/ byłyście*	*bi*·*leesh*·chye/ *bi*·*wish*·chye
they m/f	were	*byli/były*	*bi*·lee/*bi*·wi

I was homesick.
    Byłem/am stęskniony/a   bi·wem/wam stensk·*nyo*·ni/na
    za domem. m/f   za *do*·mem
    (lit: I-was-m/f longing-m/f for home)

Below are the future tense forms of *być*:

być – future tense			
I	will be	będę	*ben*·de
you sg	will be	będziesz	*ben*·jyesh
he/she/it	will be	będzie	*ben*·jye
we	will be	będziemy	*ben*·jye·mi
you pl	will be	będziecie	*ben*·jye·chye
they	will be	będą	*ben*·dom

How long will you be here for?
    Jak długo tutaj będziesz? inf   yak *dwoo*·go *too*·tai *ben*·jyesh
    (lit: how long here you-will-be)

The future tense forms of *być* are also used before imperfective infinitive verbs to form the continuous future tense (see the **future** heading in the **verbs** section for more on this).

See also **negatives**.

case

doing things · giving instructions ·
indicating location · making statements ·
naming people/things · possessing

Polish has a system of seven case endings, shown in the table on the next page, which are used to indicate the grammatical role of nouns, adjectives, pronouns and demonstratives in a sentence and their relationship to other words. The word lists and **dictionaries** in this book provide nouns in the nominative case. If you use the nominative case in any context, even when it's not grammatically correct, you'll still be understood.

nominative nom – shows the subject of a sentence

The guide will pay.
Przewodnik zapłaci.   pshe·*vod*·neek za·*pwa*·chee
(lit: guide-nom will-pay)

accusative acc – shows the direct object in affirmative sentences

I'd like to reserve a table.
Chciałam   khchow·am
zarezerwować stolik.   za·re·zer·*vo*·vach *sto*·leek
(lit: like-I reserve table-acc)

genitive gen – primarily shows possession ('of') but also indicates the direct object in negative sentences

That's my friend's seat.
To jest miejsce   to yest *myeys*·tse
mojego kolegi.   mo·*ye*·go ko·*le*·gee
(lit: this is place my-gen friend-gen)

dative dat – shows the indirect object of a sentence

I gave my son a present.
Dałem prezent   *da*·wem *pre*·zent
mojemu synowi.   mo·*ye*·moo si·*no*·vi
(lit: gave-I present to-my-dat son-dat)

instrumental inst – shows how something is done

Can we go there by car?
Czy możemy tam   chi mo·*zhe*·mi tam
dojechać samochodem?   do·*ye*·khach sa·mo·*kho*·dem
(lit: question-particle can-we there go car-inst)

locative loc – used with prepositions to show location

What should I visit in the old town?
Co powinienem zobaczyć   tso po·vee·*nye*·nem zo·*ba*·chich
na Starym Mieście?   na *sta*·rim *myesh*·chye
(lit: what should-I visit in old-loc town-loc)

vocative voc – used to address someone directly

My friend, I love it here!
Podoba mi się tu,   po·*do*·ba mee shye too
mój przyjacielu.   mooy pshi·ya·*chye*·loo
(lit: like me-dat myself here my-voc friend-voc)

demonstratives

giving instructions • indicating location • naming people/things • pointing things out

The Polish words for 'this' and 'that' agree in case, gender and number with the noun they refer to and come before the noun they refer to, eg *ta droga* ta *dro*·ga (lit: this-f-nom road-f-nom). The different forms (in the nominative case) are shown in the table below.

	singular			plural	
	m	**f**	**n**	**m personal ***	**general ***
this	*ten* ten	*ta* ta	*to* to	*ci* chee	*te* te
that	*tamten* tam·ten	*tamta* tam·ta	*tamto* tam·to	*tamci* tam·chee	*tamte* tam·te

* see **gender** below for more on these categories

gender

describing people/things • naming people/things

All Polish nouns have gender – masculine m, feminine f or neuter n. The distinction is purely grammatical and not related to a noun's meaning. You need to learn the grammatical gender for each noun as you go, but you can often recognise it by the noun's ending.

• Masculine nouns generally end in a consonant:

| *stół* m | stoow | **table** |

• Feminine nouns generally end in -*a*:

| *gazeta* f | ga·ze·ta | **newspaper** |

• Neuter nouns generally end in -*e* or -*o*:

| *słońce* n | swon'·tse | **sun** |
| *lato* n | la·to | **summer** |

In the plural, nouns, adjectives, demonstratives and possessive pronouns have only two types of ending – masculine personal (for men only and mixed groups of both men and women), and general (for women, children, animals, objects and abstract nouns). These categories are marked as m pers and general pl.

The nouns in this book's word lists, **dictionaries** and **culinary reader** have their gender marked unless they belong to the general plural category. Alternative gender endings on adjectives and verbs are separated with a slash and marked m/f/n, eg *czerwony/a/e* cher·vo·ni/na/ne (red).

have

possessing

An easy way of expressing possession in Polish is by using the verb *mieć* myech (have).

I have a tourist visa.
   Mam wizę turystyczną.   mam *vee*·ze too·ris·*tich*·nom
   (lit: have-I visa-**f-acc** tourist-**f-acc**)

The present tense forms of *mieć* are shown below. To form past and future tense forms, see **verbs**.

mieć – present tense			
I	have	*mam*	mam
you sg	have	*masz*	mash
he/she/it	has	*ma*	ma
we	have	*mamy*	*ma*·mi
you pl	have	*macie*	*ma*·chye
they	have	*mają*	*ma*·yom

See also **negatives** and **possessive pronouns**.

TOOLS

22

negatives

In Polish, negative statements are made simply by adding the word *nie* nye (not) before the verb:

I (don't) understand.
(Nie) Rozumiem.   (nye) ro·*zoo*·myem
(lit: (not) understand-I)

See also **be**, **have** and **verbs**.

personal pronouns

**doing things • making statements •
naming people/things**

Personal pronouns ('I', 'you', etc) are mostly omitted in Polish, as the subject of the sentence is indicated by the verb's ending (see **verbs**). However, they can be used for emphasis:

I will carry the bags.
Ja poniosę bagaże.   ya po·*nyo*·se ba·*ga*·zhe
(lit: I carry-will-I bags)

The pronoun 'they' has two forms. One form, *oni* o·nee, is used for men and mixed groups of both men and women and is known as the masculine personal form. The other form, *one* o·ne, is known as the general form and is used for women, children, animals, objects and abstract nouns. The nominative case forms of personal pronouns are given in the table below.

subject pronouns (nominative case)					
I	*ja*	ya	we	*my*	mi
you sg	*ty*	ti	you pl	*wy*	vi
he	*on*	on	they m personal	*oni*	o·nee
she	*ona*	o·na	they general	*one*	o·ne
it m/f/n	*on/ona/ ono*	on/o·na/ o·no			

The singular and plural forms of 'you' (*ty* ti and *wy* vi) are only used in informal situations, such as with friends, family and younger people. In more formal situations, the titles shown below are used, along with the third-person form of the verb in the singular or plural (see also **verbs**). These words mean literally 'Mr' and 'Mrs' etc but translate as 'you' in most contexts.

you – polite forms				
	masculine		feminine	
singular	*pan*	pan	*pani*	pa·nee
plural	*panowie*	pa·no·vye	*panie*	pa·nye
	państwo		pan'·stfo	

We've used the abbreviations pol and inf to indicate where you have a choice between polite and informal language. In all other cases we've chosen the appropriate form for the context.

plurals

describing people/things • naming people/things

Plurals of Polish nouns can take different forms, depending on the noun's gender and its final letter. You don't need to worry much about this, as the nouns in all phrases in this book are in the correct form, and even if you use the singular form given in the dictionaries, you'll be understood.

possessive pronouns

naming people/things • possessing

In Polish, possessive pronouns change to match the case, number and gender of the noun they describe.

That child is mine.
 To jest moje dziecko.   to yest mo·ye jyets·ko
 (lit: that-n-nom-sg child-n-nom-sg is mine-n-nom-sg)

The forms in the nominative case are on the opposite page.

	singular			plural	
	m	f	n	m personal	general
my	*mój* mooy	*moja* mo·ya	*moje* mo·ye	*moi* mo·ee	*moje* mo·ye
your sg	*twój* tfooy	*twoja* tfo·ya	*twoje* tfo·ye	*twoi* tfo·ee	*twoje* tfo·ye
his/its	*jego* ye·go				
her	*jej* yey				
our	*nasz* nash	*nasza* na·sha	*nasze* na·she	*nasi* na·shee	*nasze* na·she
your pl	*wasz* vash	*wasza* va·sha	*wasze* va·she	*wasi* va·shee	*wasze* va·she
their	*ich* eekh				

prepositions

indicating location · pointing things out

Prepositions are used to show relationships between words and come before the nouns they modify. Here are some useful ones, with the cases (see **case**) that are commonly used with them:

english	polish	transliteration	case
about	*o*	o	locative
at (place)	*na*	na	locative
at (time)	*o*	o	locative
for	*dla*	dla	genitive
from (place)	*z*	z	genitive
from (time)	*od*	od	genitive
in	*w/we*	v/ve	locative
of	*o*	o	locative
on	*na*	na	locative
to (place)	*do*	do	genitive

questions

To form a yes/no question, start the sentence with the question particle *czy* chi.

Is this seat free?

Czy to miejsce jest wolne?   chi to *myeys*·tse yest *vol*·ne
(lit: question-particle this seat is free)

Questions may also begin with a question word such as 'what', 'when' or 'where' and these come at the beginning of the sentence.

What do you recommend?

Co polecasz?   tso po·*le*·tsash
(lit: what recommend-you-inf)

question words		
How?	*Jak?*	yak
How much?	*Ile?*	*ee*·le
What?	*Co?*	tso
When?	*Kiedy?*	*kye*·di
Where?	*Gdzie?*	gjye
Which? m/f/n	*Który/a/e?*	*ktoo*·ri/ra/re
Who?	*Kto?*	kto
Why?	*Dlaczego?*	dla·*che*·go

verbs

The infinitive (or the 'dictionary form') of Polish verbs usually ends in *-ać*, *-eć*, *-ieć* or *-ować*. There are three main tenses: past, present and future.

Most Polish verbs have two infinitive forms. For example, dictionaries often have two entries for 'to read', *czytać chi*·tach and *przeczytać* pshe·*chi*·tach. The first is the 'imperfective aspect', used for unfinished, habitual or continuing actions.

I often read in Polish.
   Często czytam po polsku.   chen·sto *chi*·tam po *pol*·skoo
   (lit: often read-I-imp-pres in Polish)

The second form is the 'perfective aspect', and is used to refer to actions that have already been completed, or that are intended to be completed in the future.

I finished reading the book.
   Przeczytałam książkę.   pshe·chi·*tow*·am *ksyonzh*·ke
   (lit: read-I-perf-past book)

present

You use only the imperfective aspect in the present tense. The following table shows the present-tense endings for the four main verb groups. You drop -*ać*, -*eć*, -*ieć* and -*ować* and add the endings indicated.

present tense verb endings				
	czytać chi·tach **to read**	*umieć* oo·myech **to know**	*widzieć* vee·jyech **to see**	*pracować* pra·tso·vach **to work**
I	-*am* am	-*em* em	-*ę* e	-*uję* oo·ye
you sg	-*asz* ash	-*esz* esh	-*isz* eesh	-*ujesz* oo·yesh
he/she/it	-*a* a	-*e* e	-*i* ee	-*uje* oo·ye
we	-*amy* a·mi	-*emy* e·mi	-*imy* ee·mi	-*ujemy* oo·ye·mi
you pl	-*acie* a·chye	-*ecie* e·chye	-*icie* ee·chye	-*ujecie* oo·ye·chye
they	-*ają* a·yom	-*eją* e·yom	-*ą* om	-*ują* oo·yom

past

Both imperfective and perfective verb forms are used in the past tense. To form the past tense of both aspects remove the infinitive -*ć* ending and replace it with the endings in the table below:

past tense verb forms	m		f		n	
I	*-łem*	wem	*-łam*	wam		
you sg	*-łeś*	wesh	*-łaś*	wash		
he/she/it	*-ł*	w	*-ła*	wa	*-ło*	wo
we	*-liśmy*	leesh·mi	*-łyśmy*	wish·mi		
you pl	*-liście*	leesh·chye	*-łyście*	wish·chye		
they	*-li*	lee	*-ły*	wi		

future

A continuous action in the future is expressed by the verb *być* bich (see **be**) in the future tense followed by the imperfective infinitive of the main verb.

I will read on the plane.
> *Będę czytać w samolocie.*   ben·de *chi*·tach v sa·mo·*lo*·chye
> (lit: be-I-**fut** read-**imp** in aeroplane-**loc**)

An action that will be completed in the future is indicated by a perfective verb with endings indentical to the present tense endings shown in the table on page 27.

I will read the guidebook before I go there.
> *Przeczytam przewodnik*   pshe·*chi*·tam pshe·*vod*·neek
> *zanim tam pojadę.*   *za*·neem tam po·*ya*·de
> (lit: read-I-**fut-perf** guidebook before there go-I-**fut-perf**)

glossary

accusative (case)	type of *case marking* (usually) used to show the *direct object* of the sentence – 'she poured **the vodka**'
adjective	a word that describes something – 'the **alcoholic** content'
adverb	word that explains how an action was done – 'he drank **quickly**'
affirmative sentence	a sentence that doesn't express negation – 'I **saw** the bottle', as opposed to 'I **didn't see** the bottle'
article	the words 'a', 'an' and 'the'
aspect	Polish verbs have two aspects – *perfective* and *imperfective*
case (marking)	word ending which tells us the role of a thing or person in the sentence
dative (case)	type of *case marking* which shows the *indirect object* – 'I gave the glasses **to the pourer**'
demonstrative	a word that means 'this' or 'that'
direct object	the thing or person in the sentence that has the action directed to it – 'I read **the label**'
gender	classification of *nouns* into classes (like masculine and feminine), requiring other words (eg *adjectives*) to belong to the same class
genitive (case)	type of *case marking* which shows ownership or possession – 'the **barman's** shout'
imperfective (aspect)	*verb aspect* showing a continuous, habitual or incomplete action – 'he **was drinking** vodka all day'
indirect object	the person or thing in the sentence that is the recipient of the action – 'I gave **him** ice'
infinitive	dictionary form of a *verb* – 'we started **to drink** to his health'

a–z phrasebuilder

instrumental (case)	type of *case marking* which shows how something is done – 'she drank it down **with one gulp**'
locative (case)	type of *case marking* which shows where the *subject* is – 'the vodka is **in the freezer**'
nominative (case)	type of *case marking* used for the *subject* of the sentence – '**the drinking session** ended'
noun	a thing, person or idea – 'the **bottle**'
number	whether a word is singular or plural – 'our **hangovers** were terrible'
perfective (aspect)	*verb aspect* showing a complete action – 'they **cleared away** the party debris'
personal pronoun	a word that means 'I', 'you', etc
possessive pronoun	a word that means 'mine', 'yours', etc
preposition	a word like 'in' or 'at' in English
question particle	a word that signals a question
subject	the thing or person in the sentence that does the action – '**the inebriated people** started dancing'
tense	form of a *verb* that tells you whether the action is in the present, past or future – eg 'eat' (present), 'ate' (past), 'will eat' (future)
verb	a word that tells you what action happened – 'I **refused** another drink'
vocative (case)	type of *case marking* used to address someone directly – 'leave me alone, **you drunkard**'

Do you speak (English)?
Czy pan/pani mówi   chi pan/*pa*·nee *moo*·vee
po (angielsku)? m/f pol   po (an·*gyel*·skoo)
Czy mówisz   chi *moo*·veesh
po (angielsku)? inf   po (an·*gyel*·skoo)

Does anyone speak (English)?
Czy ktoś mówi   chi ktosh *moo*·vee
po (angielsku)?   po (an·*gyel*·skoo)

Do you understand (me)?
Czy pan/pani (mnie)   chi pan/*pa*·nee (mnye)
rozumie? m/f pol   ro·*zoo*·mye
Czy (mnie) rozumiesz? inf   chi (mnye) ro·*zoo*·myesh

Yes, I understand.
Tak, rozumiem.   tak ro·*zoo*·myem

No, I don't understand.
Nie, nie rozumiem.   nye nye ro·*zoo*·myem

I (don't) understand.
(Nie) Rozumiem.   (nye) ro·*zoo*·myem

Pardon?
Proszę?   *pro*·she

I speak (English).
Mówię po (angielsku).   *moo*·vyem po (an·*gyel*·skoo)

I don't speak (Polish).
Nie mówię po (polsku).   nye *moo*·vyem po (*pol*·skoo)

I speak a little.
Mówię trochę.   *moo*·vyem *tro*·khe

Let's speak (Polish).
Rozmawiajmy po (polsku).   roz·mav·*yai*·mi po (*pol*·skoo)

What does (nieczynne) mean?
Co to znaczy (nieczynne)?   tso to *zna*·chi (nye·*chi*·ne)

How do you …?	Jak się …?	yak shye …
pronounce this	to wymawia	to vi·*mav*·ya
write (pierogi)	pisze (pierogi)	*pee*·she (pye·*ro*·gee)
Could you please …?	Proszę …	*pro*·she …
repeat that	to powtórzyć	to pov·*too*·zhich
speak more slowly	mówić trochę wolniej	*moo*·veech *tro*·khe *vol*·nyey
write it down	to napisać	to na·*pee*·sach

tongue torture

If, like many people, you've ever been daunted by the wall-to-wall consonants of Polish, take heart! It's not really a tricky language to pronounce. The mellifluous melodies of these Polish *łamaniec językowy* wa·*ma*·nyets yen·zi·*ko*·vi (tongue twisters) should effortlessly glide off your tongue:

W Szczebrzeszynie, chrząszcz brzmi w trzcinie.
f shcheb·zhe·*shi*·nye khshonsch bzhmi f *tshtsee*·nye
(In Szczebrzeszyn a beetle buzzes in the water reeds.)

Szedł Sasza suchą szosą i suszył szare szorty.
shedw sa·sha *soo*·khom *sho*·som ee *soo*·shiw *sha*·re *shor*·ti
(Sasha walked along the highway drying his grey shorts.)

Król Karol kupił Królowej Karolinie korale koloru koralowego.
krool *ka*·rol *koo*·peew kroo·*lo*·vey ka·ro·*lee*·nye ko·*ra*·le ko·*lo*·roo ko·ra·lo·*ve*·go
(King Charles bought Queen Caroline a coral necklace in the colour coral.)

cardinal numbers

The numbers 'one' and 'two' are the only ones that take different forms for masculine, feminine and neuter words. Numbers also change form to reflect their case (see **case** in the **a–z phrasebuilder** for an explanation of this term). When counting, use *raz* ras instead of *jeden* etc for 'one'.

0	zero	ze·ro
1	jeden/jedna/ jedno m/f/n	ye·den/yed·na/ yed·no
2	dwa/dwie/ dwoje m/f/n	dva/dvye/ dvo·ye
3	trzy	tshi
4	cztery	chte·ri
5	pięć	pyench
6	sześć	sheshch
7	siedem	shye·dem
8	osiem	o·shyem
9	dziewięć	jye·vyench
10	dziesięć	jye·shench
11	jedenaście	ye·de·nash·chye
12	dwanaście	dva·nash·chye
13	trzynaście	tshi·nash·chye
14	czternaście	chter·nash·chye
15	piętnaście	pyent·nash·chye
16	szesnaście	shes·nash·chye
17	siedemnaście	shye·dem·nash·chye
18	osiemnaście	o·shem·nash·chye
19	dziewiętnaście	jye·vyet·nash·chye
20	dwadzieścia	dva·jyesh·chya
21	dwadzieścia jeden	dva·jyesh·chya ye·den
30	trzydzieści	tshi·jyesh·chee

40	*czterdzieści*	chter·*jyesh*·chee
50	*pięćdziesiąt*	pyen·*jye*·shont
60	*sześćdziesiąt*	shesh·*jye*·shont
70	*siedemdziesiąt*	shye·dem·*jye*·shont
80	*osiemdziesiąt*	o·shem·*jye*·shont
90	*dziewięćdziesiąt*	jye·vyen·*jye*·shont
100	*sto*	sto
200	*dwieście*	dvyesh·chye
300	*trzysta*	tshi·sta
400	*czterysta*	chte·*ri*·sta
500	*pięćset*	pyench·set
600	*sześćset*	sheshch·set
700	*siedemset*	shye·*dem*·set
800	*osiemset*	o·*shyem*·set
900	*dziewięćset*	jye·*vyench*·set
1000	*tysiąc*	ti·shonts
1,000,000	*milion*	mee·lyon

in the numbers

In this phrasebook you might notice that when numbers are used in combination with nouns, the form of the noun changes. So you might see, for instance, that 'a piece' is *jeden kawałek* ye·den ka·*vow*·ek, 'three pieces' is *trzy kawałki* tshi ka·*vow*·kee and 'five pieces' is *pięć kawałków* pyench ka·*vow*·koof. This morphing of noun endings happens because numbers in Polish also determine the case of the nouns that follow them (for an explanation of the term 'case', see the **a–z phrasebuilder**, page 19).

The rules for which numbers take which case and the various endings for the different cases are a little complex. You needn't worry about them because if you say the number and use the nominative (dictionary) form of the noun, people will still understand what you mean, even if it's not grammatically correct. Keep in mind that Poles are warmly appreciative of any attempt to communicate with them in their native tongue. They're also well aware of the complexities of Polish and will make allowances for less-than-perfect speech by foreigners.

ordinal numbers

The correct format of ordinal numbers is to write the number followed by a dot, eg *2. piętro* droo-gye pyen-tro (2nd floor). Ordinal numbers agree in gender and case with the noun they refer to, in much the same way as adjectives do. (See the **a–z phrasebuilder**, pages 15–30, for an explanation of these grammatical terms.)

1st	*pierwszy/a/e* m/f/n	pyerf-shi/sha/she
2nd	*drugi/a/ie* m/f/n	droo-gee/ga/gye
3rd	*trzeci/a/ie* m/f/n	tshe-chee/cha/chye
4th	*czwarty/a/e* m/f/n	chfar-ti/ta/te
5th	*piąty/a/e* m/f/n	pyon-ti/ta/te
6th	*szósty/a/e* m/f/n	shoos-ti/ta/te
7th	*siódmy/a/e* m/f/n	shyood-mi/ma/me
8th	*ósmy/a/e* m/f/n	oos-mi/ma/me
9th	*dziewiąty/a/e* m/f/n	jyev-yon-ti/ta/te
10th	*dziesiąty/a/e* m/f/n	jye-shon-ti/ta/te
11th	*jedenasty/a/e* m/f/n	ye-de-nas-ti/ta/te
12th	*dwunasty/a/e* m/f/n	dvoo-nas-ti/ta/te

decimals & fractions

Polish decimals use a *przecinek* pshe-chee-nek (comma) rather than a dot, eg *2,5*. In large numbers the digits are grouped by thousands with spaces between rather than commas, eg one million is written as 1 000 000 (as opposed to 1,000,000).

3.14	*trzy przecinek czternaście*	tshi pshe-chee-nek chter-nash-chye
4.2	*cztery przecinek dwa*	chte-ri pshe-chee-nek dva
5.1	*pięć przecinek jeden*	pyench pshe-chee-nek ye-den

a quarter	jedna czwarta	yed·na chfar·ta
a third	jedna trzecia	yed·na tshe·chya
a half	pół	poow
three-quarters	trzy czwarte	tshi chfar·te
all	całość	tsa·woshch
none	nic	neets

useful amounts

Weights smaller than a kilogram are given in *dekagramy* de·ka·*gra*·mi (decagrams), commonly abbreviated to *deko* *de*·ko, unless you want to be very precise about a given weight. You'd use decagrams, for instance, if you were ordering ham at a delicatessen. One *deko* is equal to 10 grams and there are 100 *deko* (decagrams) in a kilogram.

How much/many?	lle?	ee·le
Please give me ...	Proszę ...	pro·she ...
(100) grams	(sto) gram	(sto) gram
(10) decagrams	(10) deko	(jye·shench) de·ko
half a kilo	pół kilo	poow kee·lo
a kilo	kilo	kee·lo
a bottle	butelkę	boo·tel·ke
a jar	słoik	swo·eek
a packet	paczkę	pach·ke
a slice	plasterek	plas·te·rek
a tin	puszkę	poosh·ke
a few	kilka	keel·ka
less	mniej	mnyey
(just) a little	(tylko) trochę	(til·ko) tro·khe
a lot/many	dużo	doo·zho
more	więcej	vyen·tsey
some	trochę	tro·khe

For more amounts, see **self-catering**, page 174.

TOOLS

36

telling the time

Official times are given according to the 24-hour clock, but in everyday life people use the 12-hour clock. Rather than using cardinal numbers when referring to time, the feminine forms of ordinal numbers are used so that 'four o'clock' is *czwarta godzina* *chfar*·ta go·*jee*·na (lit: fourth hour). The word *godzina* is often left out so that four o'clock can be just *czwarta chfar*·ta (lit: fourth). Refer to **ordinal numbers** in **numbers & amounts**, page 35, for ordinal numbers to help you form time expressions.

What time is it?	*Która jest godzina?*	ktoo·ra yest go·*jee*·na
It's one o'clock.	*Pierwsza.*	*pyerf*·sha

Times 'half past' the hour refer to the coming hour rather than the current one, so that 'half past ten' is literally 'half to eleven'. The equivalents of 'past' and 'to' are the words *po* po and *za* za.

Five past (ten).	*Pięć po (dziesiątej).*	pyench po (jye·*shon*·tey)
Quarter past (ten).	*Piętnaście po (dziesiątej).*	pyent·*nash*·chye po (jye·*shon*·tey)
Half past (ten).	*Wpół do (jedenastej).*	fpoow do (ye·de·*nas*·tey)
Twenty to (eleven).	*Za dwadzieścia (jedenasta).*	za dva·*jyesh*·chya (ye·de·*nas*·ta)
Quarter to (eleven).	*Za piętnaście (jedenasta).*	za pyent·*nash*·chye (ye·de·*nas*·ta)

In conversation, to prevent any misunderstandings about whether you mean 'am' or 'pm', add the part of the day, eg 'in the morning', 'in the afternoon' or 'at night' using the expressions below. You can also use the Polish for 'am' and 'pm' (which mean literally 'morning' and 'in the afternoon'), but bear in mind that hours from 11pm to 3am or 4am are usually described as 'at night', whereas hours from roughly 6pm till 9pm or 10pm are referred to as 'in the evening'.

am	rano	ra·no
pm	po południu	po po·wood·nyoo
in the morning	rano	ra·no
in the afternooon	po południu	po po·wood·nyoo
in the evening	wieczorem	vye·cho·rem
at night	w nocy	v no·tsi
At what time?	O której godzinie?	o ktoo·rey go·jee·nye
At (five).	O (piątej).	o (pyon·tey)
At (7.57pm).	O (19.57).	o (jye·vyet·nas·tey pyen·jye·shont shye·dem)

the calendar

days

You will see the days of the week abbbreviated to *Pn., Wt., Śr., Cz., Pt., So.* and *Nd.* on timetables and signs etc.

Monday	poniedziałek m	po·nye·jya·wek
Tuesday	wtorek m	fto·rek
Wednesday	środa f	shro·da
Thursday	czwartek m	chfar·tek
Friday	piątek m	pyon·tek
Saturday	sobota f	so·bo·ta
Sunday	niedziela f	nye·jye·la

months

The names of the months are often abbreviated as follows:
Sty., Lut., Mar., Kwi., Maj., Cze., Lip., Sie., Wrz., Paź., Lis. and *Gru.*
The forms following the slashes are the forms of the months
that you'll need to use when saying dates (see below for more
on this).

January	*styczeń/stycznia* m	sti·chen´/stich·nya
February	*luty/lutego* m	loo·ti/loo·te·go
March	*marzec/marca* m	ma·zhets/mar·tsa
April	*kwiecień/ kwietnia* m	kfye·chyen´/ kfyet·nya
May	*maj/maja* m	mai/ma·ya
June	*czerwiec/czerwca* m	cher·vyets/cherf·tsa
July	*lipiec/lipca* m	lee·pyets/leep·tsa
August	*sierpień/ sierpnia* m	shyer·pyen´/ shyerp·nya
September	*wrzesień/ września* m	vzhe·shyen´/ vzhesh·nya
October	*październik/ października* m	pazh·jyer·neek/ pazh·jyer·nee·ka
November	*listopad/ listopada* m	lees·to·pat/ lees·to·pa·da
December	*grudzień/ grudnia* m	groo·jyen´/ grood·nya

dates

Ordinal numbers are used when saying dates, just as in
English. The ordinal number takes an *-ego e*·go ending, so that
13 September is *trzynastego września* tshi·nas·te·go vzhesh·nya
(lit: thirteenth of-September). The form of the month changes
from the nominative to the genitive case. Genitive case forms
are given above for each month following the slashes. See **case**
in the **a–z phrasebuilder** for an explanation of these terms.

Dates may be written in one of three ways: using Arabic
numerals (in day–month–year order) separated by dots (eg
13.09.2007), using Roman numerals for the month and no dots
(eg *13 IX 2007*), or you can write the month out longhand (eg
13 września 2007).

What date is it today?
Którego jest dzisiaj?   ktoo·*re*·go yest *jee*·shai

It's (18 October).
Jest (osiemnastego   yest (o·shem·nas·*te*·go
października).   pazh·jyer·*nee*·ka)

seasons

spring	*wiosna* f	*vyos*·na
summer	*lato* n	*la*·to
autumn/fall	*jesień* f	*ye*·shyen'
winter	*zima* f	*zhee*·ma

times past

It might be useful to know the time expressions below
(some of which are followed by their abbreviated forms)
when you're reading timetables or checking out museums,
artworks and monuments.

bieżącego roku (br.)	bye·zhon·*tse*·go *ro*·koo	this year
epoka	e·*po*·ka	era/age
godzina (godz.)	go·*jee*·na	time/hour/ o'clock
koniec	*ko*·nyets	end
okres	*o*·kres	period
początek	po·*chon*·tek	beginning
przed naszą erą (p.n.e)	pshed *na*·shom e·rom	BC
rok (r.)	rok	year
roku Pańskiego	*ro*·koo pan'·*skye*·go	AD
stulecie	stoo·*le*·chye	century
tysiąclecie	ti·shyonts·*le*·chye	millennium

present

'Today' is both *dziś* jeesh and *dzisiaj* jee·shai – there's no difference in meaning between the two.

now	*teraz*	te·ras
today	*dziś/dzisiaj*	jeesh/jee·shai
tonight	*dziś wieczorem*	jeesh vye·cho·rem
this ...		
morning	*dziś rano*	jeesh ra·no
afternoon	*dziś po południu*	jeesh po po·wood·nyoo
evening	*dziś wieczorem*	jeesh vye·cho·rem
week	*w tym tygodniu*	f tim ti·god·nyoo
month	*w tym miesiącu*	f tim mye·shon·tsoo
year	*w tym roku*	f tim ro·koo

past

day before yesterday	*przedwczoraj*	pshet·fcho·rai
(three days) ago	*(trzy dni) temu*	(tshi dnee) te·moo
since (May)	*od (maja)*	od (ma·ya)
last night	*wczoraj wieczorem*	fcho·rai vye·cho·rem
last ...	*w zeszłym ...*	v zesh·wim ...
week	*tygodniu*	ti·god·nyoo
month	*miesiącu*	mye·shon·tsoo
year	*roku*	ro·koo
yesterday ...	*wczoraj ...*	fcho·rai ...
morning	*rano*	ra·no
afternoon	*po południu*	po po·wood·nyoo
evening	*wieczorem*	vye·cho·rem

time & dates

future

day after tomorrow	*pojutrze*	po·*yoo*·tshe
in (six days)	*za (sześć dni)*	za (sheshch dnee)
until (June)	*do (czerwca)*	do (*cherf*·tsa)

next ...	*w przyszłym ...*	v *pshish*·wim ...
week	*tygodniu*	ti·*god*·nyoo
month	*miesiącu*	mye·*shon*·tsoo
year	*roku*	*ro*·koo

tomorrow ...	*jutro ...*	*yoo*·tro ...
morning	*rano*	*ra*·no
afternoon	*po południu*	po po·*wood*·nyoo
evening	*wieczorem*	vye·*cho*·rem

during the day

w ciągu dnia

afternoon	*popołudnie* n	po·po·*wood*·nye
dawn	*świt* m	shveet
day	*dzień* m	jyen'
evening	*wieczór* m	*vye*·choor
midday/noon	*południe* n	po·*wood*·nye
midnight	*północ* f	*poow*·nots
morning	*rano* n	*ra*·no
night	*noc* f	nots
sunrise	*wschód słońca* m	fskhoot swon'·tsa
sunset	*zachód słońca* m	*za*·khoot swon'·tsa

How much is it?
Ile to kosztuje?　　　　　　*ee*·le to kosh·*too*·ye

It's free.
Jest bezpłatny/a/e. m/f/n　　yest bes·*pwat*·ni/na/ne

It's (12) złotys.
To kosztuje　　　　　　　　to kosh·*too*·ye
(12) złotych.　　　　　　　　(dva·*nash*·chye) *zwo*·tikh

Can you write down the price?
Proszę napisać cenę.　　　　*pro*·she na·*pee*·sach *tse*·ne

Do I have to pay?
Czy muszę płacić?　　　　　chi *moo*·she pwa·cheech

There's a mistake in the bill/check.
Na czeku jest pomyłka.　　　na *che*·koo yest po·*miw*·ka

Do you accept ...?	*Czy mogę*	chi *mo*·ge
	zapłacić ...?	za·*pwa*·cheech ...
credit cards	*kartą*	*kar*·tom
	kredytową	kre·di·*to*·vom
debit cards	*kartą*	*kar*·tom
	debetową	de·be·*to*·vom
travellers	*czekami*	che·*ka*·mee
cheques	*podróżnymi*	pod·roozh·*ni*·mee

I'd like ..., please.	*Proszę o ...*	*pro*·she o ...
a receipt	*rachunek*	ra·*khoo*·nek
a refund	*zwrot pieniędzy*	zvrot pye·*nyen*·dzi
my change	*moją resztę*	*mo*·yom *resh*·te

Where's ...?	*Gdzie jest ...?*	gjye yest ...
an ATM	*bankomat*	ban·*ko*·mat
a foreign	*kantor walut*	*kan*·tor *va*·loot
exchange office		

I'd like to …	Chciałem/am … m/f	khchow·em/am …
cash a cheque	wymienić czek	vi·mye·neech chek
	na gotówkę	na go·toof·ke
change a travellers cheque	wymienić czek podróżny	vi·mye·neech chek po·droozh·ni
change money	wymienić pieniądze	vi·mye·neech pye·nyon·dze
get a cash advance	dostać zaliczkę na moją kartę kredytową	dos·tach za·leech·ke na mo·yom kar·te kre·di·to·vom
get change for this note	rozmienić pieniądze	roz·mye·neech pye·nyon·dze
withdraw money	wypłacić pieniądze	vi·pwa·tseech pye·nyon·dze

What's the …?	Jaki/a jest …? m/f	ya·kee/ka yest …
charge	prowizja f	pro·veez·ya
exchange rate	kurs wymiany m	koors vi·mya·ni

How much is it per …?	Ile kosztuje za …?	ee·le kosh·too·ye za …
caravan	przyczepę kampingową	pshi·che·pe kam·peen·go·vom
day	dzień	jyen'
game	grę	gre
hour	godzinę	go·jee·ne
(five) minutes	(pięć) minut	(pyench) mee·noot
night	noc	nots
page	stronę	stro·ne
person	osobę	o·so·be
tent	namiot	na·myot
week	tydzień	ti·jyen'
vehicle	samochód	sa·mo·khood
visit	wizytę	vee·zi·te

For more money-related phrases, see **banking**, page 91.

getting around

komunikacja

Which … goes to (Zakopane)?	*Który … jedzie do (Zakopanego)?*	ktoo·ri … ye·jye do (za·ko·pa·ne·go)
bus	*autobus*	ow·to·boos
minibus	*minibus*	mee·nee·boos
train	*pociąg*	po·chonk
Which … goes to (Sopot)?	*Który … jedzie do (Sopotu)?*	ktoo·ri … ye·jye do (so·po·too)
tram	*tramwaj*	tram·vai
trolleybus	*trolejbus*	tro·ley·boos

Is this the … to (Wrocław)?	*Czy to jest … do (Wrocławia)?*	chi to yest … do (vrots·wa·vya)
bus	*autobus*	ow·to·boos
minibus	*minibus*	mee·nee·boo
train	*pociąg*	po·chonk
Is this the … to (Orłowo)?	*Czy to jest … do (Orłowa)?*	chi to yest … do (or·wo·va)
tram	*tramwaj*	tram·vai
trolleybus	*trolejbus*	tro·ley·boos
When's the … (bus)?	*Kiedy jest … (autobus)?*	kye·di yest … (ow·to·boos)
first	*pierwszy*	pyerf·shi
last	*ostatni*	os·tat·nee
next	*następny*	nas·temp·ni

Which ferry goes to (Ystad)?
Który prom płynie
do (Ystad)?
ktoo·ri prom pwi·nye
do (ees·tad)

Is this the ferry to (Copenhagen)?
Czy to jest prom
do (Kopenhagi)?
chi to yest prom
do (ko·pen·kha·gee)

What time does it leave?
O której godzinie
odjeżdża?
o ktoo·rey go·jee·nye
ot·yezh·ja

What time does it get to (Toruń)?
O której godzinie
przyjeżdża do (Torunia)?
o ktoo·rey go·jee·nye
pshi·yezh·ja do (to·roo·nya)

How long will it be delayed?
Jakie będzie
opóźnienie?
ya·kye ben·jye
o·poozh·nye·nye

Is this seat free?
Czy to miejsce jest wolne?
chi to myeys·tse yest vol·ne

That's my seat.
To jest moje miejsce.
to yest mo·ye myeys·tse

Please tell me when we get to (Krynica).
Proszę mi powiedzieć
gdy dojedziemy
do (Krynicy).
pro·she mee po·vye·jyech
gdi do·ye·jye·mi
do (kri·nee·tsi)

Please stop here.
Proszę się tu zatrzymać.
pro·she shye too za·tshi·mach

How long do we stop here?
Na jak długo się
tu zatrzymamy?
na yak dwoo·go shye
too za·tshi·ma·mi

move over!

When using public transport in Poland, always offer up your seat to the elderly, pregnant women or people with a disability if there are no other seats free by saying *proszę usiąść* pro·she oo·shyonshch (please take a seat). Failure to cede your seat might just precipitate a storm of invective from the injured party.

tickets

Excuse me, where's the ticket office?

Przepraszam, gdzie jest   pshe·*pra*·sham gjye yest
kasa biletowa?   *ka*·sa bee·le·*to*·va

Where do I buy a ticket?

Gdzie mogę kupić bilet?   gjye *mo*·ge koo·peech *bee*·let

Do I need to book (well in advance)?

Czy muszę rezerwować   chi *moo*·she re·zer·*vo*·vach
(z dużym wyprzedzeniem)?   (z doo·zhim vi·pshe·*dze*·nyem)

A ... ticket (to Katowice).	*Proszę bilet ...* *(do Katowic).*	pro·she *bee*·let ... (do ka·*to*·veets)
1st-class	*pierwszej klasy*	*pyerf*·shey *kla*·si
2nd-class	*drugiej klasy*	*droo*·gyey *kla*·si
child's	*dla dziecka*	dla *jyets*·ka
one-way	*w jedną stronę*	v *yed*·nom *stro*·ne
reserved seat	*miejscówkę*	*myeys*·*tsoof*·ke
return	*powrotny*	po·*vro*·tni
student	*studencki*	stoo·*den*·tskee

I'd like a/an ... seat.	*Proszę miejsce ...*	pro·she *myeys*·tse ...
aisle	*przy* *przejściu*	pshi *pshey*·shchyoo
nonsmoking	*dla* *niepalących*	dla nye·pa·*lon*·tsikh
smoking	*dla palących*	dla pa·*lon*·tsikh
window	*przy oknie*	pshi *ok*·nye

Is there (a) ...?	*Czy jest tam ...?*	chi yest tam ...
air conditioning	*klimatyzacja*	klee·ma·ti·*za*·tsya
blanket	*koc*	kots
sick bag	*torebka na* *wymioty*	to·*rep*·ka na vi·*myo*·ti
toilet	*toaleta*	to·a·*le*·ta

How much is it?
Ile kosztuje?　　　　　　　　ee·le kosh·*too*·ye

How long does the trip take?
Ile trwa podróż?　　　　　　ee·le trfa po·droosh

Is it a direct route?
Czy to jest bezpośrednie　　chi to yest bes·po·*shred*·nye
połączenie?　　　　　　　　po·won·*che*·nye

Can I get a stand-by ticket?
Czy mogę dostać　　　　　　chi *mo*·ge *do*·stach
bilet z listy rezerwowej?　　*bee*·let z *lees*·ti re·zer·*vo*·vey

Can I get a sleeping berth?
Czy mogę dostać　　　　　　chi *mo*·ge *do*·stach
miejsce sypialne?　　　　　*myeys*·tse si·*pyal*·ne

Can I get a couchette?
Czy mogę dostać　　　　　　chi *mo*·ge *do*·stach
kuszetkę?　　　　　　　　　koo·*shet*·ke

What time should I check in?
O której godzinie　　　　　　o *ktoo*·rey go·*jee*·nye
muszę się zgłosić?　　　　　*moo*·she shye *zgwo*·sheech

I'd like to …　　　　*Chcę … mój*　　khtse … mooy
my ticket, please.　*bilet.*　　　　*bee*·let
　cancel　　　　　　*odwołać*　　　od·*vo*·wach
　change　　　　　　*zmienić*　　　*zmye*·neech
　collect　　　　　　*odebrać*　　　o·*de*·brach
　confirm　　　　　　*potwierdzić*　po·*tvyer*·jyeech

listen for …		
brak wolnych miejsc	brak *vol*·nikh myeysts	**full**
odwołany	od·vo·*wa*·ni	**cancelled**
opóźniony	o·poozh·*nyo*·ni	**delayed**
peron m	*pe*·ron	**platform**
strajk m	straik	**strike**
ten m	ten	**this one**
tamten m	*tam*·ten	**that one**

Auschwitz	*Oświęcim*	osh·*vyen*·cheem
Gdańsk	*Gdańsk*	gdan´sk
Kraków	*Kraków*	*kra*·koof
Malbork	*Malbork*	*mal*·bork
Szczecin	*Szczecin*	shche·cheen
Toruń	*Toruń*	to·roon´
Warsaw	*Warszawa*	var·*sha*·va
Wrocław	*Wrocław*	*vrots*·wav

luggage

bagaż

Where can I find (a/the) …?	*Gdzie jest …?*	gjye yest …
baggage claim	*odbiór*	od·byoor
	bagażu	ba·*ga*·zhoo
left-luggage	*przechowalnia*	pshe·kho·*val*·nya
office	*bagażu*	ba·*ga*·zhoo
luggage locker	*schowek na*	*skho*·vek na
	bagaż	ba·gazh
trolley	*wózek na bagaż*	*voo*·zek na ba·gazh

My luggage has been …	*Mój bagaż został …*	mooy ba·gazh zos·tow …
damaged	*uszkodzony*	oosh·ko·*dzo*·ni
lost	*zagubiony*	za·goo·*byo*·ni
stolen	*skradziony*	skra·*jyo*·ni

That's (not) mine.
To (nie) jest moje.   to (nye) yest *mo*·ye

Can I have some coins?
Czy mogę prosić o   chi *mo*·ge *pro*·sheech o
drobne monety?   *dro*·bne mo·*ne*·ti

Can I have some tokens?
Czy mogę prosić o żetony?   chi *mo*·ge *pro*·sheech o zhe·*to*·ni

transport

49

plane

samolot

Where's (the) …?	*Gdzie jest …?*	gjye yest …
airport shuttle	*autobus*	ow·to·boos
	lotniskowy	lot·nees·ko·vi
arrivals hall	*hala przylotów*	kha·la pshi·lo·toof
departures hall	*hala odlotów*	kha·la od·lo·toof
duty-free shop	*sklep*	sklep
	wolnocłowy	vol·no·tswo·vi
gate (5)	*wejście*	veysh·chye
	(numer pięć)	(noo·mer pyench)

Where does flight (LO125) arrive/depart?

Skąd przylatuje/ skont pshi·la·too·ye/
odlatuje lot od·la·too·ye lot
(LO125)? (el o sto dva·jyesh·chya pyench)

listen for …		
karta	*kar·ta*	**boarding pass**
pokładowa f	po·kwa·do·va	
paszport m	pash·port	**passport**
przesiadka f	pshe·shyat·ka	**transfer**
tranzyt m	tran·zit	**transit**

bus, coach, tram & trolleybus

autobus, autokar, tramwaj i trolejbus

Most of Poland's bus transport is operated by the former state bus company *PKS* pe ka es. There are two types of *PKS* bus service: *autobusy zwykłe* ow·to·boo·si zvi·kwe (local buses) and *autobusy pospieszne* ow·to·boo·si pos·pyesh·ne (fast buses) which are marked in red and cover long-distance routes.

Is this a bus stop?

Czy to jest przystanek chi to yest pshi·sta·nek
autobusowy? ow·to·boo·so·vi

How often do buses come?
Jak często przyjeżdżają autobusy?
yak *chen*·sto pshi·yezh·*ja*·yom ow·to·*boo*·si

Does it stop at (Bielsko)?
Czy się zatrzymuje w (Bielsku)?
chi shye za·tshi·*moo*·ye v (*byel*·skoo)

What's the next stop?
Jaki jest następny przystanek?
ya·kee yest nas·*tem*·pni pshi·*sta*·nek

I'd like to get off at (Gliwice).
Chcę wysiąść w (Gliwicach).
khtse *vi*·shyonshch v (glee·*vee*·tsakh)

How much is it to (Olsztyn)?
Ile kosztuje żeby dojechać do (Olsztyna)?
ee·le kosh·*too*·ye *zhe*·bi do·*ye*·khach do (ol·*shti*·na)

intercity	*międzymiastowy* m	myen·dzi·myas·*to*·vi
local bus	*lokalny autobus* m	lo·*kal*·ni ow·to·boos
hotel bus	*autobus hotelowy* m	ow·to·boos kho·te·*lo*·vi

For bus numbers, see **numbers & amounts**, page 33.

train

pociąg

What's the next station?
Jaka jest następna stacja?
ya·ka yest nas·*temp*·na *sta*·tsya

Does it stop at (Kalisz)?
Czy on się zatrzymuje w (Kaliszu)?
chi on shye za·tshi·*moo*·ye f (ka·*lee*·shoo)

Do I need to change?
Czy trzeba się przesiadać?
chi *tshe*·ba shye pshe·*shya*·dach

Is it ...?	*Czy to jest*	chi to yest
	pociąg ...?	po·chonk ...
express	*ekspresowy*	eks·pre·so·vi
a fast train	*pospieszny*	pos·pyesh·ni
an InterCity train	*InterCity*	een·ter·see·tee
a suburban train	*podmiejski*	pod·myey·skee
Which carriage	*Który wagon*	ktoo·ri va·gon
is (for) ...?	*jest ...?*	yest ...
1st class	*z pierwszą*	z pyer·fshom
	klasą	kla·som
dining	*restauracyjny*	res·tow·ra·tsiy·ni
(Kołobrzeg)	*(do*	(do
	Kołobrzegu)	ko·wo·bzhe·goo)

train timetable reader

EC. (EuroCity)	ew·ro·see·tee	EuroCity service
IC. (InterCity)	een·ter·see·tee	InterCity service
EX. (Expres)	eks·pres	express service
TLK. (Tanie Linie	*ta·nye lee·nye*	discounted
Kolejowe)	ko·le·yo·ve	intercity service
p. (pospieszny)	pos·pyesh·ni	fast train
os. (osobowy)	o·so·bo·vi	local train
codziennie	tso·jye·nye	daily
do	do	till
od	od	from
oprócz	o·prooch	except
także	tak·zhe	also

For abbreviations of the names of months and days of the
week, see **time & dates**, pages 38–39.

PRACTICAL

52

ferry

What's the sea like today?
Jaki jest dzisiaj   ya·kee yest *jee*·shai
stan morza?   stan *mo*·zha

Are there life jackets?
Czy są tam kamizelki   chi som tam ka·mee·*zel*·kee
ratunkowe?   ra·toon·*ko*·ve

I feel seasick.
Mam chorobę morską.   mam kho·*ro*·be *mor*·skom

boat	*statek* m	*sta*·tek
cabin	*kabina* f	ka·*bee*·na
captain	*kapitan* m	ka·*pee*·tan
(car) deck	*pokład*	*pok*·wad
	(samochodowy) m	(sa·mo·kho·*do*·vi)
ferry	*prom* m	prom
lifeboat	*szalupa*	sha·*loo*·pa
	ratunkowa f	ra·toon·*ko*·va
life jacket	*kamizelka*	ka·mee·*zel*·ka
	ratunkowa f	ra·toon·*ko*·va

taxi

I'd like a	*Chcę zamówić*	khtse za·*moo*·veech
taxi …	*taksówkę na …*	tak·*soof*·ke na …
now	*teraz*	*te*·ras
tomorrow	*jutro*	*yoo*·tro
at (9am)	*na (dziewiątą*	na (jye·*vyon*·tom
	rano)	*ra*·no)

Where's the taxi rank?
Gdzie jest postój taksówek?   gjye yest *pos*·tooy tak·*soo*·vek

Is this taxi available?
Czy ta taksówka jest wolna?   chi ta tak·*soof*·ka yest *vol*·na

Please take me to (this address).
Proszę mnie zawieźć
pod (ten adres).
pro·she mnye *za*·vyeshch
pod (ten *ad*·res)

Please put the meter on.
Proszę włączyć taksometr.
pro·she *vwon*·chich tak·*so*·metr

Please put the day-time rate on.
Proszę ustawić
dzienną taryfę.
pro·she oo·*sta*·veech
jyen·nom ta·*ri*·fe

How much is …?	Ile kosztuje …?	ee·le kosh·*too*·ye …
it to (Szczecin)	do (Szczecina)	(do shche·*chee*·na)
the flag fall/	złamanie	zwa·*ma*·nye
hiring charge	chorągiewki	kho·ron·*gyef*·kee

Please …	Proszę …	*pro*·she …
come back at	wrócić o	*vroo*·cheech o
(10 o'clock)	(dziesiątej)	(jye·*shon*·tey)
slow down	zwolnić	*zvol*·neech
stop here	się tu	shye too
	zatrzymać	za·*tshi*·mach

car & motorbike

samochód i motocykl

car & motorbike hire

I'd like to hire	Chcę	khtse
a/an …	wypożyczyć	vi·po·*zhi*·chich
	samochód …	sa·*mo*·khoot …
4WD	terenowy	te·re·*no*·vi
automatic	z automa-	z ow·to·ma-
	tyczną	*tich*·nom
	skrzynią biegów	*skshi*·nyom *bye*·goof
manual	z ręczną	z *rench*·nom
	skrzynią biegów	*skshi*·nyom *bye*·goof

I'd like to hire a motorbike.
Chcę wypożyczyć motocykl. khtse vi·po·*zhi*·chich mo·*to*·tsikl

PRACTICAL

54

with ...	z ...	z ...
air conditioning	klimatyzacją	klee·ma·ti·*za*·tsyom
a driver	kierowcą	kye·*rof*·tsom

How much for ... hire?	*Ile kosztuje wypożyczenie na ...?*	*ee*·le kosh·*too*·ye vi·po·zhi·*che*·nye na ...
daily	dzień	jyen´
weekly	tydzień	*ti*·jyen´

Does that include insurance?
Czy ubezpieczenie jest wliczone?　　chi oo·bes·pye·*che*·nye yest vlee·*cho*·ne

Does that include mileage?
Czy kilometry są wliczone?　　chi kee·lo·*me*·tri som vlee·*cho*·ne

Do you have a guide to the road rules (in English)?
Czy jest objaśnienie kodeksu drogowego (po angielsku)?　　chi yest ob·yash·*nye*·nye ko·*de*·ksoo dro·go·*ve*·go (po an·*gyel*·skoo)

Do you have a road map?
Czy jest mapa drogowa?　　chi yest *ma*·pa dro·*go*·va

on the road

What's the speed limit?
Jakie jest ograniczenie prędkości?　　*ya*·kye yest o·gra·nee·*che*·nye prent·*kosh*·chee

Is this the road to (Malbork)?
Czy to jest droga do (Malborka)?　　chi to yest *dro*·ga do (mal·*bor*·ka)

Where's a petrol/gas station?
Gdzie jest stacja benzynowa?　　gjye yest *sta*·tsya ben·zi·*no*·va

Can you check the ...?	*Czy może pan sprawdzić ...?*	chi *mo*·zhe pan *sprav*·jeech ...
oil	olej	*o*·ley
tyre pressure	ciśnienie w oponach	cheesh·*nye*·nye v o·*po*·nakh
water	wodę	*vo*·de

diesel	*diesel* m	*dee*·zel
leaded petrol	*benzyna ołowiowa* f	ben·*zi*·na o·wo·*vyo*·va
LPG	*gaz* m	gaz
98-octane unleaded petrol	*dziewięćdziesięcioośmio oktanowa* f	jye·vyen·jye·*shen*·cho·*osh*·myo ok·ta·*no*·va
unleaded	*bezołowiowa* f	bes·o·wo·*vyo*·va

Can I park here?
Czy można tu parkować? chi *mozh*·na too par·*ko*·vach

How long can I park here?
Jak długo można tu parkować? yak *dwoo*·go *mozh*·na too par·*ko*·vach

Do I have to pay?
Czy muszę płacić? chi *moo*·she *pwa*·cheech

problems

I need a mechanic.
Potrzebuję mechanika. po·tshe·*boo*·ye me·kha·*nee*·ka

I've had an accident.
Miałem/am wypadek. m/f myow·em/am vi·*pa*·dek

The car/motorbike has broken down at (Kozia Wólka).
Samochód/Motocykl się zepsuł w (Koziej Wólce). sa·mo·khoot/mo·to·tsikl shye zep·*soow* v (ko·zhyey *vool*·tse)

road signs		
Opłata	o·*pwa*·ta	Toll
Stop	stop	Stop
Uwaga	oo·*va*·ga	Danger
Wjazd	vyazd	Entrance
Wyjazd	*vi*·yazd	Exit

PRACTICAL

56

The car/motorbike won't start.
Samochód/Motocykl   sa·*mo*·khoot/mo·*to*·tsikl
nie chce zapalić.   nye khtse za·*pa*·leech

I have a flat tyre.
Złapałem/am gumę. m/f   zwa·*pa*·wem/wam *goo*·me

I've lost my car keys.
Zgubiłem/am   zgoo·*bee*·wem/wam
kluczyba do samochodu. m/f   kloo·*chi*·kee do sa·mo·*kho*·doo

I've locked the keys inside.
Zatrzasnąłem/   za·tsha·*sno*·wem/
Zatrzasnęłam   za·tsha·*sne*·wam
kluczyki w środku. m/f   kloo·*chi*·kee v *shrot*·koo

I've run out of petrol.
Zabrakło mi benzyny.   za·*bra*·kwo mee ben·*zi*·ni

Can you fix it (today)?
Czy może pan to   chi *mo*·zhe pan to
(dzisiaj) naprawić?   (*jee*·shai) na·*pra*·veech

How long will it take?
Ile czasu to zajmie?   ee·le *cha*·soo to *zai*·mye

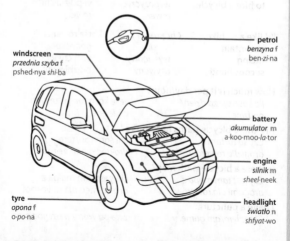

petrol
benzyna f
ben·*zi*·na

windscreen
przednia szyba f
pshed·nya *shi*·ba

battery
akumulator m
a·koo·moo·*la*·tor

engine
silnik m
sheel·neek

tyre
opona f
o·*po*·na

headlight
światło n
shfyat·wo

listen for ...		
bilet na autostradę m	*bee·let na ow·to·stra·de*	motorway pass
kilometry m pl	*ki·lo·me·tri*	kilometres
parkometr m	*par·ko·metr*	parking meter
prawo jazdy n	*pra·vo yaz·di*	driving licence

bicycle

rower

The Polish word for 'bicycle' is *rower ro·ver*. The first bicycles were imported into Poland by the British car manufacturer Rover and the name stuck.

I'd like ...	*Chcę ...*	khtse ...
my bicycle repaired	*oddać rower do naprawy*	*ot·dach ro·ver do na·pra·vi*
to buy a bicycle	*kupić rower*	*koo·peech ro·ver*
to hire a bicycle	*wypożyczyć rower*	*vi·po·zhi·chich ro·ver*

I'd like a ... bike.	*Chcę rower ...*	khtse ro·ver ...
mountain	*górski*	*goor·skee*
racing	*wyścigowy*	*vish·chee·go·vi*
secondhand	*używany*	*oo·zhi·va·ni*

How much is it per day/hour?
Ile kosztuje za dzień/ godzinę?
ee·le kosh·too·ye za jyen´/ go·jee·ne

Are there bicycle paths here/there?
Czy są tu/tam drogi dla rowerów?
chi som too/tam dro·gee dla ro·ve·roof

Is there a bicycle-path map?
Czy jest tam mapa z drogami dla rowerów?
chi yest tam ma·pa z dro·ga·mee dla ro·ve·roof

I have a puncture.
Złapałem/am gumę. m/f
zwa·pa·wem/wam goo·me

border crossing

przekraczanie granicy

I'm ...	Jestem ...	*yes·*tem ...
in transit	w tranzycie	v tran·*zi·*chye
on business	służbowo	swoozh·*bo·*vo
on holiday	na wakacjach	na va·*kats·*yakh

I'm here for ...	Będę tu przez ...	*ben·*de too pshes ...
(10) days	(dziesięć) dni	(*jye·*shench) dnee
(three) weeks	(trzy) tygodnie	(tshi) ti·*god·*nye
a month	jeden miesiąc	*ye·*den *mye·*shonts
(two) months	(dwa) miesiące	(dva) mye·*shon·*tse
(five) months	(pięć) miesięcy	(pyench) mye·*shyen·*tsi

I'm going to (Kraków).
Jadę do (Krakowa).   ya·de do (kra·*ko·*va)

I'm staying at the (Pod Różą Hotel).
Zatrzymuję się w   za·tshi·*moo·*ye shye v
(hotelu 'pod Różą').   (ho·*te·*loo pod *roo·*zhom)

The children are on this passport.
Dzieci są wpisane   *jye·*chee som fpee·*sa·*ne
do paszportu.   do pash·*por·*too

---

listen for ...

grupa f	*groo·*pa	**group**
indywidualny	een·di·vee·doo·*al·*ni	**alone**
paszport m	*pash·*port	**passport**
rodzina f	ro·*jee·*na	**family**
wiza f	*vee·*za	**visa**

at customs

I have nothing to declare.
Nie mam nic do zgłoszenia.
nye mam neets do zgwo·*she*·nya

I have something to declare.
Mam coś do zgłoszenia.
mam tsosh do zgwo·*she*·nya

Do I have to declare this?
Czy muszę to zgłosić?
chi *moo*·she to *zgwo*·sheech

That's (not) mine.
To (nie) jest moje.
to (nye) yest *mo*·ye

I didn't know I had to declare it.
Nie wiedziałem/am,
że muszę to zgłosić. m/f
nye vye·*ja*·wem/wam
zhe *moo*·she to *zgwo*·sheech

Could I please have a/an (English) interpreter?
Proszę o tłumacza (angielskiego).
pro·she o twoo·*ma*·cha (an·gyel·*skye*·go)

For phrases on payments and receipts, see **money**, page 43.

signs

Kontrola paszportowa	kon·*tro*·la pash·por·*to*·va	**Passport Control**
Kwarantanna	kfa·ran·*ta*·na	**Quarantine**
Odprawa celna	ot·*pra*·va tsel·na	**Customs**
Odprawa imigracyjna	ot·*pra*·va ee·mee·gra·*tsiy*·na	**Immigration**
Wolny od opłaty celnej	*vol*·ni od o·*pwa*·ti tsel·ney	**Duty-Free**

PRACTICAL

60

Where's a/the ...?	*Gdzie jest ...?*	gjye yest ...
bank	*bank*	bank
market	*targ*	tark
tourist office	*biuro*	*byoo*·ro
	turystyczne	too·ris·*tich*·ne

How do I get there?
Jak tam mogę   yak tam *mo*·ge
się dostać?   shye *dos*·tach

Do you know the way?
Czy znasz drogę?   chi znash *dro*·ge

How far is it?
Jak daleko to jest?   yak da·*le*·ko to yest

Can you show me (on the map)?
Czy może pan/pani   chi *mo*·zhe pan/*pa*·nee
mi pokazać (na mapie)? m/f   mee po·*ka*·zach (na *ma*·pye)

What's the address?
Jaki jest adres?   *ya*·kee yest *ad*·res

---

typical addresses

You'll probably see the words *mieszkanie*, *aleja*, *ulica*, *plac* and *osiedle* (see below) abbreviated to *m.*, *al.*, *ul.*, *pl* and *os.* respectively. A *województwo* vo·ye·*voots*·tfo (which is commonly abbreviated to *woj.*) is an administrative region of which there are 16 in Poland. In English it's translated as 'voivode'.

apartment	*mieszkanie* n	myesh·*ka*·nye
avenue	*aleja* f	a·*le*·ya
road/street	*ulica* f	oo·*lee*·tsa
square	*plac* n	plats
suburb	*osiedle* n	o·*shyed*·le
voivode	*województwo* n	vo·ye·*voots*·tfo

listen for ...		
kilometry	kee·lo·*me*·tri	**kilometres**
metry	*me*·tri	**metres**
minuty	mee·*noo*·ti	**minutes**
przecznice	pshech·*nee*·tse	**blocks**

It's ...	*Jest ...*	yest ...
behind ...	*za ...*	za ...
close	*blisko*	*blees*·ko
here	*tu*	too
in front of ...	*przed ...*	pshet ...
near ...	*koło ...*	*ko*·wo ...
next to ...	*obok ...*	*o*·bok ...
on the corner	*na rogu*	na *ro*·goo
opposite ...	*naprzeciwko ...*	nap·she·*cheef*·ko ...
straight ahead	*na wprost*	na fprost
there	*tam*	tam

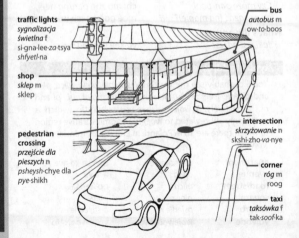

traffic lights
*sygnalizacja
świetlna* f
si·gna·lee·*za*·tsya
shfyetl·na

shop
sklep m
sklep

**pedestrian
crossing**
*przejście dla
pieszych* n
psheysh·chye dla
pye·shikh

bus
autobus m
ow·to·*boos*

intersection
skrzyżowanie n
skshi·zho·*va*·nye

corner
róg m
roog

taxi
taksówka f
tak·*soof*·ka

Turn ...	*Proszę*	*pro*·she
	skręcić ...	*skren*·cheech ...
at the corner	*na rogu*	na *ro*·goo
at the traffic lights	*na światłach*	na *shfyat*·wakh
left	*w lewo*	v *le*·vo
right	*w prawo*	v *pra*·vo
What ... is this?	*Jak się nazywa ...?*	yak shye na·*zi*·va ...
square	*ten plac*	ten plats
street	*ta ulica*	ta oo·*lee*·tsa
village	*ta miejscowość*	ta myeys·*tso*·voshch
north	*północ*	*poow*·nots
south	*południe*	po·*wood*·nye
east	*wschód*	fskhoot
west	*zachód*	*za*·khoot

writing home

When addressing a letter in Polish you use the titles *Pan* pan (Mr) or *Pani* *pa*·nee (Mrs) before the first name and then the surname, or simply the abbreviation *Sz. P.* This stands for either *Szanowny Pan* sha·*nov*·ni pan or *Szanowna Pani* sha·*nov*·na *pa*·nee – the *Szanowny/a* element means 'respected'.

If you're writing to more than one person, you just put *Sz. P* before the surname. This is an abbreviation of *Szanowni Państwo* sha·*nov*·ni pan'·stfo, *państwo* being the plural form of *pan* and the correct way of addressing a couple or family.

For the address itself, you follow the order below. The box on page 61 will give you the correct abbreviations to use.

Pan Stanisław Załęski   **Mr Stanisław Załęski**
ul. Tokarska 57 m. 1   **St. Tokarska 57 Apartment 1**
32–100 Kraków   **32–100 Kraków**

directions

The symbol for male toilets is an inverted triangle and for female toilets a circle.

Wstęp	fstemp	**Entrance**
Wyjście	viysh·chye	**Exit**
Otwarte	ot·var·te	**Open**
Zamknięte	zamk·nyen·te	**Closed**
Zakaz ...	za·kas ...	**... Prohibited**
Palenie wzbronione	pa·le·nye vzbro·nyo·ne	**No Smoking**
Toalety	to·a·le·ti	**Toilets**
Dla mężczyzn	dla menzh·chizn	**Men**
Dla kobiet	dla ko·byet	**Women**

by ...

bicycle	*rowerem*	ro·ve·rem
bus	*autobusem*	ow·to·boo·sem
foot	*pieszo*	pye·sho
minibus	*minibusem*	mee·nee·boo·sem
taxi	*taksówką*	tak·soof·kom
train	*pociągiem*	po·chon·gyem
tram	*tramwajem*	tram·va·yem

finding accommodation

Where's a/an ...?	*Gdzie jest ...?*	gjye yest ...
agritourist farm	*gospodarstwo*	gos·po·*darst*·fo
	agroturystyczne	a·gro·too·ris·*tich*·ne
bed and breakfast	*pensjonat*	pen·*syo*·nat
camping ground	*kamping*	*kam*·peeng
guesthouse	*pokoje*	po·*ko*·ye
	gościnne	gosh·*chee*·ne
hotel	*hotel*	*ho*·tel
mountain lodge	*schronisko*	skhro·*nees*·ko
	górskie	*goors*·kye
youth hostel	*schronisko*	skhro·*nees*·ko
	młodzieżowe	mwo·jye·*zho*·ve
I want something	*Chcę coś*	khtse tsosh
near the ...	*blisko ...*	*blees*·ko ...
beach	*plaży*	*pla*·zhi
city centre	*centrum*	*tsen*·troom
train station	*dworca*	*dvor*·tsa
	kolejowego	ko·le·yo·*ve*·go

country digs

If you're looking for an authentic Polish experience, consider staying in a *gospodarstwo agroturystyczne* gos·po·*darst*·fo a·gro·too·ris·*tich*·ne (agritourist farm). This term refers to accommodation in farms or country houses where owners let rooms to tourists. In most cases the rooms are simple but the prices are reasonable. To arrange a stay, contact one of the agritourist associations, known as *stowarzyszenie agroturystyczne* sto·va·zhi·*she*·nye a·gro·too·ris·*tich*·ne, which have regional offices.

Can you recommend somewhere ...?	Czy może pan/ pani polecić coś ...? m/f	chi mo·zhe pan/ pa·nee po·le·cheech tsosh ...
cheap	taniego	ta·nye·go
clean	schludnego	skhlood·ne·go
good	dobrego	do·bre·go
luxurious	ekskluzywnego	eks·kloo·ziv·ne·go
nearby	coś w pobliżu	tsosh f po·blee·zhoo
romantic	romantycznego	ro·man·tich·ne·go

Where can I find a room in a private flat?
Gdzie mogę wynająć pokój? gjye mo·ge vi·na·yonch po·kooy

What's the address?
Gdzie jest ten adres? gjye yest ten ad·res

For phrases on how to get there, see **directions**, page 61.

booking ahead & checking in

I'd like to book a room, please.
Chcę zarezerwować pokój. khtse za·re·zer·vo·vach po·kooy

I have a reservation.
Mam rezerwację. mam re·zer·va·tsye

My name's ...
Nazywam się ... na·zi·vam shye ...

For (three) nights/weeks.
Na (trzy) noce/tygodnie. na (tshi) no·tse/ti·god·nye

From (2 July) to (6 July).
Od (drugiego lipca) do (szóstego lipca). od (droo·gye·go leep·tsa) do (shoos·te·go leep·tsa)

Do I need to pay upfront?
Czy muszę płacić z góry? chi moo·she pwa·cheech z goo·ri

Do you have a ... room?	*Czy jest pokój ...?*	chi yest po·kooy ...
single	*jednoosobowy*	yed·no·o·so·bo·vi
double	*z podwójnym łóżkiem*	z pod·vooy·nim woozh·kyem
twin	*z dwoma łożkami*	z dvo·ma wozh·ka·mee

How much is it per ...?	*Ile kosztuje za ...?*	ee·le kosh·too·ye za ...
person	*osobę*	o·so·be
night	*noc*	nots
week	*tydzień*	ti·jyen'

Can I see it?	*Czy mogę go zobaczyć?*	chi mo·ge go zo·ba·chich
I'll take it.	*Wezmę go.*	vez·me go

Can I pay by ...?	*Czy mogę zapłacić ...?*	chi mo·ge za·pwa·cheech ...
credit card	*kartą kredytową*	kar·tom kre·di·to·vom
travellers cheque	*czekami podróżnymi*	che·ka·mee po·droozh·ni·mee

For other methods of payment, see **money**, page 43, and
banking, page 91.

local talk		
comfortable	*wygodny*	vi·god·ni
dive	*speluna* f	spe·loo·na
rat-infested	*nora* f	no·ra
top spot	*pierwsza klasa* f	pyerf·sha kla·sa

Łazienka	wa·*zhyen*·ka	**Bathroom**
Pralnia	*pral*·nya	**Laundry**
Brak wolnych miejsc	brak *vol*·nikh myeysts	**No Vacancy**
Wolne pokoje	*vol*·ne po·*ko*·ye	**Vacancy**

requests & queries

When is breakfast served?
O której jest śniadanie?   o *ktoo*·rey yest shnya·*da*·nye

Where is breakfast served?
Gdzie jest śniadanie?   gjye yest shnya·*da*·nye

Is there hot water all day?
Czy jest ciepła woda   chi yest *chyep*·wa *vo*·da
przez cały dzień?   pshes *tsa*·wi jyen´

Please wake me at (seven).
Proszę obudzić mnie   *pro*·she o·*boo*·jeech mnye
o (siódmej).   o (*shyood*·mey)

Do you have a laundry service?
Czy są tu usługi   chi som too oos·*woo*·gee
pralnicze?   pral·*nee*·che

Can I use the …?	*Czy mogę*	chi *mo*·ge
	używać …?	oo·*zhi*·vach …
kitchen	*kuchnię*	*kookh*·nye
laundry	*pralnię*	*pral*·nye
telephone	*telefon*	te·*le*·fon

Do you have a/an ...?	*Czy jest ...?*	chi yest ...
lift/elevator	*winda*	*veen*·da
message board	*tablica*	ta·*blee*·tsa
	ogłoszeń	o·*gwo*·shen'
safe	*sejf*	seyf
swimming pool	*basen*	*ba*·sen

Do you ... here?	*Czy tu ...?*	chi too ...
arrange tours	*organizujecie*	or·ga·nee·zoo·*ye*·chye
	wycieczki	vi·*chyech*·kee
change money	*wymieniacie*	vi·mye·*nya*·chye
	pieniądze	pye·*nyon*·dze

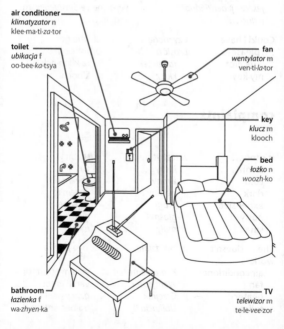

air conditioner
klimatyzator n
klee·ma·ti·*za*·tor

toilet
ubikacja f
oo·bee·*ka*·tsya

fan
wentylator m
ven·ti·*la*·tor

key
klucz m
klooch

bed
łóżko n
woozh·ko

bathroom
łazienka f
wa·*zhyen*·ka

TV
telewizor m
te·le·*vee*·zor

accommodation

69

Is there a message for me?
*Czy jest dla mnie
jakaś wiadomość?*
chi yest dla mnye
ya·kash vya·do·moshch

Can I leave a message for someone?
*Czy mogę zostawić
wiadomość dla
kogoś?*
chi mo·ge zos·ta·veech
vya·do·moshch dla
ko·gosh

I'm locked out of my room.
*Nie mogę się dostać
do mojego pokoju.*
nye mo·ge shye dos·tach
do mo·ye·go po·ko·yoo

Can I get another ...?
*Czy mogę prosić o
jeszcze jeden/jedną/
jedno ...? m/f/n*
chi mo·ge pro·sheech o
yesh·che ye·den/yed·nom/
yed·no ...

Could I have ..., please?	*Czy mogę prosić o ...?*	chi mo·ge pro·sheech o ...
a receipt	*rachunek*	ra·khoo·nek
my key	*klucz*	klooch

complaints

skargi

It's too ...	*Jest zbyt ...*	yest zbit ...
bright	*jasny*	yas·ni
cold	*zimny*	zheem·ni
dark	*ciemny*	chyem·ni
expensive	*drogi*	dro·gee
noisy	*głośny*	gwosh·ni
small	*mały*	ma·wi
The ... doesn't work.	*... nie działa.*	... nye jya·wa
air conditioner	*Klimatyzator*	klee·ma·ti·za·tor
fan	*Wentylator*	ven·ti·la·tor
heater	*Grzejnik*	gzhey·neek
toilet	*Ubikacja*	oo·bee·kats·ya

PRACTICAL

70

Who is it?	Kto tam?	kto tam
Just a moment.	Chwileczkę.	khfee·lech·ke
Come in.	Proszę wejść.	pro·she veyshch
Come back later, please.	Proszę przyjść później.	pro·she pshiyshch poozh·nyey

This ... isn't clean.
Ten/Ta/To ... nie jest czysty/a/e. m/f/n
ten/ta/to ... nye yest chis·ti/ta/te

There's no hot water.
Nie ma ciepłej wody.
nye ma *chyep·wey vo*·di

checking out

What time is checkout?
O której godzinie muszę się wymeldować?
o *ktoo*·rey go·*jye*·nye *moo*·she shye vi·mel·*do*·vach

Can you call a taxi for me (for 11 o'clock)?
Proszę zamówić mi taksówkę (na jedenastą).
pro·she za·*moo*·veech mee tak·*soof*·ke (na ye·de·*nas*·tom)

I'm leaving now.
Wyjeżdżam teraz.
vi·*yezh*·jam *te*·ras

Can I leave my bags here?
Czy mogę tu zostawić moje bagaże?
chi *mo*·ge too zo·*sta*·veech *mo*·ye ba·*ga*·zhe

There's a mistake in the bill/check.
Na czeku jest pomyłka.
na *che*·koo yest po·*miw*·ka

accommodation

71

Could I have	*Czy mogę prosić*	chi *mo*·ge *pro*·sheech
my ... please?	*o mój/moje ...? sg/pl*	o mooy/*mo*·ye ...
deposit	*depozyt sg*	de·*po*·zit
passport	*paszport sg*	*pash*·port
valuables	*kosztowności pl*	kosh·tov·*nosh*·chee

I'll be back ...	*Wrócę ...*	*vroo*·tse ...
in (three) days	*za (trzy) dni*	za (tshi) dnee
on (Thursday)	*w (czwartek)*	v (*chfar*·tek)

I had a great stay, thanks.
Miałem/am przyjemny — *myow*·em/am pshi·*yem*·ni
pobyt. Dziękuję. m/f — *po*·bit jyen·*koo*·ye

I'll recommend it to my friends.
Polecę to moim — po·*le*·tse to *mo*·yeem
znajomym. — zna·*yo*·mim

camping

kamping

How much	*Ile kosztuje*	*ee*·le kosh·*too*·ye
is it per ...?	*od ...?*	od ...
caravan	*przyczepy*	pshi·*che*·pi
	kampingowej	kam·peen·*go*·vey
person	*osoby*	o·*so*·bi
tent	*namiotu*	na·*myo*·too
vehicle	*samochodu*	sa·mo·*kho*·doo

Do you have (a) ...?	*Czy jest tu ...?*	chi yest too ...
laundry	*pralnia*	*pral*·nya
site	*miejsce pod*	*myeys*·tse pod
	namiot	na·myot
electricity	*elektryczność*	e·lek·*trich*·noshch

Do you have ...?	*Czy są tu ...?*	chi som too ...
shower facilities	*prysznice*	prish·*nee*·tse
tents for hire	*namioty do*	na·*myo*·ti do
	wynajęcia	vi·na·*yen*·chya

Can I ...?	*Czy mogę ...?*	chi *mo*·ge ...
camp here	*się tutaj*	shye *too*·tai
	rozbić	*roz*·beech
park next	*zaparkować*	za·par·*ko*·vach
to my tent	*obok mojego*	o·bok mo·*ye*·go
	namiotu	na·*myo*·too

Who do I ask to stay here?
Kogo muszę zapytać   *ko*·go *moo*·she za·*pi*·tach
o pozwolenie na nocleg?   o poz·vo·*le*·nye na *nots*·leg

Is it coin-operated?
Czy to jest na monety?   chi to yest na mo·*ne*·ti

Is the water drinkable?
Czy woda jest   chi *vo*·da yest
zdatna do picia?   *zdat*·na do *pee*·chya

Could I borrow ...?
Czy mogę pożyczyć ...?   chi *mo*·ge po·*zhi*·chich ...

renting

wynajmowanie

Do you have	*Czy jest ...*	chi yest ...
a/an ... for rent?	*do wynajęcia?*	do vi·na·*yen*·chya
apartment	*mieszkanie*	myesh·*ka*·nye
cabin	*domek*	*do*·mek
	kampingowy	kam·peen·*go*·vi
house	*dom*	dom
room	*pokój*	*po*·kooy
villa	*dom letniskowy*	dom let·nees·*ko*·vi
(partly) furnished	*(częściowo)*	(chensh·*chyo*·vo)
	umeblowany	oo·me·blo·*va*·ni
unfurnished	*nieumeblowany*	nye·oo·me·blo·*va*·ni

staying with locals

There's no need to bring gifts when staying with locals but a *butelka wina* boo·*tel*·ka *vee*·na (bottle of wine) or *bombonierka* bom·bo·*nyer*·ka (box of chocolates) would be appreciated.

Can I stay at your place?	*Czy mogę u was zostać?*	chi *mo*·ge oo vas *zos*·tach
I have my own ...	*Ja mam swój ...*	ya mam sfooy ...
mattress	*materac*	ma·*te*·rats
sleeping bag	*śpiwór*	shpee·voor
Can I ...?	*Czy mogę ...?*	chi *mo*·ge ...
bring anything for the meal	*coś przynieść do jedzenia*	tsosh pshi·nyeshch do ye·*dze*·nya
clear the table	*posprzątać ze stołu*	pos·*pshon*·tach ze *sto*·woo
do the dishes	*umyć naczynia*	oo·mich na·*chi*·nya
set the table	*nakryć stół*	na·krich stoow

Thanks for your hospitality.

Dziękuję za gościnność.   jyen·*koo*·ye za gosh·*cheen*·noshch

---

the host with the most

Poles are nothing if not hospitable. There's a saying, *Gość w dom – Bóg w dom* gosh v dom boog v dom, which translates as 'a guest in the house is like God in the house'. If you're lucky enough to be invited to someone's house, your hosts will revel in plying you with home-cooked delicacies and *wódka vood*·ka (no prizes for guessing what that is). To signal that it's time to tuck in, your hosts will probably exclaim *Smacznego!* smach·*ne*·go (Enjoy your meal!).

You'll definitely win a few hearts if you declare your appreciation of the meal in the following terms:

To było bardzo dobre!
to *bi*·wo *bar*·dzo *do*·bre   That was really tasty!

looking for ...

Are shops open on (the Corpus Christi holiday)?
Czy sklepy są otwarte   chi *skle*·pi som ot·*far*·te
w (Boże Ciało)?   v (*bo*·zhe *chya*·wo)

What hours are shops open?
W jakich godzinach   v *ya*·keekh go·*jee*·nakh
otwarte są sklepy?   ot·*far*·te som *skle*·pi

Where can I buy (a padlock)?
Gdzie mogę kupić   gjye *mo*·ge *koo*·peech
(kłódkę)?   (*kwoot*·ke)

Where's a/the ...?	*Gdzie jest ...?*	gjye yest ...
department store	*dom towarowy*	dom to·va·*ro*·vi
supermarket	*supermarket*	soo·per·*mar*·ket
24-hour shop	*sklep nocny*	sklep *nots*·ni
newsstand	*kiosk*	kyosk

For more items and shopping locations, see the **dictionary**.

service please!

Although service in shops has been improving slowly since Poland's accession to the EU, it's not always up to the standards that people from the West expect. You might need to verbally indicate that you require assistance by saying *Proszę Pana/Pani* m/f *pro*·she *pa*·na/*pa*·nee (Excuse me).

If the service happens to be slow and grumpy, don't take it personally. It's a hangover from the Communist past and a reflection of the low wages still paid in the service industry. Your most effective ally in these circumstances is a smile and an attempt at friendliness.

making a purchase

I'm just looking.
Tylko oglądam.　　　　　　　　til·ko o·*glon*·dam

I'd like to buy (an adaptor plug).
Chcę kupić (adapter　　　　khtse *koo*·peech (a·*da*·pter
do wtyczki).　　　　　　　　do *ftich*·kee)

Can I look at it?
Czy mogę to zobaczyć?　　　chi *mo*·ge to zo·*ba*·chich

How much is it?
Ile to kosztuje?　　　　　　　*ee*·le to kosh·*too*·ye

Can you write down the price?
Proszę napisać cenę.　　　　pro·she na·*pee*·sach *tse*·ne

Do you have any others?
Czy są jakieś inne?　　　　　chi som *ya*·kyesh *ee*·ne

The quality isn't good.
To nie jest dobrej　　　　　　to nye yest *do*·brey
jakości.　　　　　　　　　　　ya·*kosh*·chee

Is this (240) volts?
Czy to działa na　　　　　　　chi to *jya*·wa na
(dwieście czterdzieści)　　　　(*dvyesh*·chye chter·*jyesh*·chee)
woltów?　　　　　　　　　　　*vol*·toof

Do you accept ...?　　*Czy mogę*　　　　chi *mo*·ge
　　　　　　　　　　　　zapłacić ...?　　za·*pwa*·cheech ...
　　credit cards　　　*kartą*　　　　　*kar*·tom
　　　　　　　　　　　　kredytową　　　kre·di·*to*·vom
　　debit cards　　　*kartą*　　　　　*kar*·tom
　　　　　　　　　　　　debetową　　　de·be·*to*·vom
　　travellers　　　　*czekami*　　　　che·*ka*·mee
　　　cheques　　　　*podróżnymi*　　pod·roozh·*ni*·mee

Could I have a ..., please?	Czy moge prosić o ...?	chi *mo*·ge pro·sheech o ...
bag	torbę	*tor*·be
receipt	rachunek	ra·*khoo*·nek
I'd like ..., please.	Proszę o ...	pro·she o ...
a refund	zwrot pieniędzy	zvrot pye·*nyen*·dzi
my change	moją resztę	mo·yom *resh*·te

I don't need a bag, thanks.
*Dziękuję, nie
potrzebuję torby.*
jyen·*koo*·ye nye
po·tshe·*boo*·ye *tor*·bi

Could I have it wrapped?
Proszę zapakować.
pro·she za·pa·*ko*·vach

Does it have a guarantee?
Czy to ma gwarancję?
chi to ma gva·*ran*·tsye

Can I have it sent abroad?
*Czy mogę to wysłać
za granicę?*
chi *mo*·ge to *vi*·swach
za gra·*nee*·tse

Can you order it for me?
*Czy może pan/pani
to dla mnie zamówić?* m/f
chi *mo*·zhe pan/*pa*·nee
to dla mnye za·*moo*·veech

Can I pick it up later?
*Czy mogę odebrać
to później?*
chi *mo*·ge o·*de*·brach
to *poozh*·nyey

It's faulty.
To jest wadliwe.
to yest vad·*lee*·ve

I'd like to return this.
*Chciałem/am to
zwrócić.* m/f
khchow·em/am to
zvroo·cheech

local talk		
bargain	*okazja* f	o·*kaz*·ya
rip-off	*zdzierstwo* n	zjyerst·fo
specials	*promocja* f	pro·*mo*·tsya
sale	*wyprzedaż* m	vip·*she*·dash

bargaining

That's too expensive.
To jest za drogie. · to yest za *dro*·gye

Can you lower the price?
Czy może pan/pani · chi *mo*·zhe pan/*pa*·nee
obniżyć cenę? m/f · ob·*nee*·zhich *tse*·ne

Do you have something cheaper?
Czy jest coś tańszego? · chi yest tsosh tan'·*she*·go

What's your final price?
Jaka jest pana/pani · *ya*·ka yest *pa*·na/*pa*·nee
ostateczna cena? m/f · os·ta·*tech*·na *tse*·na

I'll give you (10 złotys).
Dam panu/pani · dam *pa*·noo/*pa*·nee
(dziesięć złotych). m/f · (*jye*·shench *zwo*·tikh)

books & reading

Do you have ...?	*Czy jest ...?*	chi yest ...
a book by	*książka*	*kshyonsh*·ka
(Ryszard	*(Ryszarda*	(ri·*shar*·da
Kapuscinski)	*Kapuściń-*	ka·poosh·cheen'·
	skiego)	*skye*·go)
an entertainment	*informator*	een·for·*ma*·tor
guide	*rozrywkowy*	roz·rif·*ko*·vi

listen for ...

W czym mogę pomóc?	
v chim *mo*·ge *po*·moots	**Can I help you?**
Czy coś jeszcze?	
chi tsosh *yesh*·che	**Anything else?**
Nie, nie ma.	
nye nye ma	**No, we don't have any.**

If you want to immerse yourself in the very essence of Polish culture, there's no better way than delving into the works of the romantic poet and patriot Adam Mickiewicz (1798–1855). Mickiewicz (pronounced meets·kye·veech) is to the Poles what Shakespeare is to the British, which is to say he's a cultural icon of the first order. His best-known work is the epic book-length poem *Pan Tadeusz* pan ta·*de*·oosh, written in 1834, which you should be able to find in English translation.

Your Polish acquaintances will be impressed no end should they discover that you're reading Mickiewicz. Much to the chagrin of Poles, the works of Mickiewicz (who's considered the greatest Slavic poet after Pushkin) are little known beyond Polish borders.

Is there an English-language …?	*Czy jest tu …* *angielski/a?* m/f	chi yest too … an·*gyel*·skee/ska
bookshop	*księgarnia* f	kshyen·*gar*·nya
section	*dział* m	jyow
I'd like a …	*Chciałem/am …* m/f	khchow·em/am …
dictionary	*słownik*	*swov*·neek
newspaper	*gazetę*	ga·*ze*·te
(in English)	*(w języku* *angielskim)*	(v yen·*zi*·koo an·*gyel*·skeem)
notepad	*notatnik*	no·*tat*·neek

Can you recommend a good book?
Czy może mi pan/pani chi *mo*·zhe mee pan/*pa*·nee
coś polecić? tsosh po·*le*·cheech

Do you have Lonely Planet guidebooks?
Czy są przewodniki chi som pshe·vod·*nee*·kee
wydawnictwa Lonely Planet? vi·dav·*neets*·tfa *lon*·li *pla*·net

Do you have Lonely Planet phrasebooks?
Czy są rozmówki chi som roz·*moof*·kee
wydawnictwa Lonely Planet? vi·dav·*neets*·tfa *lon*·li *pla*·net

shopping

79

clothes

My size is ...	*Noszę rozmiar ...*	*no·she roz·myar ...*
(40)	*(czterdzieści)*	*(chter·jyesh·chee)*
large	*L*	*el·ke*
medium	*M*	*em·ke*
small	*S*	*es·ke*

Can I try it on?
Czy mogę przymierzyć?   chi mo·ge pshi·mye·zhich

It doesn't fit.
Nie pasuje.   nye pa·soo·ye

For different types of clothing see the **dictionary**, and for sizes
see **numbers & amounts**, page 33.

hairdressing

I'd like (a) ...	*Chciałem/am ...* m/f	*khchow·em/am ...*
colour	*zafarbować*	*za·far·bo·vach*
	włosy	*vwo·si*
foils/streaks	*folie/pasemka*	*fol·ye/pa·sem·ka*
haircut	*strzyżenie*	*stshi·zhe·nye*
my beard	*podciąć*	*pod·chyonch*
trimmed	*brodę*	*bro·de*
my hair	*umyć/*	*oo·mich/*
washed/dried	*wysuszyć włosy*	*vi·soo·shich vwo·si*
shave	*golenie*	*go·le·nye*
trim	*podciąć*	*pod·chyonch*
	włosy	*vwo·si*

PRACTICAL

80

Don't cut it too short.
Proszę nie podcinać
za krótko.
*pro·she nye pod·chee·nach
za kroot·ko*

Please use a new blade.
Proszę użyć nowe ostrza.
pro·she oo·zhich no·ve ost·sha

Shave it all off!
Proszę ogolić „na zero".
pro·she o·go·leech na ze·ro

I (don't) like it!
(Nie) Podoba mi się!
(nye) po·do·ba mee shye

I should never have come here!
Żałuję że tu
przyszedłem/przyszłam! m/f
*zha·woo·ye zhe too
pshi·shed·wem/pshi·shwam*

music & DVDs

I'd like a ...
Chciałem/am ... m/f
khchow·em/am ...
- **blank tape** czystą taśmę *chis·tom tash·me*
- **CD** płytę CD *pwi·te tse de*
- **DVD** płytę DVD *pwi·te dee vee dee*
- **video tape** taśmę wideo *tash·me vee·de·o*

I'm looking for something by (Henryk Górecki).
Szukam czegoś
(Henryka Góreckiego).
*shoo·kam che·gosh
(hen·ri·ka goo·rets·kye·go)*

What's their best recording?
Jakie jest ich
najlepsze nagranie?
*ya·kye yest eekh
nai·lep·she na·gra·nye*

Can I listen to this?
Czy mogę tego posłuchać?
chi mo·ge te·go po·swoo·khach

Will this work on any DVD player?
Czy to będzie grało na
każdym odtwarzaczu?
*chi to ben·jye gra·wo na
kazh·dim odt·fa·zha·choo*

Is this for a (PAL/NTSC) system?
Czy to jest na system
(PAL/NTSC)?
*chi to yest na sis·tem
(pal/en te es tse)*

shopping

81

video & photography

... camera	aparat ... m	a·pa·rat ...
digital	cyfrowy	tsi·fro·vi
disposable	jednorazowy	yed·no·ra·zo·vi
underwater	wodoszczelny	vo·dosh·chel·ni
video camera	kamera wideo f	ka·me·ra vee·de·o
Can you ...?	Czy może pan/ pani ...? m/f	chi mo·zhe pan/ pa·nee ...
develop this film	wywołać ten film	vi·vo·wach ten film
enlarge this photo	powiększyć to zdjęcie	po·vyenk·shich to zdyen·chye
load my film	założyć film	za·wo·zhich film
print digital photos	zrobić odbitki zdjęcia cyfrowe	zro·beech od·beet·kee zdyen·cha tsif·ro·ve
recharge the battery for my digital camera	naładować baterię do mojego aparatu cyfrowego	na·wa·do·vach ba·te·rye do mo·ye·go a·pa·ra·too tsif·ro·ve·go
transfer photos from my camera to CD	skopiować zdjęcia z mojego aparatu na płytę kompaktową	sko·pyo·vach zdyen·chya z mo·ye·go a·pa·ra·too na pwi·te kom·pak·to·vom
Do you have ... for this camera?	Czy są ... do tego aparatu?	chi som ... do te·go a·pa·ra·too
batteries	baterie	ba·te·rye
flashbulbs	żarówki	zha·roof·kee
(zoom) lenses	soczewki	so·chef·kee
light meters	światłomierze	shfyat·wo·mye·zhe
memory cards	karty pamięci	kar·ti pa·myen·chee

I need ... film for this camera.	Potrzebuję film ... do tego aparatu.	po·tshe·*boo*·ye film ... do *te*·go a·pa·*ra*·too
APS	APS	a pe es
B&W	panchromatyczny	pan·khro·ma·*tich*·ni
colour	kolorowy	ko·lo·*ro*·vi
slide	do slajdów	do *slai*·doof
(200) ASA	(200) ASA	(dvyesh·chye) *a*·sa

I need a cable to connect my camera to a computer.
Potrzebuję kabel do podłączenia aparatu do komputera.
po·tshe·*boo*·ye *ka*·bel do pod·won·*che*·nya a·pa·*ra*·too do kom·poo·*te*·ra

I need a cable to recharge this battery.
Potrzebuję kabel do ładowania tej baterii.
po·tshe·*boo*·ye *ka*·bel do wa·do·*va*·nya tey ba·*ter*·yee

I need a video cassette for this camera.
Potrzebuję taśmę wideo do tej kamery.
po·tshe·*boo*·ye *tash*·me vee·*de*·o do tey ka·*me*·ri

When will it be ready?
Na kiedy będzie gotowe?
na *kye*·di *ben*·jye go·*to*·ve

How much is it?
Ile to kosztuje?
ee·le to kosh·*too*·ye

I need a passport photo taken.
Chciałem/am zrobić zdjęcie paszportowe. m/f
khchow·em/am *zro*·beech *zdyen*·chye pash·por·*to*·ve

I'm not happy with these photos.
Nie jestem zadowolony/a z tych zdjęć. m/f
nye *ye*·stem za·do·vo·*lo*·ni/na z tikh zdyench

I don't want to pay the full price.
Nie chcę płacić pełnej ceny.
nye khtse *pwa*·cheech *pew*·ney *tse*·ni

repairs

Can I have my … repaired here?

Czy mogę tu oddać …
do naprawy?

chi *mo*·ge too *ot*·dach …
do na·*pra*·vi

When will my ... be ready?	*Na kiedy będzie gotowy/a ...? m/f*	na *kye*·di *ben*·jye go·to·vi/va ...
backpack	*mój plecak* m	mooy *ple*·tsak
bag	*moja torba* f	*mo*·ya *tor*·ba
(video) camera	*moja kamera (wideo)* f	*mo*·ya ka·*me*·ra (vee·*de*·o)

When will my ... be ready?	*Na kiedy będą gotowe ...?*	na *kye*·di *ben*·dom go·to·ve ...
(sun)glasses	*moje okulary (przeciw-słoneczne)*	*mo*·ye o·koo·*la*·ri (pshe·*cheef*·swo·*nech*·ne)
shoes	*moje buty*	*mo*·ye *boo*·ti

---

souvenirs

If it's Polish crafts you're after, seek out the network of shops that sell the artefacts made by local artisans which are known as *Cepelia* tse·*pe*·lya.

amber jewellery	*biżuteria z bursztynu* f	bee·zhoo·*ter*·ya z boorsh·*ti*·noo
Ćmielów porcelain	*porcelana ćmielowska* f	por·tse·*la*·na chmye·*lof*·ska
folk art	*sztuka ludowa* f	*shtoo*·ka loo·*do*·va
painted glass	*kolorowe szkło* n	ko·lo·*ro*·ve shkwo
posters	*plakaty* pl	pla·*ka*·ti
Silesian cut glass	*kryształy śląskie* pl	krish·*ta*·wi *shlons*·kye
Toruń gingerbread	*pierniki toruńskie* pl	pyer·*nee*·kee to·*roon*´·skye

the internet

internet

Where's the local internet café?
Gdzie jest kawiarnia gjye yest ka·*vyar*·nya
internetowa? een·ter·ne·*to*·va

I'd like to ...	*Chciałem/am ...* m/f	khchow·em/am ...
check my	*sprawdzić*	*sprav*·jeech
email	*mój email*	mooy *ee*·mayl
burn a CD	*wypalić*	vi·*pa*·leech
	kompakt	*kom*·pakt
download my	*pobrać moje*	*po*·brach *mo*·ye
photos	*zdjęcia*	*zdyen*·chya
get internet	*podłączyć się*	pod·*won*·chich shye
access	*do internetu*	do een·ter·*ne*·too
use a printer	*użyć*	*oo*·zhich
	drukarki	droo·*kar*·kee
use a scanner	*użyć skaner*	*oo*·zhich *ska*·ner
Do you have ...?	*Czy ma pan/*	chi ma pan/
	pani ...? m/f	*pa*·nee ...
Macs	*Mcintosha*	ma·keen·*to*·sha
PCs	*peceta*	pe·*tse*·ta
a Zip drive	*napęd Zip*	*na*·pend zeep
Can I connect	*Czy mogę*	chi *mo*·ge
my ... to this	*podłączyć ... do*	pod·*won*·chich ... do
computer?	*tego komputera?*	*te*·go kom·poo·*te*·ra
camera	*aparat*	a·*pa*·rat
media player	*odtwarzacz*	odt·*fa*·zhach
	multimedialny	mool·tee·me·*dyal*·ni
portable hard	*zewnętrzny*	zev·*nentsh*·ni
drive	*dysk twardy*	disk *tfar*·di
USB drive	*dysk USB*	disk oo es be

communications

How much per ...?	*Ile kosztuje za ...?*	*ee·le kosh·too·ye za ...*
hour	*godzinę*	*go·jee·ne*
(five) minutes	*(pięć) minut*	*(pyench) mee·noot*
page	*stronę*	*stro·ne*

How do I log on?	*Jak się mam zalogować?*	*yak shye mam za·lo·go·vach*
Bloody internet!	*Cholerny internet!*	*kho·ler·ni een·ter·net*
It's crashed.	*Zawiesił się.*	*za·vye·sheew shye*
I've finished.	*Skończyłem/ am.* m/f	*skon·chi·wem/ wam*

mobile/cell phone

telefon komórkowy

What are the call rates?
Jakie są stawki za rozmowy?
ya·kye som staf·kee za roz·mo·vi

(Two złotys) per (30) seconds.
(Dwa złote) za (trzydzieści) sekund.
(dva zwo·te) za (tshi·jyesh·chee) se·koond

I'd like a ...	*Chciałem/am ...* m/f	*khchow·em/am ...*
charger for my phone	*ładowarkę do mojego telefonu*	*wa·do·var·ke do mo·ye·go te·le·fo·noo*
mobile/cell phone for hire	*wypożyczyć telefon komórkowy*	*vi·po·zhi·chich te·le·fon ko·moor·ko·vi*
prepaid mobile/ cell phone	*telefon komórkowy na konto z przedpłatą*	*te·le·fon ko·moor·ko·vi na kon·to z pshet·pwa·tom*
SIM card for your network	*kartę SIM na waszą sieć*	*kar·te seem na va·shom shyech*
(flat) battery	*(wyczerpana) bateria* f	*(vi·cher·pa·na) ba·ter·ya*
(send an) SMS	*(wysłać) SMS* m	*(vi·swach) es em es*

phone

What's your phone number?

Jaki jest pana/pani numer telefonu? m/f pol	*ya·*kee yest *pa·*na/*pa·*nee *noo·*mer te·le·*fo·*noo
Jaki jest twój numer telefonu? inf	*ya·*kee yest tfooy *noo·*mer te·le·*fo·*noo

Where's the nearest public phone?

Gdzie jest najbliższy telefon?	gjye yest nai·*bleezh·*shi te·*le·*fon

Can I look at a phone book?

Czy mogę zobaczyć książkę telefoniczną?	chi *mo·*ge zo·*ba·*chich *kshyonzh·*ke te·le·fo·*neech·*nom

Can I have some coins/tokens?

Czy mogę prosić o kilka monet/żetonów?	chi *mo·*ge *pro·*sheech o *keel·*ka *mo·*net/zhe·*to·*noof

I want to …	*Chciałem/am …* m/f	khchow·em/am …
buy a chip phonecard	*kupić czipową kartę telefoniczną*	*koo·*peech chee·*po·*vom *kar·*te te·le·fo·*neech·*nom
call (Singapore)	*zadzwonić do (Singapuru)*	zad·*zvo·*neech do (seen·ga·*poo·*roo)
make a (local) call	*zadzwonić (pod lokalny numer)*	zad·*zvo·*neech (pod lo·*kal·*ni *noo·*mer)
reverse the charges	*zamówić rozmowę na koszt odbiorcy*	za·*moo·*veech roz·*mo·*ve na kosht od·*byor·*tsi
send an email/ SMS	*wysłać email/ SMS*	*vi·*swach *e·*mayl/ es em es
speak for (five) minutes	*rozmawiać przez (pięć) minut*	roz·*ma·*vyach pshes (pyench) *mee·*noot

phone talk

Here are a few useful informal words and phrases for telephone conversations, some of which you might see in SMS messages:

Cze/Cz.	che	Hi.
Dam znać.	dam znach	I'll let you know.
Dozo.	do·zo	See you later.
Hej/Witam.	hey/*vee*·tam	Hi.
Hello.	he·lo	Hello.
Nara.	na·ra	See you later.
Nawzajem.	nav·*za*·yem	Same to you.
Odezwę się.	o·*dez*·ve shye	I'll be in touch.
Oki.	o·kee	OK.
Spoko.	spo·ko	No worries.

How much does ... cost?   *Ile kosztuje ...?*   ee·le kosh·*too*·ye ...

a (three)-minute call	*rozmowa (trzy) minutowa*	roz·*mo*·va (tshi) mee·noo·*to*·va
each extra minute	*każda dodatkowa minuta*	*kazh*·da do·dat·*ko*·va mee·*noo*·ta

What's the country code for (New Zealand)?
Jaki jest numer kierunkowy do (Nowej Zelandii)?
ya·kee yest noo·mer kye·roon·ko·vi do (no·vey ze·lan·dyee)

It's engaged.
Jest zajęty.
yest za·*yen*·ti

The connection's bad.
Jakość połączenia jest zła.
ya·koshch po·won·*che*·nya yest zwa

I've been cut off.
Zostałem/łam rozłączony/na. m/f
zo·*sta*·wem/wam roz·won·*cho*·ni/na

Hello.
Halo.
ha·lo

Can I speak to (Wojtek)?

Czy mogę rozmawiać z (Wojtkiem)?

chi *mo*·ge roz·*ma*·vyach z (*voyt*·kyem)

It's …

Tu …

too …

Please tell him/her I called.

Proszę mu/jej powiedzieć, że dzwoniłem/am. m/f

pro·she moo/yey po·*vye*·jyech zhe dzvo·*nee*·wem/wam

Can I leave a message?

Czy mogę zostawić wiadomość?

chi *mo*·ge zos·*ta*·veech vya·*do*·moshch

My number is …

Mój numer telefonu jest …

mooy *noo*·mer te·le·*fo*·noo yest …

I don't have a contact number.

Nie mam numeru telefonicznego.

nye mam noo·*me*·roo te·le·fo·neech·*ne*·go

I'll call back later.

Zadzwonię później.

zad·*zvo*·nye *poozh*·nyey

---

listen for …

Chwileczkę.	khfee·*lech*·ke	**One moment.**
Kto mówi?	kto *moo*·vee	**Who's calling?**
Nie ma (go/jej).	nye ma (go/yey)	**(He/She) isn't here.**
Pomyłka.	po·*miw*·ka	**Wrong number.**

---

post office

poczta

I want to send a …	*Chciałem/am wysłać … m/f*	*khchow*·em/am *vis*·wach …
fax	*faks*	faks
letter	*list*	leest
parcel	*paczkę*	*pach*·ke
postcard	*pocztówkę*	poch·*toof*·ke

communications

89

I want to buy a/an ...	Chciałem/am kupić ... m/f	khchow·em/am koo·peech ...
(padded) envelope	kopertę (bąbelkową)	ko·per·te (bom·bel·ko·vom)
stamp	znaczek	zna·chek
customs declaration	deklaracja celna f	de·kla·ra·tsya tsel·na
domestic	krajowy	kra·yo·vi
fragile	kruchy	kroo·khi
international	zagraniczny	za·gra·neech·ni
mail	przesyłka f	pshe·siw·ka
postcode	kod pocztowy m	kod poch·to·vi
PO box	skrytka pocztowa f	skrit·ka poch·to·va

Please send it by air/surface mail to (Australia).

Proszę wysłać to pocztą lotniczą/lądową do (Australii).

pro·she vis·wach to poch·tom lot·nee·chom/lon·do·vom do (aus·tra·lyee)

It contains (souvenirs).

Zawiera (upominki).

za·vye·ra (oo·po·meen·kee)

Where's the poste restante section?

Gdzie jest dział z poste restante?

gjye yest jyow z pos·te res·tant

Is there any mail for me?

Czy jest dla mnie jakaś korespondencja?

chi yest dla mnye ya·kash ko·res·pon·den·tsya

snail mail		
by ... mail	pocztą ...	poch·tom ...
express	ekspresową	eks·pre·so·vom
registered	poleconą	po·le·tso·nom
sea	morską	mor·skom
surface	lądową	lon·do·vom
by airmail	pocztą lotniczą	poch·tom lot·nee·chom

banking

w banku

Popular places to change money are the *kantor walut kan·tor va·loot* (small foreign exchange offices), as they usually offer a better rate than banks. Unlike a bank, a *kantor* (as they're commonly called) doesn't charge a commission or require any paperwork.

What times/days is the bank open?

W jakich godzinach/ — v ya·keekh go·jee·nakh/
dniach jest bank otwarty? — dnyakh yest bank ot·far·ti

Where can I …?	Gdzie mogę …?	gjye mo·ge …
I'd like to …	Chciałem/am … m/f	khchow·em/am …
cash a cheque	wymienić czek	vi·mye·neech chek
	na gotówkę	na go·toof·ke
change a travellers cheque	wymienić czek podróżny	vi·mye·neech chek po·droozh·ni
change money	wymienić pieniądze	vi·mye·neech pye·nyon·dze
get a cash advance	dostać zaliczkę na moją kartę kredytową	dos·tach za·leech·ke na mo·yom kar·te kre·di·to·vom
get change for this note	rozmienić pieniądze	roz·mye·neech pye·nyon·dze
withdraw money	wypłacić pieniądze	vi·pwa·cheech pye·nyon·dze
Where's …?	Gdzie jest …?	gjye yest …
an ATM	bankomat	ban·ko·mat
a foreign exchange office	kantor walut	kan·tor va·loot

banking

91

The ATM took my card.
Bankomat połknął — ban·ko·mat *powk·*now
moją kartę. — mo·yom kar·te

I've forgotten my PIN.
Zapomniałem/am — za·pom·*nyow·*em/am
mój numer PIN. m/f — mooy noo·mer peen

Can I use my credit card to withdraw money?
Czy mogę użyć — chi mo·ge oo·zhich
kartę kredytową do — kar·te kre·di·to·vom do
wypłacenia pieniędzy? — vi·pwa·tse·nya pye·nyen·dzi

Has my money arrived yet?
Czy doszły już moje — chi dosh·wi yoosh mo·ye
pieniądze? — pye·nyon·dze

How long will it take to arrive?
Ile czasu zajmie — ee·le cha·soo zai·mye
przesyłka? — pshe·siw·ka

What's the …? — *Jaki/a jest …?* m/f — ya·kee/ka yest …
  exchange rate — *kurs wymiany* m — koors vi·mya·ni
  charge for that — *prowizja* f — pro·veez·ya

For other useful phrases, see **money**, page 43.

For other useful phrases, see **money**, page 43.

listen for …		
dokument	do·koo·ment	**identification**
tożsamości m	tozh·sa·mosh·chee	
paszport m	pash·port	**passport**

Jest pewien problem.
yest pe·vyen prob·lem — **There's a problem.**

Nie ma pan/pani pieniędzy na koncie. m/f
nye ma pan/pa·nee — **You have no funds left.**
pye·nyen·dzi na kon·chye

Nie możemy tego zrobić.
nye mo·zhe·mi te·go zro·beech — **We can't do that.**

Proszę tu podpisać.
pro·she too pod·pee·sach — **Sign here.**

PRACTICAL

92

I'd like a/an …	*Chciałem/am …* m/f	khchow·em/am …
audio set	*zestaw audio*	zes·taf ow·dyo
catalogue	*broszurę*	bro·shoo·re
guidebook	*przewodnik*	pshe·vod·neek
(in English)	*(po angielsku)*	(po an·gyel·skoo)
(local) map	*mapę (okolic)*	ma·pe (o·ko·leets)

Do you have information on … sights?	*Czy jest informcja o miejscach o szczególnych walorach …?*	chi yest een·for·ma·tsya o myeys·tsakh o shche·gool·nikh va·lo·rakh …
cultural	*kulturowych*	kool·too·ro·vikh
historical	*historycznych*	khees·to·rich·nikh
religious	*religijnych*	re·lee·geey·nikh

I'd like to see …
Chciałem/am obejrzeć … m/f khchow·em/am o·bey·zhech …

What's that?
Co to jest? tso to yest

Who built/made it?
Kto to zbudował/zrobił? kto to zboo·do·vow/zro·beew

How old is it?
Ile to ma lat? ee·le to ma lat

Could you take a photo of me?
Czy może pan/pani zrobić mi zdjęcie? m/f chi mo·zhe pan/pa·nee zro·beech mee zdyen·che

Could you take a photo of us?
　　Czy może pan/pani zrobić　　　chi *mo*·zhe pan/*pa*·ni
　　nam zdjęcie? m/f　　　　　　　*zro*·beech nam *zdyen*·chye

Can I take a photo (of you)?
　　Czy mogę (panu/pani)　　　　chi *mo*·ge (*pa*·noo/*pa*·nee)
　　zrobić zdjęcie? m/f　　　　　*zro*·beech *zdyen*·chye

I'll send you the photo.
　　Przyślę panu/pani　　　　　　*pshi*·shle *pa*·noo/*pa*·nee
　　zdjęcie. m/f　　　　　　　　　*zdyen*·chye

---

skansen hopping

High on any sightseeing agenda in Poland is a visit to a *skansen skan*·sen. *Skansen* is a word of Scandinavian origin referring to an open-air ethnographic museum. Aimed at preserving traditional folk culture and architecture, a *skansen* gathers together a selection of typical, mostly wooden rural buildings, collected from a region and reassembled to look like a village. The buildings are furnished and decorated in their traditional style. Visiting one is a little like a time-capsule travel experience, giving visitors insights into the life, work and customs of bygone days.

The term *skansen* is a collective term and museums of this kind may be given one of the following three specific designations as well: *muzeum budownictwa ludowego* moo·ze·oom boo·dov·*neets*·tva loo·do·*ve*·go (museum of folk architecture), *muzeum wsi* moo·ze·oom fshee (museum of the village) or *park etnograficzny* park et·no·gra·*feech*·ni (ethnographic park).

---

getting in

wstęp

What time does it open?
　　O której godzinie jest　　　o *ktoo*·rey go·*jee*·nye yest
　　otwarte?　　　　　　　　　ot·*far*·te

What time does it close?
　　O której godzinie jest　　　o *ktoo*·rey go·*jee*·nye yest
　　zamknięte?　　　　　　　zam·*knyen*·te

What's the admission charge?
Ile kosztuje wstęp?   ee·le kosh·*too*·ye fstemp

Is there a discount for ...?	*Czy jest zniżka dla...?*	chi yest *zneezh*·ka dla ...
children	*dzieci*	*jye*·chee
families	*rodzin*	*ro*·jeen
groups	*grup*	groop
older people	*osób starszych*	*o*·soob *star*·shikh
pensioners	*emerytów*	e·me·*ri*·toof
students	*studentów*	stoo·*den*·toof

tours

When's the next ...?	*Kiedy jest następna wycieczka ...?*	*kye*·di yest nas·*temp*·na vi·*chyech*·ka ...
boat trip	*statkiem*	*stat*·kyem
day trip	*jednodniowa*	yed·no·*dnyo*·va
(sightseeing) tour	*krajoznawcza*	kra·yo·*znaf*·cha

Is … included?	Czy … wliczone?	chi … vlee·*cho*·ne
accommodation	noclegi są	nots·*le*·gee som
food	wyżywienie jest	vi·zhi·*vye*·nye yest

Is transport included?
Czy transport jest wliczony?   chi *trans*·port yest vlee·*cho*·ni

Can you recommend (a tour)?
Czy może pan/pani polecić (jakąś wycieczkę)? m/f   chi *mo*·zhe pan/*pa*·nee po·*le*·cheech (*ya*·komsh vi·*chyech*·ke)

How long is the tour?
Jak długo trwa wycieczka?   yak *dwoo*·go trfa vi·*chyech*·ka

The guide will pay.
Przewodnik zapłaci.   pshe·*vod*·neek zap·*wa*·chee

What time should we be back?
O której godzinie powinniśmy wrócić?   o *ktoo*·rey go·*jee*·nye po·vee·*neesh*·mi *vroo*·cheech

I've lost my group.
Zgubiłem/am moją grupę. m/f   zgoo·*bee*·wem/wam *mo*·yom *groo*·pe

---

money talks

The Polish currency is the *złoty* zwo·ti, which is also a masculine adjective meaning 'golden'. *Złoty* is often abbreviated to *zł.* but in official documents and banks the abbreviations *PLZ* or *PLN* are used. The final letter in the latter acronym stands for nowy *no*·vi (new) because the currency was revalued after rampant inflation in the '80s.

One *złoty* is the equivalent of 100 *groszy* gro·shi (abbreviated to *gr.*). The word *grosz*, adopted in the 14th century, is said to have entered Polish via Czech from the Middle High German word *grosse* (thick), which was in turn an adaption of the Latin word *grossus* with the same meaning. There's a Polish proverb encouraging thrift that goes:

Grosz do grosza, a będzie kokosza.
grosh do *gro*·sha a *ben*·jye ko·*ko*·sha
(Save your pennies and you'll buy a hen.)

I'm attending a …	Jestem na …	yes·tem na …
conference	konferencji	kon·fe·ren·tsyee
course	kursie	koor·shye
meeting	spotkaniu	spot·ka·nyoo
trade fair	targach	tar·gakh

I'm with …	Jestem …	yes·tem …
(LOT)	zatrudniony/a w (Locie) m/f	za·trood·nyo·ni/na v (lo·chye)
my colleague	z kolegą/ koleżanką m/f	z ko·le·gom/ ko·le·zhan·kom
my colleagues	z kolegami	z ko·le·ga·mee
(two) others	z (dwoma) innymi osobami	z (dvo·ma) ee·ni·mee o·so·ba·mee

I'm alone.
Podróżuję samotnie. po·droo·zhoo·ye sa·mot·nye

I have an appointment with (Mr Mossakowski).
Mam umówione spotkanie z (panem Mossakowskim). mam oo·moo·vyo·ne spot·ka·nye z (pa·nem mo·sa·kof·skeem)

I'm here for (two) days/weeks.
Będę tu przez (dwa) dni/tygodnie. ben·de too pshes (dva) dnee/ti·god·nye

---

oiling the wheels

A verb in common usage in Polish and that might come in handy in business circles is *kombinować* kom·bee·no·vach. It's a product of a complicated history and is virtually untranslatable into English but means something along the lines of: 'to achieve your aim by a mixture of subterfuge, cunning and knowing people in the right places or being able to charm them into acquiescence'.

Here's my ...	Tu jest mój ...	too yest mooy ...
What's your ...?	Jaki jest pana/ pani ...? m/f	ya·kee yest pa·na/ pa·nee ...
address	adres	a·dres
mobile/cell number	numer telefonu komórkowego	noo·mer te·le·fo·noo ko·moor·ko·ve·go
email address	adres emailowy	a·dres e·mai·lo·vi
fax number	numer faksu	noo·mer fak·soo
pager number	numer pagera	noo·mer pey·je·ra
work number	numer telefonu do pracy	noo·mer te·le·fo·noo do pra·tsi

Where's the ...?	Gdzie jest ...?	gjye yest ...
business centre	centrum handlowe	tsen·troom hand·lo·ve
conference	konferencja	kon·fe·ren·tsya
meeting	spotkanie	spot·ka·nye

I need (a/an) ...	Potrzebuję ...	po·tshe·boo·yem ...
computer	komputer	kom·poo·ter
internet connection	połączenie do internetu	po·won·che·nye do een·ter·ne·too
interpreter	tłumacza	twoo·ma·cha
to send a fax	wysłać faks	vis·wach faks

Can I please have your business card?
Czy mogę prosić o pana/ pani wizytówkę? m/f — chi mo·ge pro·sheech o pa·na/ pa·nee vee·zi·toof·ke

That went very well.
Dobrze poszło. — dob·zhe posh·wo

Thank you for your time.
Dziękuję za poświęcony mi czas. — jyen·koo·ye za posh·vyen·tso·ni mee chas

Shall we go for a drink?
Pójdziemy na drinka? — pooy·jye·mi na dreen·ka

Shall we go for a meal?
Pójdziemy coś zjeść? — pooy·jye·mi tsosh zyeshch

It's on me.
Ja funduję. — ya foon·doo·ye

senior & disabled travellers
osoby starsze i niepełnosprawne

I have a disability.
Jestem
niepełnosprawny/a. m/f
yes·tem
nye·pew·no·*sprav*·ni/na

I need assistance.
Potrzebuję pomocy.
po·tshe·*boo*·ye po·*mo*·tsi

Are there disabled toilets?
Czy są toalety dla osób
niepełnosprawnych?
chi som to·a·*le*·ti dla *o*·soob
nye·pew·no·*sprav*·nikh

Is there wheelchair access?
Czy da się wjechać
wózkiem inwalidzkim?
chi da shye *vye*·khach
vooz·kyem een·va·*leets*·keem

How wide is the entrance?
Jak szerokie jest wejście?
yak she·*ro*·kye yest *veysh*·chye

I'm deaf.
Jestem głuchy/a. m/f
yes·tem *gwoo*·khi/kha

I have a hearing aid.
Mam aparat słuchowy.
mam a·*pa*·rat swoo·*kho*·vi

My companion's blind.
Moja osoba
towarzysząca jest
niewidoma.
mo·ya o·*so*·ba
to·va·zhi·*shon*·tsa yest
nye·vee·*do*·ma

Are guide dogs permitted?
Czy psy przewodniki
są dozwolone?
chi psi pshe·vod·*nee*·kee
som doz·vo·*lo*·ne

How many steps are there?
Ile tam jest schodów?
ee·le tam yest *skho*·doof

Is there an lift/elevator?
Czy jest winda?
chi yest *veen*·da

Are there rails in the bathroom?
Czy są poręcze
w łazience?
chi som po·*ren*·che
v wa·*zhyen*·tse

senior & disabled

99

Could you call me a disabled taxi?

Proszę zamówić dla mnie taksówkę dla osób niepełnosprawnych.

pro·she za·*moo*·veech dla mnye tak·*soof*·ke dla o·soob nye·pew·no·*sprav*·nikh

Could you help me cross the street safely?

Proszę mnie przeprowadzić przez ulicę.

pro·she mnye pshe·pro·*va*·jeech pshes oo·*lee*·tse

Is there somewhere I can sit down?

Czy mogę gdzieś usiąść?

chi *mo*·ge gjyesh oo·shyonshch

older person	*osoba starsza* f	o·*so*·ba *star*·sha
person with	*osoba*	o·*so*·ba
a disability	*niepełnosprawna* f	nye·pew·no·*sprav*·na
ramp	*rampa* f	*ram*·pa
walking frame	*rama do chodzenia* f	*ra*·ma do kho·*dze*·nya
walking stick	*laska* f	*las*·ka
wheelchair	*wózek*	*voo*·zek
	inwalidzki m	een·va·*leets*·kee

it's all about you

When speaking Polish you need to use either polite or informal language (indicated in this book by the abbreviations pol and inf). Informal forms use the *ty* ti form of 'you' in the singular and the *wy* vi form in the plural and the corresponding second-person verb forms. As pronouns are often left out, you might just see these verb forms.

Polite language uses the words *pan* pan and *pani* pa·nee for men and women respectively (lit: 'Mr' and 'Mrs') and *państwo* pan'·stfo in the plural. These all translate as 'you' so you'll get very used to hearing them. You use third-person singular verb forms (the same forms as for 'he' and 'she') with *pan* and *pani* and third-person plural forms with *państwo*. For more information, see the **a–z phrasebuilder**, page 23.

In this book we've chosen the appropriate form for the situations that the phrase is used in. For phrases where either form might be suitable, we've given both forms.

travelling with children

podróżowanie z dziećmi

Is there a …?	Czy jest …?	chi yest …
baby change room	przebieralnia dla dzieci	pshe·bye·ral·nya dla jye·chee
child's portion	porcja dla dziecka	por·tsya dla jye·tska
crèche	przedszkole	pshet·shko·le
discount for children	zniżka dla dziecka	zneezh·ka dla jye·tska
family ticket	bilet rodzinny	bee·let ro·jee·ni
I need a/an …	Potrzebuję …	po·tshe·boo·ye …
baby seat	fotelik dla dziecka	fo·te·leek dla jye·tska
(English-speaking) babysitter	opiekunkę do dziecka (mówiącą po angielsku)	o·pye·koon·ke do jye·tska (moo·vyon·tsom po an·gyel·skoo)
booster seat	podstawkę podwyższa-jącą dla dziecka	pod·staf·ke pod·vizh·sha·yon·tsom dla jye·tska
cot	łóżeczko	woo·zhech·ko
highchair	wysokie krzesełko dla dziecka	vi·so·kye kshe·sew·ko dla jye·tska
plastic bag	torbę plastykową	tor·be plas·ti·ko·vom
potty	nocnik	nots·neek
pram	wózek głęboki	voo·zek gwem·bo·kee
pushchair/stroller	wózek spacerowy	voo·zek spa·tse·ro·vi
sick bag	torbę na wymioty	tor·be na vi·myo·ti

Do you sell …?	Czy sprzedajecie …?	chi spshe·da·ye·chye …
baby wipes	chusteczki pielęgnacyjne	khoos·tech·kee pye·leng·na·tsiy·ne
disposable nappies	pieluszki jednorazowe	pye·loosh·kee yed·no·ra·zo·ve
painkillers for infants	środki przeciw-bólowe dla niemowląt	shrod·kee pshe·cheev·boo·lo·ve dla nye·mov·lont
tissues	chusteczki higieniczne	khoos·tech·kee khee·gye·neech·ne

Where's the nearest …?	Gdzie jest najbliższy/e …? m/n	gjye yest nai·bleezh·shi/she …
park	park m	park
playground	plac zabaw m	plats za·baf
swimming pool	basen m	ba·sen
tap	kran m	kran
theme park	wesołe miasteczko n	ve·so·we myas·tech·ko
toyshop	sklep zabawkowy m	sklep za·baf·ko·vi

Is there a child-minding service?
Czy są usługi
pilnowania dzieci?
chi som oos·woo·gee
peel·no·va·nya jye·chee

Are there any good places to take children around here?
Czy są niedaleko jakieś
ciekawe miejsca
dla dzieci?
chi som nye·da·le·ko ya·kyesh
chye·ka·ve myeys·tsa
dla jye·chee

Is there space for a pram?
Czy jest miejsce na wózek?
chi yest myeys·tse na voo·zek

Are children allowed?
Czy dzieci mogą
wchodzić?
chi jye·chee mo·gom
fkho·jeech

Where can I change a nappy/diaper?
Gdzie mogę zmienić
pieluchę?
gjye mo·ge zmye·neech
pye·loo·khe

Do you mind if I breast-feed here?

    Czy będzie panu/pani/   chi *ben·jye pa·*noo/*pa·*nee/
    państwu przeszkadzało   *panst·*foo pshesh·ka·*dza·*wo
    jeśli będę karmiła   yesh·lee ben·de kar·mee·wa
    piersią? m/f/pl   *pyer·*shom

Could I have some paper and pencils, please?

    Czy mogę prosić o   chi *mo·*ge *pro·*sheech o
    papier i kredki?   *pa·*pyer ee *kred·*kee

Is this suitable for (six)-year-old children?

    Czy jest to odpowiednie   chi yest to od·pov·*yed·*nye
    dla dziecka które ma   dla *jye·*tska *ktoo·*re ma
    (sześć) lat?   (sheshch) lat

Do you know a dentist/doctor who is good with children?

    Czy pan/pani zna dobrego   chi pan/*pa·*nee zna do·*bre·*go
    dentystę/lekarza   den·*tis·*te/le·*ka·*zha
    dla dzieci? m/f   dla *jye·*chee

If your child is sick, see **health**, page 193.

talking with children

rozmawianie z dziećmi

What's your name?

    Jak masz na imię?   yak mash na *ee·*mye

How old are you?

    Ile masz lat?   *ee·*le mash lat

When's your birthday?

    Kiedy masz urodziny?   *kye·*di mash oo·ro·*jee·*ni

Do you go to school/kindergarten?

    Czy chodzisz do szkoły/   chi *kho·*jeesh do *shko·*wi/
    przedszkola?   pshet·*shko·*la

Do you like …?	Czy lubisz …?	chi *loo*·beesh …
school	szkołę	*shko*·we
sport	sport	sport
your teacher	swojego	svo·*ye*·go
	nauczyciela	na·oo·chi·*chye*·la

talking about children

When's the baby due?
Kiedy urodzi się dziecko? kye·di oo·*ro*·jee shye *jyet*·sko

What are you going to call the baby?
Jak dziecko będzie yak *jyet*·sko ben·jye
miało na imię? *myow*·o na ee·mye

How many children do you have?
Ile pan/pani ma ee·le pan/*pa*·nee ma
dzieci? m/f *jye*·chee

What a beautiful child!
Ależ piękne dziecko! *a*·lesh pyenk·ne *jyet*·sko

Is it a boy or a girl?
Czy to jest chłopiec czy chi to yest *khwo*·pyets chi
dziewczynka? jev·*chin*·ka

How old is he/she?
Ile ma lat? ee·le ma lat

How many months is he/she?
Ile ma miesięcy? ee·le ma mye·*shyen*·tsi

Does he/she go to school?
Czy on/ona chodzi chi on/*o*·na *kho*·jee
do szkoły? do *shko*·wi

What's his/her name?
Jak ma na imię? yak ma na ee·mye

He/She …	On/Ona …	on/o·na …
has your eyes	ma pana/pani	ma *pa*·na/*pa*·nee
	oczy m/f	o·chi
looks like you	jest podobny/a	yest po·*dob*·ni/na
	do pana/pani m/f	do *pa*·na/*pa*·nee

1# SOCIAL > meeting people

spotkania z ludźmi

basics

podstawy

Yes.	*Tak.*	tak
No.	*Nie.*	nye
Please.	*Proszę.*	*pro*·she
Thank you (very much).	*Dziękuję (bardzo).*	jyen·*koo*·ye (*bar*·dzo)
You're welcome.	*Proszę.*	*pro*·she
Excuse me/Sorry.	*Przepraszam.*	pshe·*pra*·sham

greetings & goodbyes

powitania i pożegnania

Be prepared to shake hands often in Poland as it's the usual manner of greeting. Etiquette dictates that a handshake be initiated by a woman (if one is present), the older party or a superior at work. Family members or close friends also kiss each other three times on the cheeks in the French manner on special occasions such as parties, welcomes or farewells.

Hello/Hi.	*Cześć.*	cheshch
Good afternoon/ day/morning.	*Dzień dobry.*	jyen´ *do*·bri
Good evening.	*Dobry wieczór.*	*do*·bri *vye*·choor
How are you?	*Jak pan/pani się miewa?* m/f pol	yak pan/*pa*·nee shye *mye*·va
	Jak się masz? inf	yak shye mash
Fine. And you?	*Dobrze.*	*dob*·zhe
	A pan/pani? m/f pol	a pan/*pa*·nee
	Dobrze. A ty? inf	*dob*·zhe a ti

meeting people

105

What's your first name?

Jak pan/pani ma
na imię? m/f pol

yak pan/*pa*·nee ma
na *ee*·mye

Jak masz na imię? inf

yak mash na *ee*·mye

My first name is …

Mam na imię …

mam na *ee*·mye …

What's your (full) name?

Jak się pan/pani
nazywa? m/f pol

yak shye *pa*·na/*pa*·nee
na·*zi*·va

Jakie się nazywasz? inf

yak shye na·*zi*·vash

My (full) name is …

Nazywam się …

na·*zi*·vam shye …

I'd like to introduce you to …

Chciałem/am pana/
panią przedstawić … m/f pol

khchow·em/am *pa*·na/
pa·nyom pshet·*sta*·veech …

Chciałem/am cię
przedstawić … inf

khchow·em/am chye
pshet·*sta*·veech …

I'm pleased to meet you.

Miło mi pana/
panią poznać. m/f pol

mee·wo mee *pa*·na/
pa·nyom *po*·znach

Miło mi
ciebie poznać. inf

mee·wo mee
chye·bye *po*·znach

hi there!

It's best not to use the informal *cześć!* cheshch (hi) with
people who are older than you as it could be construed
as impolite. Use *dzień dobry* jyen' *do*·bri (lit: good day) as
the all-purpose greeting in the morning, daytime and
early evening. In the late evening use *dobry wieczór* do·bri
vye·choor (lit: good evening).

SOCIAL

106

This is my ...	To jest mój/moja/	to yest mooy/mo·ya/
	moje ... m/f/n	mo·ye ...
child	dziecko n	jye·tsko
colleague	kolega/	ko·le·ga/
	koleżanka m/f	ko·le·zhan·ka
friend	przyjaciel/	pzhi·ya·chyel/
	przyjaciółka m/f	pzhi·ya·chyoow·ka
husband	mąż m	monzh
partner	partner/	part·ner/
(intimate)	partnerka m/f	part·ner·ka
wife	żona f	zho·na

See you later.	Do zobaczenia.	do zo·ba·che·nya
Bye.	Pa.	pa
Goodbye.	Do widzenia.	do vee·dze·nya
Good night.	Dobranoc.	do·bra·nots

---

knights ahoy!

Sisters, don't panic if an older man kisses you on the hand. This rather antiquated custom, known as *całowanie w rękę* tsa·wo·*va*·nye v *ren*·ke, was once the usual cross-gender greeting and is still practised by chivalrous members of the older generation.

---

addressing people

Polish society tends to be quite conservative and formal. One manifestation of this is the rules for addressing people. Never address a person who's older than you or senior to you by their first name unless you're invited to. An invitation to do so is called *bruderszaft* broo·der·shaft and is often quite a formal occasion officially completed with a toast of vodka. If you're the older party it's OK to use a person's first name, as it is with your peers. In all other cases, address people by their professional title, a selection of which are given on the next page.

chairperson	*Panie Prezesie/*	*pa·nye pre·ze·shye/*
	Pani Prezes m/f	*pa·nee pre·zes*
director	*Panie Dyrektorze/*	*pa·nye di·rek·to·zhe/*
	Pani Dyrektor m/f	*pa·nee di·rek·tor*
doctor/dentist	*Panie Doktorze/*	*pa·nye dok·to·zhe/*
	Pani Doktor m/f	*pa·nee dok·tor*
engineer	*Panie*	*pa·nye*
	Inżynierze/	*een·zhi·nye·zhe/*
	Pani Inżynier m/f	*pa·nee een·zhi·nyer*
professor/high-school teacher	*Panie Profesorze/*	*pa·nye pro·fe·so·zhe/*
	Pani Profesor m/f	*pa·nee pro·fe·sor*

In everyday situations such as in the street or in shops, address people by using the forms below. While they translate literally as 'Mr', 'Mrs' etc, they're used just as you'd use 'you' in English.

Mr/Sir	*Pan*	pan
Ms/Mrs/Madam	*Pani*	*pa·nee*
Miss	*Panna*	*pa·na*

making conversation

rozpoczynanie rozmowy

You can converse freely on most topics with Poles but tread lightly when it comes to the holy-of-holies – the Catholic Church.

What's new?
  Co tam nowego? tso tam no·ve·go

What a beautiful day!
  Co za piękny dzień! tso za *pyenk*·ni jyen´

Nice/Awful weather, isn't it?
  Piękna/Okropna *pyenk*·na/o·*kro*·pna
  pogoda, prawda? po·*go*·da *prav*·da

Do you live here?
  Czy pan/pani tu chi pan/*pa*·nee too
  mieszka? m/f pol *myesh*·ka
  Czy tu mieszkasz? inf chi too *myesh*·kash

Where are you going?

Dokąd pan/pani idzie? m/f pol
do·kond pan/pa·nee ee·jye

Dokąd idziesz? inf
do·kond ee·jyesh

What are you doing?

Co pan/pani robi? m/f pol
tso pan/pa·nee ro·bee

Co robisz? inf
tso ro·beesh

Do you like it here?

Czy się panu/pani tu podoba? m/f pol
chi shye pa·noo/pa·nee too po·do·ba

Czy ci się tu podoba? inf
chi chee shye too po·do·ba

I love it here.

Bardzo mi się tu podoba.
bar·dzo mee shye too po·do·ba

What's this called?

Jak się to nazywa?
yak shye to na·zi·va

That's (beautiful), isn't it?

To jest (piękne), prawda?
to yest (pyenk·ne) prav·da

How long are you here for?

Jak długo pan/pani tutaj będzie? m/f pol
yak dwoo·go pan/pa·nee too·tai ben·jye

Jak długo tutaj będziesz? inf
yak dwoo·go too·tai ben·jyesh

I'm here for (four) weeks/days.

Będę tutaj przez (cztery) tygodnie/dni.
ben·de too·tai pshes (chte·ri) ti·go·dnye/dnee

I'm here ...	Jestem tutaj ...	yes·tem too·tai ...
for a holiday	na wakacjach	na va·kats·yakh
on business	służbowo	swoozh·bo·vo
to study	na studiach	na stood·yakh

Hey!	*Cześć!*	cheshch
Great!	*Świetnie!*	shvyet·nye
Just a minute.	*Chwileczkę.*	khfee·lech·ke
Just joking.	*Żartuję.*	zhar·too·ye
It's OK.	*W porządku.*	v po·zhont·koo
Maybe.	*Może.*	mo·zhe
No problem.	*Nie ma sprawy.*	nye ma spra·vi
No way!	*W żadnym bądź razie.*	v zhad·nim bonj ra·zhye
Sure.	*Pewnie.*	pev·nye

nationalities

narodowości

Where are you from?
  Skąd pan/pani jest? m/f pol   skont pan/pa·nee yest
  Skąd jesteś? inf   skont yes·tesh

I'm from …	*Jestem z …*	yes·tem z …
Australia	*Australii*	ow·stra·lyee
Canada	*Kanady*	ka·na·di
Singapore	*Singapuru*	seen·ga·poo·roo

For more nationalities, see the **dictionary**.

age

wiek

How old is …?	*Ile lat ma …?*	ee·le lat ma …
your son	*pana/i*	pa·na/nee
	syn m/f pol	sin
	twój syn inf	tfooy sin
your daughter	*pana/i córka* pol	pa·na/nee tsoor·ka
	twoja córka inf	tfo·ya tsoor·ka

How old are you?
Ile pan/pani ma lat? m/f pol   *ee*·le pan/*pa*·nee ma lat
Ile masz lat?   *ee*·le mash lat

I'm … years old.
Mam … lat.   mam … lat

He/She is … years old.
On/Ona ma … lat.   on/*o*·na ma … lat

I'm younger than I look.
Jestem młodszy/a   *yes*·tem *mwod*·shi/sha
niż wyglądam. m/f   neesh vi·*glon*·dam

For your age, see **numbers & amounts**, page 33.

occupations & studies

What's your occupation?
Jaki jest pana/pani   *ya*·kee yest *pa*·na/*pa*·nee
zawód? m/f pol   *za*·vood
Jaki jest twój zawód? inf   *ya*·kee yest tfooy *za*·vood

I'm a/an …	*Jestem …*	*yes*·tem …
architect	*architektem* m&f	ar·khee·*tek*·tem
chef	*kucharzem/*	koo·*kha*·zhem/
	kucharką m/f	koo·*khar*·kom
dentist	*dentystą/*	den·*tis*·tom/
	dentystką m/f	den·*tist*·kom
doctor	*lekarzem* m&f	le·*ka*·zhem
engineer	*inżynierem* m&f	een·zhi·*nye*·rem
farmer	*rolnikiem* m&f	rol·*nee*·kyem
journalist	*dziennikarzem/*	jyen·nee·*ka*·zhem/
	dziennikarką m/f	jyen·nee·*kar*·kom
lawyer	*prawnikiem* m&f	prav·*nee*·kyem
miner	*górnikiem* m&f	goor·*nee*·kyem
nurse	*pielęgniarzem/*	pye·leng·*nya*·zhem/
	pielęgniarką m/f	pye·leng·*nyar*·kom
teacher	*nauczycielem/*	na·oo·chi·*chye*·lem/
	nauczycielką m/f	na·oo·chi·*chyel*·kom

meeting people

111

I work in ...	Pracuję w ...	pra·*tsoo*·ye v ...
administration	*admini-stracji*	ad·mee·nee·*stra*·tsyee
health	*służbie zdrowia*	*swoozh*·bye *zdro*·vya
sales & marketing	*marketingu*	mar·ke·*teen*·goo

I'm ...	Jestem ...	*yes*·tem ...
retired	*emerytem/ emerytką* m/f	e·me·*ri*·tem/ e·me·*rit*·kom
self-employed	*samozatrud-niony/a* m/f	sa·mo·za·*trood*·*nyo*·ni/nom
unemployed	*bezrobotny/a* m/f	bez·ro·*bot*·ni/nom

I'm studying ...	Studiuję ...	stood·*yoo*·ye ...
humanities	*humanistykę*	khoo·ma·nees·*ti*·ke
Polish	*polonistykę*	po·lo·nees·*ti*·ke
science	*nauki ścisłe*	na·*oo*·kee *shchee*·swe

What are you studying?

Co pan/pani studiuje? m/f pol	tso pan/*pa*·nee stoo·*dyoo*·ye
Co studiujesz? inf	tso stoo·*dyoo*·yesh

well-wishing

Congratulations!
Gratulacje! — gra·too·*la*·tsye

Good luck!
Powodzenia! — po·vo·*dze*·nya

Happy birthday!
Wszystkiego najlepszego (w dniu urodzin)! — fshist·*kye*·go nai·lep·*she*·go (v dnyoo oo·*ro*·jeen)

Happy name day!
Wszystkiego najlepszego (z okazji imienin)! — fshist·*kye*·go nai·lep·*she*·go (z o·*kaz*·yee ee·*mye*·neen)

SOCIAL

112

family

Do you have a …?	*Czy pan/pani*	chi pan/*pa*·nee
	ma …? m/f pol	ma …
	Czy masz …? inf	chi mash …
I have a …	*Mam …*	mam …
brother	*brata*	*bra*·ta
daughter	*córkę*	tsoor·ke
family	*rodzinę*	ro·*jee*·ne
father	*ojca*	*oy*·tsa
granddaughter	*wnuczkę*	vnooch·ke
grandfather	*dziadka*	*jyad*·ka
grandmother	*babcię*	*bab*·chye
grandson	*wnuczka*	*vnooch*·ka
husband	*męża*	*men*·zha
mother	*matkę*	*mat*·ke
partner	*partnera/*	part·*ne*·ra/
(intimate)	*partnerkę* m/f	part·*ner*·ke
sister	*siostrę*	*shyos*·tre
son	*syna*	*si*·na
wife	*żonę*	*zho*·ne
I don't have a …	*Nie mam …*	nye mam …
brother	*brata*	*bra*·ta
daughter	*córki*	tsoor·kee
family	*rodziny*	ro·*jee*·ni
father	*ojca*	*oy*·tsa
granddaughter	*wnuczki*	vnooch·kee
grandfather	*dziadka*	*jyad*·ka
grandmother	*babci*	*bab*·chee
grandson	*wnuczka*	*vnooch*·ka
husband	*męża*	*men*·zha
mother	*matki*	*mat*·kee
partner	*partnera/*	part·*ne*·ra/
(intimate)	*partnerki* m/f	part·*ner*·kee
sister	*siostry*	*shyos*·tri
son	*syna*	*si*·na
wife	*żony*	*zho*·ni

meeting people

Are you married? (addressed to a man)
Czy jest pan żonaty? pol   chi yest pan zho·*na*·ti
Czy jesteś żonaty? inf   chi *yes*·tesh zho·*na*·ti

Are you married? (addressed to a woman)
Czy jest pani zamężna? pol   chi yest *pa*·nee za·*menzh*·na
Czy jesteś zamężna? inf   chi *yes*·tesh za·*menzh*·na

I live with someone.
Mieszkam z kimś.   *myesh*·kam z keemsh

I'm ...	*Jestem ...*	*yes*·tem ...
married	*żonaty/ zamężna* m/f	zho·*na*·ti/ za·*menzh*·na
separated	*w separacji*	f se·pa·*ra*·tsyee
single	*nieżonaty/ niezamężna* m/f	nye·zho·*na*·ti/ nye·za·*menzh*·na

farewells

pożegnania

Tomorrow is my last day here.
Jutro jest tu mój   *yoo*·tro yest too mooy
ostatni dzień.   os·*ta*·tnee jyen´

Keep in touch!
Bądźmy w kontakcie!   *bonj*·mi v kon·*tak*·chye

It's been great meeting you.
Miło było pana/   *mee*·wo *bi*·wo *pa*·na/
pania poznać. m/f pol   *pa*·nyom *poz*·nach
Miło było cię poznać. inf   *mee*·wo *bi*·wo chye *poz*·nach

Here's my ...	*Tu jest mój ...*	too yest mooy ...
What's your ...?	*Jaki jest pan/ pani ...?* m/f pol	*ya*·kee yest pan/ *pa*·nee ...
	Jaki jest twój ...? inf	*ya*·kee yest tfooy ...
address	*adres*	*ad*·res
email address	*adres emailowy*	*ad*·res e·mai·*lo*·vi
phone number	*numer telefonu*	*noo*·mer te·le·*fo*·noo

In this chapter we've given informal verb forms. If you're not sure what this means, see the **a-z phrasebuilder**, page 24.

common interests

wspólne zainteresowania

What do you do in your spare time?
Co robisz w wolnym czasie? tso *ro*·beesh v *vol*·nim *cha*·shye

Do you like …?	*Czy lubisz …?*	chi *loo*·beesh …
I (don't) like …	*(Nie) Lubię …*	(nye) *loo*·bye …
computer games	*grać na komputerze*	grach na kom·poo·*te*·zhe
cooking	*gotować*	go·*to*·vach
dancing	*tańczyć*	*tan'*·chich
drawing	*rysować*	ri·*so*·vach
gardening	*zajmować się ogródkiem*	zai·*mo*·vach shye o·*grood*·kyem
ice skating	*jeździć na łyżwach*	*yezh*·jeech na *wizh*·vakh
painting	*malować*	ma·*lo*·vach
photography	*fotografować*	fo·to·gra·*fo*·vach
reading	*czytać*	*chi*·tach
surfing the Internet	*żeglować po internecie*	zhe·*glo*·vach po een·ter·*ne*·chye
travelling	*podróżować*	po·droo·*zho*·vach

Do you like ...?	*Czy lubisz ...?*	chi *loo*·beesh ...
I like ...	*Lubię ...*	*loo*·bye ...
films	*oglądać filmy*	o·*glon*·dach *feel*·mi
hiking	*piesze*	*pye*·she
	wycieczki	vi·*chyech*·kee
music	*muzykę*	moo·*zi*·ke
playing cards	*grać w karty*	grach f *kar*·ti
shopping	*chodzić po*	*kho*·jeech po
	sklepach	*skle*·pakh
socialising	*spędzać czas z*	*spend*·zach chas z
	przyjaciółmi	pshi·ya·*chyoow*·mee
sport	*sport*	sport
watching TV	*oglądać*	o·*glon*·dach
	telewizję	te·le·*veez*·ye
I don't like ...	*Nie lubię ...*	nye *loo*·bye ...
films	*oglądać*	o·*glon*·dach
	filmów	*feel*·moof
hiking	*pieszych*	*pye*·shikh
	wycieczek	vi·*chye*·chek
music	*muzyki*	moo·*zi*·kee
playing cards	*grać w karty*	grach f *kar*·ti
shopping	*chodzić po*	*kho*·jeech po
	sklepach	*skle*·pakh
socialising	*spędzać czasu z*	*spend*·zach *cha*·soo z
	przyjaciółmi	pshi·ya·*chyoow*·mee
sport	*sportu*	*spor*·too
watching TV	*oglądać*	o·*glon*·dach
	telewizji	te·le·*veez*·yee

going solo

In our pronunciation guides you'll notice the single consonants f, v, s and z. They might look like mistakes but in fact f and v represent the preposition *w* (meaning 'in') and s and z represent *z* (meaning 'with'), which are words in their own right. Don't get tongue-tied over these single-consonant syllables – as you're pronouncing them try linking them with the word that comes after them.

music

Do you ...?	Czy ...?	chi ...
dance	tańczysz	tan'-chish
go to concerts	chodzisz na koncerty	kho-jeesh na kon-tser-ti
listen to music	słuchasz muzyki	swoo-khash moo-zi-kee
play an instrument	grasz na jakimś instrumencie	grash na ya-keemsh een-stroo-men-chye
sing	śpiewasz	shpye-vash

What ... do you like?	... lubisz?	... loo-beesh
bands	Jakie zespoły	ya-kye zes-po-wi
music	Jaką muzykę	ya-kom moo-zi-ke
performers	Jakich wykonawców	ya-keekh vi-ko-naf-tsoof
singers	Jakich piosenkarzy	ya-keekh pyo-sen-ka-zhi

classical music	muzyka klasyczna f	moo-zi-ka kla-sich-na
blues	blues m	bloos
electronic music	muzyka elektroniczna f	moo-zi-ka e-lek-tro-nee-chna
folk music	muzyka ludowa f	moo-zi-ka loo-do-va
jazz	jazz m	jez
pop	muzyka popularna f	moo-zi-ka po-poo-lar-na
rock	rock m	rok
traditional music	muzyka tradycyjna f	moo-zi-ka tra-di-tsiy-na
world music	muzyka świata f	moo-zi-ka shvya-ta

Planning to go to a concert? See **tickets**, page 47, and **going out**, page 127.

interests

117

cinema & theatre

Did you like the …?	*Czy ci się podobał/ podobała …?* m/f	chi chee shye … po-*do*-bow/ po-*do*-bow-a …
ballet	*balet* m	*ba*-let
film	*film* m	feelm
opera	*opera* f	o-*pe*-ra
play	*sztuka* f	*shtoo*-ka

I feel like going to (a ballet).
Mam ochotę pójść na (balet).
mam o-*kho*-te pooyshch na (*ba*-let)

What's showing at the cinema/theatre tonight?
Co grają dzisiaj wieczorem w kinie/ teatrze?
tso *gra*-yom *jee*-shai vye-*cho*-rem v *kee*-nye/ te-*a*-tshe

Is it in (English)?
Czy to jest po (angielsku)?
chi to yest po (an-*gyel*-skoo)

Does it have (English) subtitles?
Czy ma (angielskie) napisy?
chi ma (an-*gyel*-skye) na-*pee*-si

Do you have tickets for …?
Czy są bilety na …?
chi som bee-*le*-ti na …

Are there any extra tickets?
Czy są dodatkowe bilety?
chi som do-dat-*ko*-ve bee-*le*-ti

I'd like the cheapest tickets.
Chciałem/am najtańsze miejsca. m/f
khchow-em/am nai-*tan'*-she *myeys*-tsa

I'd like the best tickets.
Chciałem/am najlepsze miejsca. m/f
khchow-em/am nai-*lep*-she *myeys*-tsa

Is there a matinée show?
Czy jest seans popołudniowy?
chi yest *se*-ans po-po-wood-*nyo*-vi

Is this seat taken?
Czy to miejsce jest zajęte?
chi to *myeys*-tse yest za-*yen*-te

gender reminder

In all the phrases in this book the gender markers m and f signal who the subject of the sentence is. For instance, when you see the English phrase 'I'd like …' you'll see it translated in Polish as *Chciałbym/Chciałabym* … m/f khchow·bim/khchow·*a*·bim … The gender markers indicate that if you're a man you select the first option and if you're a woman you select the second one.

Have you seen (*Man of Marble*)?
   Czy widziałeś/aś   chi vee·*jya*·wesh/wash
   (Człowieka z marmuru)? m/f   (chwo·*vye*·ka z mar·*moo*·roo)

Who's in it?
   Kto tam występuje?   kto tam vis·tem·*poo*·ye

It stars (Piotr Adamczyk).
   Występuje   vis·tem·*poo*·ye
   (Piotr Adamczyk).   (pyotr a·*dam*·chik)

I thought it was …   *Myślę, że to było …*   *mish*·le zhe to *bi*·wo …
   excellent   *wspaniałe*   fspa·*nya*·we
   long   *za długie*   za *dwoo*·gye
   OK   *niezłe*   *nye*·zwe

interests

119

I like ...	Lubię ...	*loo*·bye ...
action movies	*filmy akcji*	*feel*·mi *ak*·tsyee
animated films	*filmy*	*feel*·mi
	animowane	a·nee·mo·*va*·ne
comedies	*komedie*	ko·*me*·dye
documentaries	*filmy*	*feel*·mi
	dokumentalne	do·koo·men·*tal*·ne
drama	*dramaty*	dra·*ma*·ti
(Polish) cinema	*(polskie) kino*	*(pol*·skye) *kee*·no
horror movies	*horrory*	ho·*ro*·ri
sci-fi	*fantastykę*	fan·tas·*ti*·ke
	naukową	now·*ko*·vom
short films	*filmy*	*feel*·mi
	krótkometra-	kroot·ko·me·tra·
	żowe	zho·ve
thrillers	*thrillery*	tree·*le*·ri
war movies	*filmy wojenne*	*feel*·mi vo·*ye*·ne
I don't like ...	Nie lubię ...	nye *loo*·bye ...
action movies	*filmów akcji*	*feel*·moof *ak*·tsyee
animated films	*filmów*	*feel*·moof
	animowanych	a·nee·mo·*va*·nikh
comedies	*komedii*	ko·*me*·dyee
documentaries	*filmów*	*feel*·moof
	dokumentalnych	do·koo·men·*tal*·nikh
drama	*dramatów*	dra·*ma*·toof
(Polish) cinema	*(polskiego)*	*(pol*·*skye*·go)
	kina	*kee*·na
horror movies	*horrorów*	ho·*ro*·roof
sci-fi	*fantastyki*	fan·tas·*ti*·kee
	naukowej	now·*ko*·vey
short films	*filmów*	*feel*·moof
	krótkometra-	kroot·ko·me·tra·
	żowych	zho·vikh
thrillers	*thrillerów*	tree·*le*·roof
war movies	*filmów*	*feel*·moof
	wojennych	vo·*ye*·nikh

feelings

uczucia

Are you …?	*Czy jest pan/ pani …?* m/f pol	chi yest pan/ *pa*·nee …
	Czy jesteś …? inf	chi *yes*·tesh …
I'm (not) …	*(Nie) Jestem …*	(nye) *yes*·tem …
annoyed	*zły/zła* m/f	zwi/zwa
cold	*zmarznięty/a* m/f	zmar·*znyen*·ti/ta
disappointed	*rozczarowany/a* m/f	roz·cha·ro·*va*·ni/na
embarrassed	*zakłopotany/a* m/f	zak·wo·po·*ta*·ni/na
happy	*szczęśliwy/a* m/f	shchen·*shlee*·vi/va
homesick	*stęskniony/a*	stensk·*nyo*·ni/na
	za domem m/f	za *do*·mem
hungry	*głodny/a* m/f	*gwod*·ni/na
sad	*smutny/a* m/f	*smoot*·ni/na
surprised	*zaskoczony/a* m/f	za·sko·*cho*·ni/na
thirsty	*spragniony/a* m/f	sprag·*nyo*·ni/na
tired	*zmęczony/a* m/f	zmen·*cho*·ni/na
worried	*zmartwiony/a* m/f	zmart·*fyo*·ni/na

I'm (not) hot.	*(Nie) Jest mi gorąco.*	(nye) yest mee go·*ron*·tso
I'm (not) in a hurry.	*(Nie) Śpieszę się.*	(nye) *shpye*·she shye
I'm (not) well.	*(Nie) Czuje się dobrze.*	(nye) *choo*·ye shye *dob*·zhe

If you're not feeling well, see **health**, page 193.

how are you really?		
not at all	*wcale*	*ftsa·le*
I don't care at all.	*Wcale mnie to nie obchodzi.*	*ftsa·le mnye to nye ob·kho·jee*
a little	*trochę*	*tro·khe*
I'm a little sad.	*Trochę mi smutno.*	*tro·khe mee smoot·no*
very	*bardzo*	*bar·dzo*
I feel very lucky.	*Czuję się bardzo szczęśliwy/a.* m/f	*choo·ye shye bar·dzo shchen·shlee·vi/va*

opinions

opinie

Did you like it?
Czy się to panu/panii podobało? m/f pol
chi shye to *pa·noo/pa·nee* po·do·*bow*·o
Czy ci się to podobało? inf
chi chee shye to po·do·*bow*·o

What do you think of it?
Co pan/pani o tym myśli? m/f pol
tso pan/*pa·nee* o tim *mish*·lee
Co o tym myślisz? inf
tso o tim *mish*·leesh

I thought it was …	*Myślę, że to było …*	*mish·le zhe to bi·wo …*
It's …	*To jest …*	*to yest …*
awful	*okropne*	*o·krop·ne*
beautiful	*piękne*	*pyenk·ne*
boring	*nudne*	*nood·ne*
great	*wspaniałe*	*fspa·nya·we*
interesting	*interes-ujące*	*een·te·re·soo·yon·tse*
OK	*dobre*	*dob·re*
original	*oryginalne*	*o·ri·gee·nal·ne*
strange	*dziwne*	*jeev·ne*
too expensive	*za drogie*	*za dro·gye*

politics & social issues

The major political preoccupations of Poles these days are *bezrobocie* bez·ro·bo·chye (unemployment) and *korupcja* ko·roo·ptsya (corruption) in government – both problems symptomatic of the difficult transition the country has made from communist rule to a market economy. Another hot social issue in ultra-Catholic Poland is *aborcja* a·bor·tsya (abortion), which is illegal in most cases.

Who do you vote for?

Na kogo pan/pani głosuje? **m/f pol**	na ko·go pan/pa·nee gwo·soo·ye
Na kogo głosujesz? **inf**	na ko·go gwo·soo·yesh

I support the ... party.

Popieram partię ...	po·pye·ram par·tye ...

I'm a member of the ... party.

	Jestem członkiem partii ...	yes·tem chwon·kyem par·tyee ...
communist	*komunistycznej*	ko·moo·nees·tich·ney
conservative	*konserwatywnej*	kon·ser·va·tiv·ney
democratic	*demokratycznej*	de·mo·kra·tich·ney
green	*zielonych*	zhye·lo·nikh
liberal	*liberalnej*	lee·be·ral·ney
social	*socjal-*	so·tsyal·
democratic	*demokratycznej*	de·mo·kra·tich·ney
socialist	*socjalistycznej*	so·tsya·lee·sti·chney

the eyes have it

Pulling the lower eyelid down with the index finger indicates ironic disbelief in what someone else is saying. You can also simultaneously say *Czy jedzie mi tu czołg?* chi ye·jye mee too chowg (Do you see a tank driving here?) – a colourful equivalent of the English expression 'pull the other leg'.

proverbial polish wisdom

Gdzie dwóch Polaków, tam trzy opinie.
gje dvookh po·*la*·koov tam tzhi o·*pee*·nye
(Where there are two Poles there are three opinions.)

Mądry Polak po szkodzie.
mon·dri *po*·lak po *shko*·jye
(A Pole is wise after the damage has been done.)

Włażąc między wrony, krakaj jak i one.
vwa·zhach myen·dzi *vro*·ni *kra*·kai yak ee *o*·ne
(If you hang out with crows, then squawk like them –
ie when in Rome …)

Did you hear about …?
Czy słyszał pan o …? m pol	chi *swi*·show pan o …
Czy słyszała pani o …? f pol	chi swi·*sha*·wa *pa*·nee o …
Czy słyszałeś/aś o …? m/f inf	chi swi·*sha*·wesh/wash o …

Do you agree with it?
Czy pan/pani zgadza się z tym? m/f pol	chi pan/*pa*·nee *zga*·dza shye z tim
Czy zgadzasz się z tym? inf	chi *zga*·dzash shye z tim

I (don't) agree with …
(Nie) Zgadzam się z …	(nye) *zga*·dzam shye z …

How do people feel about …?
Co ludzie myślą o …?	tso *loo*·jye *mish*·lom o …

How can we protest against …?
Jak możemy zaprotestować przeciwko …?	yak mo·*zhe*·mi za·pro·tes·*to*·vach pshe·*cheef*·ko …

How can we support …?
Jak możemy wspomóc …?	yak mo·*zhe*·mi *fspo*·moots …

abortion	*aborcja* f	a·*bor*·tsya
animal rights	*prawa*	*pra*·va
	zwierząt pl	zvye·zhont
corruption	*korupcja* f	ko·*roo*·ptsya
crime	*przestępstwo* n	pshe·*stemp*·stfo
discrimination	*dyskryminacja* f	dis·kri·mee·*na*·tsya
drugs	*narkotyki* pl	nar·ko·*ti*·kee
the economy	*gospodarka* f	gos·po·*dar*·ka
education	*edukacja* f	e·doo·*ka*·tsya
the environment	*środowisko* n	shro·do·*vees*·ko
equal opportunity	*równo-*	roov·no·
	uprawnienie n	oo·prav·*nye*·nye
euthanasia	*eutanazja* f	ew·ta·*na*·zya
globalisation	*globalizacja* f	glo·ba·lee·*za*·tsya
human rights	*prawa*	*pra*·va
	człowieka pl	chwo·*vye*·ka
immigration	*imigracja* f	ee·mee·*gra*·tsya
inequality	*nierówność* f	nye·*roov*·noshch
poverty	*ubóstwo* n	oo·*boos*·tfo
privatisation	*prywatyzacja* f	pri·va·ti·*za*·tsya
racism	*rasizm* m	*ra*·sheezm
religious	*fundamentalizm*	foon·da·men·*ta*·leezm
fundamentalism	*religijny*	re·lee·*geey*·ni
sexism	*seksizm* m	*sek*·sheezm
terrorism	*terroryzm* m	te·ro·*ri*·zm
social welfare	*świadczenia*	shvyad·*che*·nya
	socjalne pl	so·*tsyal*·ne
unemployment	*bezrobocie* n	bez·ro·*bo*·chye
war (in Iraq)	*wojna*	*voy*·na
	(w Iraku) f	(v ee·*ra*·koo)
Is there help	*Czy jest pomoc*	chi yest *po*·mots
for (the) …?	*dla …?*	dla …
aged	*osób starszych*	o·soob *star*·shikh
beggars	*żebrzących*	zheb·*zhon*·tsikh
disabled	*niepełno-*	nye·pew·no·
	sprawnych	*sprav*·nikh
homeless	*bezdomnych*	bez·*dom*·nikh
street kids	*uliczników*	oo·leech·*nee*·koof

środowisko

Is there a ... problem here?
  Czy jest tam problem ...?   chi yest tam *pro*·blem ...

What should be done about ...?
  Co powinno się   tso po·*vi*·no shye
  zrobić aby ...?   *zro*·beech *a*·bi ...

acid rain	*kwaśny deszcz* m	*kvash*·ni deshch
deforestation	*ogołacenie z*	o·go·wa·*tse*·nye z
	lasów n	*la*·soof
drought	*susza* f	*soo*·sha
endangered	*zagrożone*	za·gro·*zho*·ne
species	*gatunki* pl	ga·*toon*·kee
genetically	*żywność*	*zhiv*·noshch
modified food	*zmodyfikowana*	zmo·di·fee·ko·*va*·na
	genetycznie f	ge·ne·*tich*·nye
hunting	*polowanie* n	po·lo·*va*·nye
hydroelectricity	*hydroelektryczność* f	hi·dro·e·lek·*trich*·noshch
irrigation	*nawadnianie* n	na·vad·*nya*·nye
nuclear energy	*energia*	e·*ner*·gya
	jądrowa f	yon·*dro*·va
ozone layer	*warstwa*	*vars*·tfa
	ozonowa f	o·zo·*no*·va
pesticides	*pestycydy* pl	pes·ti·*tsi*·di
pollution	*zanieczyszczenie* n	za·nye·chish·*che*·nye
recycling	*program*	*pro*·gram
programme	*recyklingowy* m	re·tsi·kleen·*go*·vi
toxic waste	*odpady*	od·*pa*·di
	toksyczne pl	tok·*sich*·ne
water supply	*zapasy wody* pl	za·*pa*·si *vo*·di

Is this a	*Czy ten ...*	chi ten ...
protected ...?	*jest chroniony?*	yest khro·*nyo*·ni
forest	*las*	las
park	*park*	park
species	*gatunek*	ga·*too*·nek

In this chapter we've given informal forms. If you're not sure what this means, see the **a-z phrasebuilder**, page 24.

where to go

dokąd iść

What's there to do in the evenings?
Co można tu robić
wieczorami?
tso *mozh*·na too *ro*·beech
vye·cho·*ra*·mee

What's on …?	Co jest ciekawego …?	tso yest chye·ka·*ve*·go …
locally	tu na miejscu	too na *myeys*·tsoo
today	dzisiaj	*jee*·shai
tonight	dzisiaj wieczorem	*jee*·shai vye·*cho*·rem
this weekend	podczas weekendu	*pod*·chas wee·*ken*·doo

Where can I find …?	Gdzie mogę znaleźć …?	gjye *mo*·ge *zna*·lezhch …
clubs	kluby nocne	*kloo*·bi *nots*·ne
gay/lesbian venues	kluby dla gejów/lesbijek	*kloo*·bi dla ge·yoof/les·*bee*·yek
places to eat	miejsce gdzie można coś zjeść	*myeys*·tse gjye *mozh*·na tsosh zyeshch
pubs	puby	*pa*·bi

Is there a local ... guide?	Czy jest lokalny informator ...?	chi yest lo·kal·ni een·for·ma·tor ...
entertainment	rozrywkowy	roz·riv·ko·vi
film	filmowy	feel·mo·vi
gay/lesbian	dla gejów/ lesbijek	dla ge·yoof/ les·bee·yek
music	muzyczny	moo·zi·chni
I feel like going to a ...	Mam ochotę pójść ...	mam o·kho·te pooyshch ...
ballet	na balet	na ba·let
bar	do baru	do ba·roo
café	do kawiarnii	do ka·vyar·nee
concert	na koncert	na kon·tsert
film	na film	na feelm
karaoke bar	do baru karaoke	do ba·roo ka·ra·o·ke
nightclub	do klubu nocnego	do kloo·boo nots·ne·go
party	na imprezę	na eem·pre·ze
performance	na przedstawienie	na pshet·sta·vye·nye
play	na sztukę	na shtoo·ke
pub	do pubu	do pa·boo
restaurant	do restauracji	do res·tow·ra·tsyee

bottoms up!

Wherever there's a social gathering in Poland it's a fairly safe bet that the *wódka* vood·ka (vodka) will be flowing freely. Before you make an idiot of yourself, remember that the national beverage is *not* sipped but downed in a single gulp, or *do dna* do dna (to the bottom) as the Poles say. A sip of water, juice or coke is the usual chaser and there'll often be some kind of snack on hand to help line your stomach, such as *śledź* shlej (pickled herring) or a plate of *grzyby marynowane* gzhi·bi ma·ri·no·va·ne (marinated wild mushrooms), a much-prized local delicacy.

Remember to say *Na zdrowie!* na zdro·vye (To your health!) or *Sto lat!* sto lat (lit: 100 years) as you down your firewater.

invitations

What are you doing now?
Co teraz robisz?   tso *te*·ras *ro*·beesh

What are you doing tonight?
Co będziesz robić   tso *ben*·jyesh *ro*·beech
wieczorem?   vye·*cho*·rem

What are you doing this weekend?
Co będziesz robić w   tso *ben*·jyesh *ro*·beech v
czasie weekendu?   cha·shye wee·*ken*·doo

Would you like to go (for a) …?	*Czy chciałbyś/ chciałabyś iść …?* m/f	chi *khchow*·bish/ khchow·*a*·bish eeshch …
I feel like going (for a) …	*Mam ochotę pójść …*	mam o·*kho*·te pooyshch …
coffee	*na kawę*	na *ka*·ve
dancing	*potańczyć*	po·*tan'*·chich
drink	*na drinka*	na *dreen*·ka
meal	*coś zjeść*	tsosh zyeshch
out somewhere	*gdzieś*	gjyesh
walk	*na spacer*	na *spa*·tser

My round.
Ja funduję.   ya foon·*doo*·ye

Do you know a good restaurant?
Czy znasz jakąś   chi znash *ya*·komsh
dobrą restaurację?   *do*·brom res·tow·*ra*·tsye

Do you want to come to the concert with me?
Czy chcesz pójść ze   chi khtsesh pooyshch ze
mną na koncert?   mnom na *kon*·tsert

We're having a party.
Organizujemy imprezę.   or·ga·nee·zoo·*ye*·mi eem·*pre*·ze

You should come.
Powinieneś/Powinnaś   po·vee·*nye*·nesh/po·*vee*·nash
przyjść. m/f   pshiyshch

hip-hop polish style

If you're in the mood to go clubbing in Poland chances are that your eardrums will experience a strangely dislocating phenomenon: hip-hop in Polish. The Polish hip-hop scene was born in the early '90s when American exports MC Hammer and Vanilla Ice became popular, inspiring a raft of home-grown Polish rappers. Hip-hop music is now firmly ensconced in the mainstream and is just about the only form of Polish music to permeate beyond Polish borders.

Though the lyrics might be foreign, the themes are not unfamiliar. They express the alienation and anger of the *blokersi* blo·*ker*·shee (young white working-class men) from the *bloki* blo·kee (communist-era high-rise housing estates) who've missed out on the prosperity of post-Communist Poland. If you don't speak any Polish, you won't be able to make much sense of what you hear but you should recognise the popular swearword *kurwa* koor·va ('whore' or 'slut') amid a sprinkling of American slang.

responding to invitations

odpowiadanie na zaproszenia

Sure!
  Oczywiście!   o·chi·*veesh*·chye

Yes, I'd love to.
  Tak, z przyjemnością.   tak z pzhi·yem·*nosh*·chyom

That's very kind of you.
  To miło z twojej strony.   to mee·wo z *tfo*·yey *stro*·ni

Where shall we go?
  Gdzie pójdziemy?   gjye *pooy*·jye·mi

No, I'm afraid I can't.
Niestety, nie mogę. nye·*ste*·ti nye *mo*·ge

Sorry, I can't sing/dance.
Przepraszam, ale nie pshe·*pra*·sham *a*·le nye
śpiewam/tańczę. shpye·vam/*tan'*·che

What about tomorrow?
A może jutro? a *mo*·zhe *yoo*·tro

arranging to meet

What time will we meet?
O której godzinie o *ktoo*·rey go·*jee*·nye
się spotkamy? shye spot·*ka*·mi

Where will we meet?
Gdzie się spotkamy? gjye shye spot·*ka*·mi

I'll pick you up.
Przyjadę po ciebie. pshi·*ya*·de po *chye*·bye

Are you ready?
Czy jesteś gotowy/a? m/f chi *yes*·tesh go·*to*·vi/va

I'm ready.
Jestem gotowy/a. m/f *yes*·tem go·*to*·vi/va

I'll be coming later.
Przyjdę później. *pshiy*·de *poozh*·nyey

Where will you be?
Gdzie będziesz? gjye *ben*·jyesh

If I'm not there by (nine), don't wait for me.
Jeśli nie będzie mnie tu *yesh*·lee nye *ben*·jye mnye too
do (dziewiątej) to do (jye·*vyon*·tey) to
nie czekaj na mnie. nye *che*·kai na mnye

Let's meet at … *Umówmy się …* oo·*moov*·mi shye …
  (eight) o'clock *o (ósmej)* o (*oos*·mey)
  the (entrance) *przy (wejściu)* pshi (*veysh*·chyoo)

OK!
Dobrze.

*dob·*zhe

I'll see you then.
To do zobaczenia.

to do zo·ba·*che*·nya

See you later/tomorrow.
Do zobaczenia/jutra.

do zo·ba·*che*·nya/*yoo*·tra

I'm looking forward to it.
*Czekam na to z
niecierpliwością.*

che·kam na to z
nye·chyer·plee·*vosh*·chyom

Sorry I'm late.
*Przepraszam za
spóźnienie.*

pshe·*pra*·sham za
spoozh·*nye*·nye

Never mind.
Nic nie szkodzi.

neets nye *shko*·jee

drugs

narkotyki

Do you have a light?
Czy masz zapalniczkę?

chi mash za·pal·*neech*·ke

Do you want to have a smoke?
Czy chcesz zapalić?

chi khtsesh za·*pa*·leech

I take ... occasionally.
Czasem wezmę ...

cha·sem *vez*·me ...

I don't take drugs.
Nie zażywam narkotyków.

nye za·*zhi*·vam nar·ko·*ti*·koof

I'm high.
Jestem na haju.

yes·tem na *ha*·yoo

If the police are talking to you about drugs, see **police**, page 190, for useful phrases.

SOCIAL

132

In this chapter we've given informal verb forms. If you're not sure what this means, see the **a–z phrasebuilder**, page 24.

asking someone out

Where would you like to go (tonight)?
Gdzie byś chciał/chciała   gjye bish *khchow/khchow*·a
pójść (dzisiaj   pooyshch (*jee*·shai
wieczorem)? m/f   vye·*cho*·rem)

Would you like to do something (tomorrow)?
Czy chciałbyś/chciałabyś   chi *khchow*·bish/khchow·*a*·bish
(jutro) coś zrobić?   (*yoo*·tro) tsosh *zro*·beech

Yes, I'd love to.
Tak, bardzo bym   tak *bar*·dzo bim
chciał/chciała. m/f   khchow/*khchow*·a

Sorry, I can't.
Przepraszam, ale nie mogę.   pshe·*pra*·sham *a*·le nye *mo*·ge

pick-up lines

I'll buy you a drink.
Kupię ci drinka.   koo·pye chee *dreen*·ka

You look like someone I know.
Kogoś mi   ko·gosh mee
przypomianasz.   pshi·po·*mee*·nash

You're a fantastic dancer.
Świetnie tańczysz.   shvyet·nye *tan'*·chish

He's a babe.	*On jest słodki.*	on yest *swod*·kee
He's hot.	*On jest boski.*	on yest *bo*·skee
He's a bastard.	*On jest skurwielem.*	on yest skoor·*vye*·lem
He gets around.	*On się puszcza.*	on shye *poosh*·cha
She's a babe.	*Ona jest słodka.*	o·na yest *swod*·ka
She's hot.	*Ona jest fajna foczka.*	o·na yest *fai*·na *foch*·ka
	(lit: she's a cute seal)	
She's a bitch.	*Ale z niej suka.*	*a*·le z nyey *soo*·ka
She gets around.	*Ona się puszcza.*	o·na shye *poosh*·cha

Can I ...?	*Czy mogę ...?*	chi *mo*·ge ...
dance with you	*z tobą zatańczyć*	z *to*·bom za·*tan'*·chich
sit here	*tu usiąść*	too oo·*shyonshch*
take you home	*odprowadzić cię do domu*	od·pro·*va*·jeech chye do *do*·moo

rejections

No, thank you.
Nie dziękuję.   nye jyen·*koo*·ye

I'd rather not.
Raczej nie.   *ra*·chey nye

I'm here with my girlfriend.
Jestem z moją dziewczyną.   *yes*·tem z *mo*·yom jyev·*chi*·nom

I'm here with my boyfriend.
Jestem z moim chłopakiem.   *yes*·tem z *mo*·yeem khwo·*pa*·kyem

Excuse me, I have to go now.
Przepraszam, ale muszę już iść.   pshe·*pra*·sham ale *moo*·she yoosh eeshch

getting closer

Offering someone *kwiaty* kfya·ti (flowers) is a common sign of a romantic interest. Your bunch of flowers – preferably *róże* roo·zhe (roses) – should contain an odd number of flowers as an even number is considered bad luck. Colour choice is of the essence too: white for innocence, yellow for jealousy and red for love is the local mantra.

I really like you.
Bardzo cię lubię.   bar·dzo chye loo·bye

You're great.
Jesteś cudowny/a. m/f   yes·tesh tsoo·dov·ni/na

Can I kiss you?
Czy mogę cię pocałować?   chi mo·ge chye po·tsa·wo·vach

Do you want to come inside for a while?
Czy chcesz wejść na   chi khtsesh veysh na
chwilę do środka?   khvee·le do shrod·ka

Do you want a massage?
Czy zrobić ci masaż?   chi zro·beech chee ma·sash

Would you like to stay over?
Czy chcesz zostać na noc?   chi khtsesh zos·tach na nots

Can I stay over?
Czy mogę zostać na noc?   chi mo·ge zos·tach na nots

---

local talk

I have a headache.
Boli mnie głowa.   bo·lee mnye gwo·va

Leave me alone!
Zostaw mnie w spokoju   zos·tav mnye v spo·ko·yoo

sex

seks

Kiss me.	*Pocałuj mnie.*	po·tsa·wooy mnye
I want you.	*Pragnę ciebie.*	prag·ne chye·bye
Let's go to bed.	*Chodźmy do łóżka.*	khoj·mi do woozh·ka
Touch me here.	*Dotknij tu mnie.*	dot·kneey too mnye
Do you like this?	*Czy lubisz to?*	chi loo·beesh to
I (don't) like that.	*(Nie) Lubię tego.*	(nye) loo·bye te·go

I think we should stop now.
Myślę, że powinniśmy przestać.
mish·le zhe po·vi·neesh·mi pshes·tach

Do you have a (condom)?
Czy masz (prezerwatywę)?
chi mash (pre·zer·va·ti·ve)

Let's use a (condom).
Musimy użyć (prezerwatywę).
moo·shee·mi oo·zhich (pre·zer·va·ti·ve)

I won't do it without protection.
Nie chcę tego robić bez zabezpieczenia.
nye khtse te·go ro·beech bes za·bes·pye·che·nya

It's my first time.
To jest mój pierwszy raz. to yest mooy *pyerf*·shi ras

Don't worry, I'll do it myself.
Nie przejmuj się, sam/ nye *pshey*·mooy shye sam/
sama sobie to zrobię. m/f *sa*·ma *so*·bye to *zro*·bye

It helps to have a sense of humour.
Dobre poczucie *do*·bre po·*choo*·chye
humoru bardzo khoo·*mo*·roo *bar*·dzo
pomaga. po·*ma*·ga

Oh my god!	*Ach!*	akh
That's great.	*To jest cudowne.*	to yest tsoo·*dov*·ne
faster	*szybciej*	*shib*·chyey
harder	*mocniej*	*mots*·nyey
slower	*wolniej*	*vol*·nyey
softer	*delikatniej*	de·lee·*kat*·nyey
That was ...	*To było ...*	to *bi*·wo ...
amazing	*niesamowite*	nye·sa·mo·*vee*·te
romantic	*romantyczne*	ro·man·*tich*·ne
wild	*szalone*	sha·*lo*·ne

---

pillow talk

Common terms of endearment are *kochanie* ko·*kha*·nye (my love) and *skarbie* *skar*·bye (my treasure). Other more exotic names for your Polish paramour are gender-specific.

Addressed to a man:

little tiger	*tygrysku*	ti·*gris*·koo
little worm	*robaczku*	ro·*bach*·koo
teddy bear	*misiu*	*mee*·shyoo

Addressed to a woman:

little cat	*kotku*	*kot*·koo
little crumb	*kruszynko*	kroo·*shin*·ko
little fish	*rybko*	*rip*·ko
little frog	*żabko*	*zhab*·ko
little mouse	*myszko*	*mish*·ko

love

I think we're good together.
Myślę, że dobrze — mish·le zhe dob·zhe
nam razem. — nam ra·zem

I love you.
Kocham cię. — ko·kham chye

Will you …?	*Czy …?*	chi …
go out with me	*umówisz się ze mną*	oo·moo·veesh shye ze mnom
marry me (said by a man)	*wyjdziesz za mnie*	viy·jyesh za mnye
marry me (said by a woman)	*ożenisz się ze mną*	o·zhe·neesh shye ze mnom
meet my parents	*poznasz moich rodziców*	poz·nash mo·yeekh ro·jee·tsoof

problems

I don't think it's working out.
Nie wydaje mi się — nye vi·da·ye mee shye
żeby to miało sens. — zhe·bi to myow·o sens

Are you seeing someone else?
Czy spotykasz się — chi spo·ti·kash shye
z kimś innym? — z keemsh ee·nim

He/She is just a friend.
To tylko przyjaciel/ — to til·ko pshi·ya·chyel/
przyjaciółka. m/f — pshi·ya·chyoow·ka

I never want to see you again.
Nie chcę się już więcej — nye khtse shye yoosh vyen·tsey
z tobą spotykać. — z to·bom spo·ti·kach

We'll work it out.
Zaczniemy od nowa. — zach·nye·mi od no·va

religion

What's your religion?
Jakiego jesteś wyznania? ya·*kye*·go *yes*·tesh viz·*na*·nya

I'm not religious.
Nie jestem zbyt nye *yes*·tem zbit
religijny/a. m/f re·lee·*geey*·ni/na

I'm ...	Jestem ...	yes·tem ...
agnostic	*agnostykiem/*	ag·nos·*ti*·kyem/
	agnostyczką m/f	ag·nos·*tich*·kom
Buddhist	*buddystą/*	bood·*dis*·tom/
	buddystką m/f	bood·*dist*·kom
Catholic	*katolikiem/*	ka·to·*lee*·kyem/
	katoliczką m/f	ka·to·*leech*·kom
Christian	*chrześcijaninem/*	khshesh·chee·ya·*nee*·nem/
	chrześcijanką m/f	khshesh·chee·*yan*·kom
Hindu	*hinduistą/*	heen·doo·*ees*·tom/
	hinduistką m/f	heen·doo·*eest*·kom
Jewish	*żydem/*	*zhi*·dem/
	żydówką m/f	zhi·*doof*·kom
Muslim	*muzułmaninem/*	moo·zoow·ma·*nee*·nem/
	muzułmanką m/f	moo·zoow·*man*·kom
Orthodox	*prawosławnym/*	pra·vo·*swav*·nim/
	prawosławną m/f	pra·vo·*swav*·nom
Protestant	*protestantem/*	pro·test·*tan*·tem/
	protestantką m/f	pro·test·*tant*·kom

I (don't) believe in ...	*(Nie) Wierzę w ...*	(nye) *vye*·zhe v ...
astrology	*astrologię*	a·stro·*lo*·gye
fate	*przeznaczenie*	pshez·na·*che*·nye
God	*Boga*	*bo*·ga

Can I ... here?	*Czy mogę tu gdzieś ...?*	chi *mo*·ge too gjyesh ...
Where can I ...?	*Gdzie mogę ...?*	gjye *mo*·ge ...
attend mass	*iść na mszę*	eeshch na mshe
attend a service	*uczestniczyć w nabożeństwie*	oo·chest·*nee*·chich v na·bo·*zhen'ts*·fye
pray	*się pomodlić*	shye po·*mod*·leech
worship	*uczestniczyć w nabożeństwie*	oo·chest·*nee*·chich v na·bo·*zhenst*·fye

cultural differences

różnice kulturowe

I didn't mean to do anything wrong.
Nie chciałem/am zrobić nic złego. m/f
nye *khchow*·em/am *zro*·beech neets *zwe*·go

I didn't mean to say anything wrong.
Nie chciałem/am powiedzieć nic złego. m/f
nye *khchow*·em/am po·*vye*·jyech neets *zwe*·go

Is this a local or national custom?
Czy to jest miejscowy czy ogólnopolski zwyczaj.
chi to yest myeys·*tso*·vi chi o·gool·no·*pol*·skee zvi·chai

I don't want to offend you.
Nie chcę cię urazić.
nye khtse chye oo·*ra*·zheech

I'm not used to this.
Nie jestem do tego przyzwyczajony/a. m/f
nye *yes*·tem do *te*·go pshi·zvi·cha·*yo*·ni/na

Easter   *Wielkanoc*   vyel·*ka*·nots

Easter Sunday is the most important religious celebration in Poland and the culmination of *Wielki Tydzień* vyel·kee *ti*·jyen´ (Holy Week). The day's celebrations kick off with a *śniadanie wielkanocne* shnya·*da*·nye vyel·ka·*nots*·ne (Easter breakfast) where food (including hand-painted eggs) that has been blessed on Easter Saturday is shared. Easter Monday, known as *Dyngus din*·goos or *Lany Poniedziałek la*·ni po·nye·*jya*·wek, concludes the celebrations in a wet way as young people observe the tradition of pouring water on passers-by.

Christmas Eve   *Boże Narodzenie*   bo·zhe na·ro·dze·nye

Although technically the 24th of December isn't a public holiday, it's one of the most joyous celebrations in Poland. Most people fast for the whole day but when the first star shines in the sky a sumptuous supper begins. After some prayers and exchanging the Christmas greeting *Wesołych Świąt!* ve·so·wikh shvyont, an *opłatek* o·*pwa*·tek (a wafer symbolising bread) is eaten. This is followed by the Christmas dinner itself, where no less than 12 different dishes are served, followed by a selection of desserts.

It's around this time that children start looking expectantly towards the *choinka* kho·*een*·ka (Christmas tree) hoping that presents will finally appear under it. This miracle, however, doesn't take place until the family sing some carols together and the children are sent outside to look for *Święty Mikołaj* shvyen·ti mee·ko·wai (St Nicholas). With the children safely outdoors the presents magically appear under the tree.

New Year   *Nowy Rok*   no·vi rok

New Year celebrations start on New Year's Eve, which is known as *Sylwester* sil·*ves*·ter. Most people see in the New Year at large alcohol-fuelled parties but in the larger cities there are open-air celebrations in the *rynek główny ri*·nek *gwoov*·ni (main marketplace).

beliefs & cultural differences

I'd rather not join in.
Wolałbym/Wolałabym się   vo·*low*·bim/vo·low·*a*·bim shye
nie przyłączać. m/f   nye pshi·*won*·chach

I'll try it.
Spróbuję.   sproo·*boo*·ye

I'm sorry, it's	*Przepraszam, ale*	pshe·*pra*·sham *a*·le
against my …	*to jest wbrew*	to yest vbrev
	mojej …	*mo*·yey …
beliefs	*wierze*	*vye*·zhe
religion	*religii*	re·*lee*·gyee

This is …	*To jest …*	to yest …
different	*inne*	*ee*·ne
fun	*fajne*	*fai*·ne
interesting	*interesujące*	een·te·re·soo·*yon*·tse

---

what's in a name?

If you look at a Polish calendar you'll see that every day of the year has a name attached to it. These are the names of the Catholic saints whose feast days fall on a given day but, more importantly, they also indicate *imieniny* ee·mye·*nee*·ni (name days), the Polish equivalent of a birthday.

Polish babies are traditionally named after a particular saint. A child by the name of Barbara takes her name from *Święta Barbara* shvyen·ta bar·*ba*·ra (Saint Barbara), for instance. Up until the age of 13 or so the child will celebrate her *urodziny* oo·ro·*jee*·ni (birthday) on the day of her actual birth. Beyond this age she'll celebrate her *imieniny* on Saint Barbara's feast day instead, along with all the other Barbaras in Poland.

Name days are celebrated with special gatherings of family and friends. If gifts are given they're usually small and often consist of flowers or chocolates. The traditional name-day greeting is *Wszystkiego najlepszego!* fshist·*kye*·go nai·lep·*she*·go (All the best!), and a congratulatory song called *Sto Lat* sto lat (100 years) is sung wishing the person a long life. More often than not, the well-wishing is washed down with a little vodka.

When's the ...	Kiedy jest ...	kye·di yest ...
open?	otwarty/a/e? m/f/n	ot·far·ti/ta/te
gallery	galeria f	ga·le·rya
museum	muzeum n	moo·ze·oom
skansen	skansen m	skan·sen

What's in the collection?
Co jest w zbiorach?	tso yest v zbyo·rakh

It's an exhibition of ...
To jest wystawa ...	to yest vi·sta·va ...

What kind of art are you interested in?
Jakim rodzajem sztuki	ya·keem ro·dza·yem shtoo·kee
pan/pani się	pan/pa·nee shye
interesuje? m/f pol	een·te·re·soo·ye
Jakim rodzajem sztuki	ya·keem ro·dza·yem shtoo·kee
się interesujesz? inf	shye een·te·re·soo·yesh

What do you think of ...?
Co pan/pani myśli	tso pan/pa·nee mish·lee
o ...? m/f pol	o ...
Co myślisz o ...? inf	tso mish·leesh o ...

I'm interested in ...
Interesuję się ...	een·te·re·soo·ye shye ...

I like the works of ...
Lubię prace ...	loo·bye pra·tse ...

It reminds me of ...
To mi przypomina ...	to mee pshi·po·mee·na ...

... art	... sztuka f	... shtoo·ka
baroque	barokowa	ba·ro·ko·va
impressionist	impresjonis-	eem·pre·syo·nees·
	tyczna	tich·na
modern	nowoczesna	no·vo·ches·na
Renaissance	Renesansowa	re·ne·san·so·va
surrealist	surrealistyczna	soor·re·a·lees·tich·na

architecture	architektura f	ar·khee·tek·too·ra
art	sztuka f	shtoo·ka
artwork	dzieło sztuki n	jye·wo shtoo·kee
avant-garde	awangarda f	a·van·gar·da
curator	kustosz m	koos·tosh
design	projekt m	pro·yekt
etching	kwasoryt m	kva·so·rit
exhibit	wystawa f	vis·ta·va
exhibition hall	hala wystawowa f	kha·la vis·ta·vo·va
fabric	tkanina f	tka·nee·na
installation	instalacja f	een·sta·la·tsya
opening	otwarcie n	ot·far·chye
painter	malarz m	ma·lash
painting (artwork)	obraz m	o·bras
painting (technique)	malarstwo n	ma·lars·tfo
period	okres m	o·kres
permanent collection	wystawa stała f	vis·ta·va sta·wa
Polish poster school	polska szkoła plakatu f	pol·ska shko·wa pla·ka·too
Poster Museum	Muzeum Plakatu m	moo·ze·oom pla·ka·too
print	druk m	drook
sculptor	rzeźbiarz m	zhezh·byash
sculpture	rzeźba f	zhezh·ba
statue	pomnik m	pom·neek
studio	pracownia f	pra·tsov·nya
style	styl m	stil

superstitious poles

Keep your eyes peeled for *kominarze* ko·mee·na·zhe (chimney sweeps) on the streets. These men, clad in dusty-black overalls and sprouting a number of oddly shaped brushes and containers, look a bit like apparitions from the 19th century. Superstition has it that if you clasp a button anywhere on your clothing as soon as you see one and make a wish it will invariably be fulfilled.

SOCIAL

In this chapter we've given informal forms. If you're not sure what this means, see the **a–z phrasebuilder**, page 24.

sporting interests

zainteresowania sportowe

What sport do you play?
Jaki sport uprawiasz?   *ya·kee* sport oo·*pra·*vyash

What sport do you follow?
Jakim sportem się   *ya·*keem *spor·*tem shye
interesujesz?   een·te·re·*soo·*yesh

I play/do ...	*Gram ...*	gram ...
I follow ...	*Interesuję się ...*	een·te·re·*soo·*ye shye ...
Alpine skiing	*narciarstwem*	nar·*chyarst·*fem
	zjazdowym	zyaz·*do·*vim
athletics	*lekkoatletyką*	le·ko·at·le·*ti·*kom
basketball	*koszykówką*	ko·shi·*koof·*kom
cycling	*kolarstwem*	ko·*larst·*fem
football (soccer)	*piłką nożną*	*peew·*kom *nozh·*nom
karate	*karate*	ka·*ra·*te
scuba diving	*nurkowaniem*	noor·ko·*va·*nyem
tennis	*tenisem*	te·*nee·*sem
volleyball	*siatkówką*	shyat·*koof·*kom

For more sports, see the **dictionary**.

popular polish sports

koszykówka f   ko·shi·*koof*·ka
Basketball: this is a school sport. The women's national team has had some success in European competitions.

narciarstwo zjazdowe n   nar·*chyar*·stfo zyaz·*do*·ve
Alpine skiing: every winter weekend masses of keen skiers head for the mountains for their dose of adrenaline.

piłka nożna f   *peew*·ka *nozh*·na
Football: this is by far the most popular sport in Poland.

siatkówka f   shyat·*koof*·ka
Volleyball: this a very popular sport taught in primary schools as part of physical education.

żużel m   *zhoo*·zhel
Speedway: surprisingly, this is the second most-watched sport in Poland. Four drivers or motorcyclists race it out on an oval track.

I …		
cycle	*Jeżdżę na rowerze.*	*yezh*·je na ro·*ve*·zhe
run	*Biegam.*	*bye*·gam
walk	*Chodzę.*	*kho*·dze

Do you like (tennis)?
Czy lubisz (tenis)?   chi *loo*·beesh (*te*·nees)

Yes, very much.
Tak. Bardzo.   tak. *bar*·dzo

Not really.
Nie specjalnie.   nye spe·*tsyal*·nye

I like watching it.
Lubię oglądać.   *loo*·bye o·*glon*·dach

Who's your favourite sportsperson?
Kto jest twoim   kto yest *tfoy*·eem
ulubionym sportowcem?   oo·loo·*byo*·nim spor·*tof*·tsem

What's your favourite team?
Jaka jest twoja   *ya*·ka yest *tfo*·ya
ulubiona drużyna?   oo·loo·*byo*·na droo·*zhi*·na

going to a game

Would you like to go to a game?
Czy chcesz iść na mecz?   chi khtsesh eeshch na mech

Who are you supporting?
Komu kibicujesz?   ko·moo kee·bee·tsoo·yesh

Who's ...?	Kto ...?	kto ...
playing	gra	gra
winning	wygrywa	vi·gri·va

That was a ... game!	To był ... mecz!	to biw ... mech
bad	słaby	swa·bi
boring	nudny	noo·dni
great	wspaniały	vspa·nya·wi

playing sport

Do you want to play?
Czy chcesz grać?   chi khtsesh grach

Can I join in?
Czy mogę dołączyć?   chi mo·ge do·won·chich

That would be great.
To by było świetnie!   to bi bi·wo shvyet·nye

I can't.
Nie mogę.   nye mo·ge

I have an injury.
Mam kontuzję.   mam kon·too·zye

Your/My point.
Punkt dla ciebie/mnie. poonkt dla *chye*·bye/mnye

Kick/Pass it to me!
Podaj do mnie! *po*·dai do mnye

You're a good player.
Jesteś dobrym graczem. yes·tesh *do*·brim *gra*·chem

Thanks for the game.
Dziękuję za grę. jyen·*koo*·ye za gre

Where's a good place to …?	*Gdzie jest dobre miejsce …?*	gjye yest *do*·bre myeys·tse …
fish	*do łowienia ryb*	do wo·*vye*·nya rib
go horse riding	*do jazdy konnej*	do *yaz*·di *kon*·ney
go sailboarding	*na windsurfing*	na weend·*ser*·feeng
run	*do biegania*	do bye·*ga*·nya
ski	*do jazdy na nartach*	do *yaz*·di na *nar*·takh

Where's the nearest …?	*Gdzie jest … najbliższy/a?* m/f	gjye yest … nai·*blizh*·shi/sha
gym	*siłownia* f	shee·*wov*·nya
swimming pool	*basen* m	*ba*·sen
tennis court	*kort tenisowy* m	kort te·nee·*so*·vi

Do I have to be a member to attend?
Czy muszę być chi *moo*·she bich
członkiem by wejść? *chwon*·kyem bi veyshch

Is there a women-only session?
Czy jest sesja tylko chi yest *ses*·ya *til*·ko
dla kobiet? dla *ko*·byet

Where are the changing rooms?
Gdzie są szatnie? gjye som *shat*·nye

scoring

What's the score?	*Jaki jest wynik?*	*ya·*kee yest *vi·*neek
draw/even	*remis*	*re·*mees
love (zero)	*zero*	*ze·*ro
match-point	*meczbol*	*mech·*bol
nil	*zero*	*ze·*ro

What's the charge per …?	*Jaka jest opłata za …?*	*ya·*ka yest o·*pwa·*ta za …
day	*dzień*	jyen´
game	*grę*	gre
hour	*godzinę*	go·*jee·*ne
visit	*wizytę*	vee·*zi·*te

Can I hire (a) …?	*Czy mogę wypożyczyć …?*	chi *mo·*ge vi·po·*zhi·*chich …
ball	*piłkę*	*peew·*ke
bicycle	*rower*	*ro·*ver
court	*kort*	kort
racquet	*rakietę*	ra·*kye·*te
kayak	*kajak*	*ka·*yak
yacht	*yacht*	yakht
skis	*narty*	*nar·*ti

skiing

na nartach

How much is a pass?
Ile kosztuje bilet? ee·le kosh·*too·*ye bee·let

Can I take lessons?
Czy mogę zamówić lekcję? chi *mo·*ge za·*moo·*veech lek·tsye

I'd like to hire (a) ...	Chciałbym/ Chciałabym wypożyczyć ... m/f	khchow·bim/ khchow·a·bim vi·po·zhi·chich ...
boots	buty	boo·ti
gloves	rękawice	ren·ka·vee·tse
goggles	gogle	go·gle
poles	kijki	keey·kee
skis	narty	nar·ti
ski suit	kombinezon narciarski	kom·bee·ne·zon nar·chyar·skee

Is it possible to go ...?	Czy jest możliwe aby pojechać na ...?	chi yest mozh·lee·ve a·bi po·ye·khach na ...
Alpine skiing	narty	nar·ti
cross-country skiing	biegówki	bye·goof·kee
snowboarding	snowboard	snow·bord
tobogganing	sanki	san·kee

What are the conditions like ...?	Jakie są warunki ...?	ya·kye som va·roon·kee ...
at (Kasprowy)	na (Kasprowym)	na (kas·pro·vim)
on that run	na tej trasie	na tey tra·shye
higher up	tam wyżej	tam vi·zhey

Which are the ... slopes?	Który zjazd jest dla ...?	ktoo·ri zyazd yest dla ...
beginner	początkujących	po·chont·koo·yon·tsikh
intermediate	średniozaawansowanych	shred·nyo·za·a·van·so·va·nikh
advanced	zaawansowanych	za·a·van·so·va·nikh

cable car	*kolejka linowa* f	ko·*ley*·ka lee·*no*·va
chairlift	*wyciąg*	vi·chyonk
	krzesełkowy m	kshe·sew·*ko*·vi
instructor	*instruktor* m	een·*strook*·tor
resort	*ośrodek*	osh·ro·dek
	narciarski m	nar·*chyar*·skee
ski lift	*wyciąg*	vi·chyonk
	narciarski m	nar·*chyar*·skee
sled	*sanki* pl	*san*·kee

soccer/football

piłka nożna

Who plays for (Legia Warszawa)?
Kto gra w (Legii Warszawa)? kto gra v (le·gyee var·*sha*·va)

He's a great (player).
On jest świetnym (graczem). on yest *shfyet*·nim (*gra*·chem)

He played brilliantly in the match against (Italy).
On grał wspaniale w on grow fspa·*nya*·le v
meczu z (Włochami). me·choo z (vwo·*kha*·mee)

Which team is at the top of the league?
Która drużyna jest *ktoo*·ra droo·*zhi*·na yest
na szczycie tabeli? na *shchi*·chye ta·*be*·lee

What a great/terrible team!
Co za wspaniały/ tso za vspa·*nya*·wi/
beznadziejny zespół! bez·na·*jyey*·ni *zes*·poow

sports talk		
What a ...!	*Co za ... !*	tso za ...
goal	*gol*	gol
hit	*uderzenie*	oo·de·*zhe*·nye
kick	*strzał*	stshow
pass	*podanie*	po·*da*·nye
performance	*występ*	*vis*·temp

sport

151

ball	*piłka* f	peew·ka
coach n	*trener* m	tre·ner
corner (kick) n	*róg* m	roog
expulsion	*usunięcie* n	oo·soo·nyen·chye
fan	*kibic* m	kee·beets
foul n	*faul* m	faool
free kick	*rzut wolny* m	zhoot vol·ni
goal (structure)	*bramka* f	bram·ka
goalkeeper	*bramkarz* m	bram·kash
manager	*menedżer* m	me·ne·jer
offside	*spalony* m	spa·lo·ni
penalty	*rzut karny* m	zhoot kar·ni
player	*zawodnik* m	za·vod·neek
red card	*czerwona kartka* f	cher·vo·na kart·ka
referee	*sędzia* m	sen·jya
striker	*napastnik* m	na·past·neek
throw in n	*wrzut z autu* m	vzhoot z ow·too
yellow card	*żółta kartka* f	zhoow·ta kart·ka

Off to see a match? Check out **going to a game**, page 147.

ups and down

If you're at a match and want to be vocal in the support of a particular team or howl the opposition down, try out these phrases:

Go ...!	... *pany!*	... *pa·ni*
Down with ...!	... *dziady!*	... *jya·di*
A goal for (Poland)!	*(Polska) gola!*	*(pol·ska) go·la*

SOCIAL

152

outdoors
na wolnym powietrzu

hiking

wycieczki piesze

Where can I …?	*Gdzie mogę …?*	gjye *mo*·ge …
buy supplies	*kupić*	koo·peech
	zaopatrzenie	za·o·pa·*tshe*·nye
find someone	*znaleźć*	zna·leshch
who knows	*kogoś kto*	ko·gosh kto
this area	*zna okolicę*	zna o·ko·*lee*·tse
get a map	*dostać mapę*	dos·tach ma·pe
hire hiking gear	*wypożyczyć*	vi·po·*zhi*·chich
	sprzęt	spshent
	turystyczny	too·ris·*tich*·ni

How …?	*Jak …?*	yak …
high is the	*długie jest*	*dwoo*·gye yest
climb	*podejście*	po·*deysh*·chye
long is the	*długi jest*	*dwoo*·gee yest
trail	*szlak*	shlak

Do we need a guide?
Czy potrzebujemy przewodnika?
chi po·tshe·boo·*ye*·mi pshe·vod·*nee*·ka

Are there guided treks?
Czy są tam wyznaczone szlaki?
chi som tam viz·na·*cho*·ne *shla*·kee

Is it safe?
Czy to jest bezpieczne?
chi to yest bes·*pyech*·ne

Is there a hut/shelter?
Czy jest tam chatka/ schronisko?
chi yest tam *khat*·ka/ skhro·*nees*·ko

When does it get dark?
Kiedy robi się ciemno?
kye·di ro·bee shye *chyem*·no

outdoors

153

Do we need to take ...?	Czy musimy zabrać ...?	chi moo·shee·mi za·brach ...
a sleeping bag	śpiwór	shpee·voor
a mat	materac	ma·te·rats
food	żywność	zhiv·noshch
water	wodę	vo·de

Is the track ...?	Czy droga jest ...?	chi dro·ga yest ...
(well-)marked	(dobrze) oznaczona	(dob·zhe) oz·na·cho·na
open	otwarta	ot·far·ta
scenic	widowiskowa	vee·do·vees·ko·va

Which is the ... route?	Która droga jest ...?	ktoo·ra dro·ga yest ...
easiest	najłatwiejsza	nai·wat·fyey·sha
most interesting	najciekawsza	nai·chye·kaf·sha
shortest	najkrótsza	nai·kroot·sha

Where can I find the ...?	Gdzie jest/są ...? sg/pl	gjye yest/som ...
camping ground	kamping sg	kam·peeng
nearest village	najbliższa wieś sg	nai·bleezh·sha vyesh
showers	prysznice pl	prish·nee·tse
toilets	toalety pl	to·a·le·ti

Where have you come from?
Skąd pan/pani przyszedł/przyszła? m/f pol — skont pan/pa·nee pshi·shedw/pshi·shwa
Skąd przyszedłeś/przyszłaś? m/f — skont pshi·shed·wesh/pshi·shwash

How long did it take?
Ile czasu to zajęło? — ee·le cha·soo to za·ye·wo

Does this path go to (Kudowa)?
Czy ta droga prowadzi do (Kudowy)?
chi ta *dro*·ga pro·*va*·jee do (koo·*do*·vi)

Can I go through here?
Czy mogę tędy przejść?
chi *mo*·ge *ten*·di psheyshch

Is the water OK to drink?
Czy woda jest zdatna do picia?
chi *vo*·da yest *zdat*·na do *pee*·chya

I'm lost.
Zgubiłem/am się. m/f
zgoo·*bee*·wem/wam shye

beach

plaża

Beaches along Poland's Baltic coastline are either *płatne* pwat·ne (paying) or *dzikie* jee·kye (lit: wild, but meaning 'free of charge') and you'll see signage to this effect. Another sign you may see is one that reads *strzeżone* stshe·*zho*·ne (guarded), indicating that there is a lifeguard. Facilities such as toilets are usually present at these beaches too.

Where's the … beach?	*Gdzie jest …?*	gjye yest …
best	*najlepsza plaża*	nai·*lep*·sha *pla*·zha
nearest	*najbliższa plaża*	nai·*bleezh*·sha *pla*·zha
nudist	*plaża dla nudystów*	*pla*·zha dla noo·*dis*·toof
Is it safe to … here?	*Czy tu można bezpiecznie …?*	chi too *mozh*·na bes·*pyech*·nye …
dive	*nurkować*	noor·*ko*·vach
swim	*pływać*	*pwi*·vach

beach & pool signs		
No Diving	*Skakanie wzbronione*	ska·*ka*·nye vzbro·*nyo*·ne
No Swimming	*Zakaz kąpieli*	*za*·kaz kom·*pye*·lee

outdoors

155

What time is high/low tide?
  O której godzinie   o ktoo·rey go·*jee*·nye
  jest przypływ/odpływ?   yest pshi·pwiv/*od*·pwiv

Do we have to pay?
  Czy musimy płacić?   chi moo·*shee*·mi *pwa*·cheech

How much to	*Ile kosztuje*	*ee·*le kosh·*too*·ye
rent a/an …?	*wypożyczenie …?*	vi·po·zhi·*che*·nye …
chair	*krzesła*	*kshes*·wa
umbrella	*parasola*	pa·ra·*so*·la

weather

pogoda

What's the weather like?
  Jaka jest pogoda?   *ya*·ka yest po·*go*·da

What will the weather be like tomorrow?
  Jaka jutro będzie pogoda?   *ya*·ka *yoo*·tro *ben*·jye po·*go*·da

wet sense of humour

Want to sound like a local? Here are a couple of amusing
Polish idioms you can trot out in inclement weather:

Leje jak z cebra.
le·ye yak z *tse*·bra
(It's raining cats and dogs – lit: it's pouring from a bucket.)

Przemokłem/am do suchej nitki. m/f
pzhe·*mok*·wem/wam do *soo*·khey *neet*·kee
(I'm soaked to the bone – lit: to be wet right through to
your dry threads.)

It's ...		
raining	*Pada deszcz.*	*pa*·da deshch
snowing	*Pada śnieg.*	*pa*·da shnyeg

It's ...	*Jest ...*	yest ...
cloudy	*pochmurnie*	pokh·*moor*·nye
cold	*zimno*	*zheem*·no
fine	*pogodnie*	po·*god*·nye
freezing	*lodowato*	lo·do·*va*·to
hot	*gorąco*	go·*ron*·tso
sunny	*słonecznie*	swo·*nech*·nye
warm	*ciepło*	*chyep*·wo
windy	*wietrznie*	*vyetzh*·nye

Where can I buy a/an ...?	*Gdzie mogę kupić ...?*	gjye *mo*·ge *koo*·peech ...
rain jacket	*kurtkę przeciw deszczową*	*koort*·ke *pshe*·cheef desh·*cho*·vom
umbrella	*parasol*	pa·*ra*·sol

flora & fauna

flora i fauna

What ... is that?	*Co to jest za ...?*	tso to yest za ...
animal	*zwierzę*	*zvye*·zhe
flower	*kwiat*	kfyat
plant	*roślina*	rosh·*lee*·na
tree	*drzewo*	*dzhe*·vo

Is it ...?	*Czy to jest ...?*	chi to yest ...
common	*pospolite*	pos·po·*lee*·te
dangerous	*niebezpieczne*	nye·bes·*pyech*·ne
endangered	*pod ochroną*	pod okh·*ro*·nom
poisonous	*trujące*	troo·*yon*·tse
protected	*chronione*	khro·*nyo*·ne

What's it used for?
Do czego się to używa? do *che*·go shye to oo-*zhi*·va

Can you eat the fruit?
Czy ten owoc jest jadalny? chi ten *o*·vots yest ya-*dal*·ni

For geographical and agricultural terms, and the names of animals and plants, see the **dictionary**.

local animals & plants

The Polish word for 'bear', *niedźwiedź nyej*·vyej, is derived from the common Slavic words *medu* (meaning 'honey') and *ed* ('to eat'). Thus *niedźwiedź* originally meant 'honey eater'. This eumphemistic derivation came about because naming the fearful beast was once taboo. Here are some other examples of Polish flora and fauna:

bear	*niedźwiedź* m	*nyej*·vyej
bison	*żubr* m	zhoobr
oak	*dąb* m	domb
pine	*sosna* f	*sos*·na
white stork	*bocian* m	*bo*·chyan
wolf	*wilk* m	veelk

Breakfast might seem a bit heavy by Western standards. It usually includes bread and butter, various types of cheese, ham and eggs, washed down with tea or coffee. Around 11am morning tea is served. This generally consists of various types of sandwiches and fruit. The next and main meal of the day is dinner in the early afternoon which usually features soup, a main course and a dessert. The last meal of the day is supper which is relatively light and is served around 6 to 7pm.

basics

podstawy

breakfast	*śniadanie* n	shnya·*da*·nye
morning tea	*drugie*	droo·gye
	śniadanie n	shnya·*da*·nye
dinner (late lunch)	*obiad* m	o·byad
supper	*kolacja* f	ko·*la*·tsya
snack	*przekąska* f	pshe·*kons*·ka
menu	*jadłospis* m	ya·*dwo*·spees
eat	*jeść*	yeshch
drink v	*pić*	peech
I'd like ...	*Chciałbym/*	khchow·bim/
	Chciałabym ... m/f	khchow·*a*·bim ...
Please.	*Proszę.*	*pro*·she
Thank you.	*Dziękuję.*	jyen·*koo*·ye
I'm starving!	*Umieram z głodu!*	oo·*mye*·ram z *gwo*·doo

finding a place to eat

Your best option for dining out in Poland is a meal at a *restauracja* res·tow·*rats*·ya (restaurant). These run the gamut from unpretentious eateries to luxury establishments. A *bar mleczny* bar *mlech*·ni (lit: milk bar) is a no-frills self-service cafeteria with a large portion of the menu made up of dairy-derived dishes, as the name suggests. The place to go for coffee, snacks and light meals is a *kawiarna* ka·*vyar*·na (café).

Can you recommend a …?	*Czy może pan/ pani polecić …?* m/f	chi *mo*·zhe pan/ *pa*·nee po·*le*·cheech …
bar	*bar*	bar
café	*kawiarnię*	ka·*vyar*·nye
restaurant	*restaurację*	res·tow·*rats*·ye
self-service cafeteria	*bar mleczny*	bar *mlech*·ni
Where would you go for …?	*Dokąd byś poszedł/ poszła …?* m/f	do·kond bish po·shedw/ po·shwa …
a celebration	*by coś uczcić*	bi tsosh *ooch*·tseech
a cheap meal	*na tani posiłek*	na *ta*·nee po·*shee*·wek
local specialities	*na miejscowe specjały*	na myeys·*tso*·ve spe·*tsya*·wi
I'd like to reserve a table for …	*Chciałem/am zarezerwować stolik …* m/f	khchow·em/am za·re·zer·*vo*·vach *sto*·leek …
(two) people	*dla (dwóch) osób*	dla (dvookh) o·soob
(eight) o'clock	*na (ósmą)*	na (*oos*·mom)

Are you still serving food?
Czy można jeszcze zamawiać jedzenie?
chi *mo*·zhna *yesh*·che za·*ma*·vyach ye·*dze*·nye

How long is the wait?
Jak długo trzeba czekać? yak *dwoo*·go *tshe*·ba *che*·kach

listen for ...

Już jest zamknięte.
yoosh yest zamk·*nyen*·te

We're closed.

Nie ma wolnych miejsc.
nye ma *vol*·nikh myeysts

We're full.

Chwileczkę.
khfee·*lech*·ke

One moment.

at the restaurant

w restauracji

Leaving a *napiwek* na·*pee*·vek (tip) is advisable but not strictly necessary. Worth sampling is *bigos* *bee*·gos, the national dish, made from sauerkraut and a variety of meats slow-simmered together.

What would you recommend?
Co by pan/pani
polecił/poleciła? m/f
tso bi pan/*pa*·nee
po·*le*·cheew/po·le·*chee*·wa

What's in that dish?
Co jest w tym daniu?
tso yest v tim *da*·nyoo

What's that called?
Jak się to nazywa?
yak shye to na·*zi*·va

I'll have that.
Zamówię to.
za·*moo*·vye to

Does it take long to prepare?
Czy długo trwa
przyrządzenie tego?
chi *dwoo*·go trfa
pshi·zhon·*dze*·nye tego

Is it self-serve?
Czy tu jest samoobsługa?
chi too yest sa·mo·ob·*swoo*·ga

eating out

161

Is there a cover/service charge?
Czy jest opłata za   chi yest o-*pwa*-ta za
wstęp/obsługę?   fstemp/ob-*swoo*-ge

Is service included in the bill?
Czy obsługa jest   chi ob-*swoo*-ga yest
wliczona do rachunku?   vlee-*cho*-na do ra-*khoon*-koo

Are these complimentary?
Czy to jest bezpłatne?   chi to yest bes-*pwa*-tne

Could I please see the wine list?
Czy mogę prosić o   chi *mo*-ge *pro*-sheech o
listę win?   *lees*-te veen

I'd like (a/the) …, *Proszę …*	*pro*-she …
please.	
children's menu	*o jadłospis*	o ya-*dwo*-spees
	dla dzieci	dla *jye*-chee
drink list	*o spis napojów*	o spees na-*po*-yoof
half portion	*o pół porcji*	o poow *ports*-yee
local speciality	*o miejscową*	o myeys-*tso*-vom
	specjalność	spe-*tsyal*-noshch
meal fit for	*o królewski*	o kroo-*lef*-skee
a king	*posiłek*	po-*shee*-wek
menu	*o jadłospis*	o ya-*dwo*-spees
(in English)	*(po angielsku)*	(po an-*gyel*-skoo)
nonsmoking	*dla*	dla
	niepalących	nye-pa-*lon*-tsikh
smoking	*dla palących*	dla pa-*lon*-tsikh
table for (five)	*o stolik na*	o *sto*-leek na
	(pięć osób)	(pyench o-soob)
that dish	*to danie*	to *da*-nye

I'd like it with …	*Chciałbym/ Chciałabym to z …* m/f	khchow·bim/ khchow·a·bim to z …
cheese	*serem*	se·rem
chilli	*chili*	chee·lee
chilli sauce	*sosem chili*	so·sem chee·lee
garlic	*czosnkiem*	chosn·kyem
ketchup	*keczupem*	ke·choo·pem
nuts	*orzechami*	o·zhe·kha·mee
oil	*oliwą*	o·lee·vom
pepper	*pieprzem*	pyep·shem
salt	*solą*	so·lom
tomato sauce	*sosem pomidorowym*	so·sem po·mee·do·ro·vim
vinegar	*octem*	ots·tem
I'd like it without …	*Chciałbym/ Chciałabym to bez …* m/f	khchow·bim/ khchow·a·bim to bes …
cheese	*sera*	se·ra
chilli	*chili*	chee·lee
chilli sauce	*sosu chili*	so·soo chee·lee
garlic	*czosnku*	chosn·koo
ketchup	*keczupu*	ke·choo·poo
nuts	*orzechów*	o·zhe·khoof
oil	*oliwy*	o·lee·vee
pepper	*pieprzu*	pyep·shoo
salt	*soli*	so·lee
tomato sauce	*sosu pomidorowego*	so·soo po·mee·do·ro·ve·go
vinegar	*octu*	ots·too

For other specific meal requests, see **vegetarian & special meals**, page 177.

For other specific meal requests, see **vegetarian & special meals**, page 177.

listen for …

Polecam …	po·le·tsam …	I suggest the …
Proszę bardzo!	pro·she bar·dzo	Here you go!
Smacznego.	smach·ne·go	Enjoy your meal.

eating out

Poland has for centuries been a cosmopolitan country, and its food has been influenced by the cuisines of its neighbours. Polish food is hearty and rich in meat, if not vegetables. Vegetarians should find *dania jarskie* da·nya yar·skye or vegetable dishes on the menu in most places. The price of a main course doesn't usually include side orders, which you should select from the *dodatki* do·dat·kee section of the menu. Below is a selection of other common menu terms:

Przekąski	pshe·*kons*·kee	Appetisers
Zupy	*zoo*·pi	Soups
Entrée	*an*·tre	Entrées
Sałatki	sa·*wat*·kee	Salads
Drugie Dania	*droo*·gye da·nya	Main Courses
Dania Mięsne	da·nya *myens*·ne	Meat Dishes
Dania Rybne	da·nya *rib*·ne	Fish Dishes
Drób	droob	Poultry
Dania Jarskie	da·nya *yar*·skye	Vegetarian Dishes
Dodatki	do·*dat*·kee	Side Dishes
Desery	de·*se*·ri	Desserts
Aperitify	a·pe·ree·*tee*·fi	Apéritifs
Drinki	*dreen*·kee	Drinks
Napoje	na·*po*·ye	Soft Drinks
Alkohole	al·ko·*ho*·le	Spirits
Piwa	*pee*·va	Beers
Alkohole	al·ko·*ho*·le	Digestifs
Poprawiające	po·pra·vya·*yon*·tse	
Trawienie	tra·*vye*·nye	
Wina ...	*vee*·na ...	... Wines
Musujące	moo·soo·*yon*·tse	Sparkling
Białe	*bya*·we	White
Czerwone	cher·*vo*·ne	Red
Deserowe	de·se·*ro*·ve	Dessert

For additional items, see the **culinary reader**, page 179.

at the table

Please bring (a/the) …	Proszę o …	pro·she o …
bill/check	rachunek	ra·khoo·nek
cutlery	sztućce	shtooch·tse
(wine)glass	kieliszek	kye·lee·shek
	(do wina)	(do vee·na)
serviette	serwetkę	ser·vet·ke
tablecloth	obrus	o·broos

This is …	To jest …	to yest …
burnt	przypalone	pshi·pa·lo·ne
(too) cold	(za) zimne	(za) zheem·ne
(too) spicy	(za) pikantne	(za) pee·kant·ne
(too) salty	(za) słone	(za) swo·ne
stale	nieświeże	nye·shvye·zhe
superb	pyszne	pish·ne
spicy	ostre	os·tre

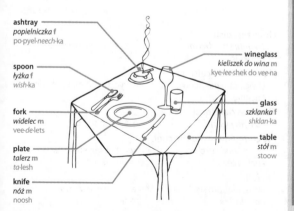

ashtray
popielniczka f
po·pyel·neech·ka

spoon
łyżka f
wish·ka

fork
widelec m
vee·de·lets

plate
talerz m
ta·lesh

knife
nóż m
noosh

wineglass
kieliszek do wina m
kye·lee·shek do vee·na

glass
szklanka f
shklan·ka

table
stół m
stoow

Try some of these treats while you're out and about:

gofry pl   go·fri
waffles with whipped cream – as delicious as they sound

obwarzanek m   ob·va·*zha*·nek
bagel – legend has it that these originated in Poland

oscypek m   os·*tsi*·pek
smoked sheep's-milk cheese – an important symbol of
Poland's culinary heritage hailing from the Tatra Mountains

placki ziemniaczane pl   *plats*·kee zhyem·nya·*cha*·ne
potato pancakes – fried cakes of grated potato and egg
flavoured with onion

zapiekanki pl   za·pye·*kan*·kee
split baguette topped with cheese, mushrooms and ketchup

talking food

komentowanie posiłku

I love this dish.
To danie bardzo mi   to *da*·nye *bar*·dzo mee
smakuje.   sma·*koo*·ye

I love the local cuisine.
Uwielbiam miejscową   oo·*vyel*·byam myeys·*tso*·vom
kuchnię.   *kookh*·nye

That was delicious!
To było pyszne.   to *bi*·wo *pish*·ne

My compliments to the chef.
Proszę podziękować   *pro*·she po·jyen·*ko*·vach
kucharzowi.   koo·kha·*zho*·vee

I'm full.
Najadłem/am się   na·*yad*·wem/wam shye
do syta. m/f   do *si*·ta

methods of preparation

I'd like it ...	Chciałbym/	khchow·bim/
	Chciałabym	khchow·a·bim
	to ... m/f	to ...
boiled	gotowane	go·to·va·ne
deep-fried	smażone	sma·zho·ne
	w oleju	v o·le·yoo
fried	usmażone	oo·sma·zho·ne
grilled	z rusztu	z roosh·too
mashed	purée	pee·re
medium	średnio	shred·nyo
	przyrządzone	pshi·zhon·dzo·ne
rare	lekko	le·ko
	przyrządzone	pshi·zhon·dzo·ne
reheated	odgrzane	od·gzha·ne
steamed	na parze	na pa·zhe
well done	dobrze	dob·zhe
	przyrządzone	pshi·zhon·dzo·ne
without ...	bez ...	bes ...
I don't want it ...	Nie chcę tego ...	nye khtse te·go ...
boiled	ugotowanego	oo·go·to·va·ne·go
deep-fried	smażonego w	sma·zho·ne go v
	oleju	o·le·yoo
fried	usmażonego	oo·sma·zho·ne·go
grilled	z rusztu	z roosh·too
mashed	purée	pee·re
medium	średnio	shred·nyo
	przyrządzonego	pshi·zhon·dzo·ne·go
rare	lekko	le·ko
	przyrządzonego	pshi·zhon·dzo·ne·go
reheated	odgrzanego	od·gzha·ne·go
steamed	na parze	na pa·zhe
well done	dobrze	dob·zhe
	przyrządzonego	pshi·zhon·dzo·ne·go

nonalcoholic drinks

... water	*woda* f ...	*vo*·da ...
mineral	*mineralna*	mee·ne·*ral*·na
sparkling	*gazowana*	ga·zo·*va*·na
still	*niegazowana*	nye·ga·zo·*va*·na
(orange) juice	*sok*	sok
	(pomarańczowy) m	(po·ma·ran'·*cho*·vi)
soft drink	*napój* m	*na*·pooy
(hot) water	*(gorąca) woda* f	(go·*ron*·tsa) *vo*·da
cup of tea	*filiżanka herbaty*	fee·lee·*zhan*·ka her·*ba*·ti
(with lemon)	*(z cytryną)*	(z tsi·*tri*·nom)
cup of coffee/	*filiżanka kawy/*	fee·lee·*zhan*·ka *ka*·vi/
tea ...	*herbaty* ...	her·*ba*·ti ...
with milk	*z mlekiem*	z *mle*·kyem
without milk	*bez mleka*	bes *mle*·ka
with sugar	*z cukrem*	z *tsoo*·krem
without sugar	*bez cukru*	bez *tsoo*·kroo

anyone for coffee?

Coffee *po turecku* po too·*rets*·koo (lit: in the Turkish manner) is, much like its namesake, thick, black and sweet with a sludge of grounds at the bottom. It's made by putting a couple of teaspoons of coffee grounds directly into a glass and topping it up with water. This brew also goes by the name of *kawa parzona* *ka*·va pa·*zho*·na.

black coffee	*czarna kawa* f	*char*·na *ka*·va
decaffeinated	*kawa bez*	*ka*·va bes
coffee	*kafeiny* f	ka·fe·*ee*·ni
iced coffee	*kawa mrożona* f	*ka*·va mro·*zho*·na
strong	*mocna* f	*mots*·na
strong black	*kawa po*	*ka*·va po
coffee	*turecku* f	too·*rets*·koo
weak	*słaba* f	*swa*·ba

alcoholic drinks

napoje alkoholowe

(cold) beer	(zimne) piwo n	(zheem·ne) pee·vo
brandy	brandy m	bren·di
champagne	szampan m	sham·pan
cocktail	koktail m	kok·tail
Goldwasser (herbal liqueur)	goldwasser m	gold·va·ser
grape brandy	winiak m	vee·nyak
honey liqueur	krupnik m	kroop·neek

a shot of ...	kieliszek ...	kye·lee·shek ...
gin	dżinu	jee·noo
rum	rumu	roo·moo
tequila	tequili	te·kee·lee
vodka	wódki	vood·kee
whisky	whisky	wis·kee

a bottle/glass of ... wine	butelka/ kieliszek wina ...	boo·tel·ka/ kye·lee·shek vee·na ...
dessert	deserowego	de·se·ro·ve·go
red	czerwonego	cher·vo·ne·go
rosé	rose	ro·se
sparkling	musującego	moo·soo·yon·tse·go
white	białego	bya·we·go

a ... of beer	... piwa	... pee·va
glass	szklanka	shklan·ka
pint	kufel	koo·fel
small bottle	mała butelka	ma·wa boo·tel·ka
large bottle	duża butelka	doo·zha boo·tel·ka

For additional items, see the **culinary reader**, page 179, and the **dictionary**.

eating out

in the bar

The most popular drink by far in Poland is *wódka* vood·ka (vodka), which is served neat in 25ml or 50ml glasses (or 100ml for heavy drinkers). Only Russians or Finns can match the prodigious vodka consumption of the Poles, so pace yourself carefully if you're joining in with the locals. Some of the best brands of vodka are *Belvedere* bel·ve·der, *Wyborowa* vi·bo·ro·va and *Żubrówka* zhoo·broof·ka. *Piwo* pee·vo (beer) is also good quality and popular. Try these brands: *Tyskie* tis·kye, *Okocim* o·ko·cheem, *Lech* lekh and *Żywiec* zhi·vyets.

Excuse me!
  Przepraszam!   pshe·*pra*·sham

I'm next.
  Ja jestem następny w   ya *yes*·tem nas·*temp*·ni v
  kolejce.   ko·*ley*·tse

I'll have (vodka).
  Proszę (wódkę).   pro·she (vood·ke)

Same again, please.
  Proszę jeszcze raz to samo.   pro·she yesh·che ras to *sa*·mo

No ice, thanks.
  Proszę bez lodu.   pro·she bes lo·doo

I'll buy you a drink.
  Czy mogę panu/pani   chi mo·ge pa·noo/*pa*·nee
  kupić drinka? m/f pol   koo·peech dreen·ka
  Kupię ci drinka. inf   koo·pye chee dreen·ka

---

listen for ...

Co mogę panu/pani/państwu podać? m/f/pl
tso mo·ge pa·noo/pa·nee/   **What are you having?**
pan'·stfoo po·dach

Myślę, że panu/i już wystarczy.
mish·le zhe pa·noo/nee   **I think you've had**
yoosh vis·tar·chi   **enough.**

What would you like?
    Co mogę dla pana/pani   tso *mo*·ge dla *pa*·na/*pa*·nee
    zamówić? m/f pol   za·*moo*·veech
    Co zamówić dla ciebie? inf   tso za·*moo*·veech dla *chye*·bye

I don't drink alcohol.
    Nie piję alkoholu.   nye *pee*·ye al·ko·*kho*·loo

It's my round.
    Ja stawiam.   ya *sta*·vyam

How much is that?
    Ile to kosztuje?   *ee*·le to kosh·*too*·ye

Do you serve meals here?
    Czy można tu coś   chi *mozh*·na too tsosh
    zjeść?   zyeshch

drinking up

The gesture for indicating inebriation is an outstretched palm making a repeated chopping action on the side of the neck.

Cheers!
    Na zdrowie!   na *zdro*·vye

I feel fantastic!
    Czuję się wspaniale!   *choo*·ye shye fspa·*nya*·le

I think I've had one too many.
    Chyba wypiłem/am   *khi*·ba vi·*pee*·wem/wam
    o jeden za dużo. m/f   o *ye*·den za *doo*·zho

I'm feeling drunk.
    Jestem pijany/a. m/f   *yes*·tem pee·*ya*·ni/na

I'm pissed.
    Jestem zalany/a. m/f   *yes*·tem za·*la*·ni/na

I feel ill.
    Niedobrze mi.   nye·*do*·bzhe mee

Where's the toilet?
    Gdzie jest ubikacja?   gje yest oo·bee·*ka*·tsya

I'm tired, I'd better go home.

Jestem zmęczony/a,   yes·tem zmen·*cho*·ni/na
lepiej już pójdę   le·pyey yoosh *pooy*·de
do domu. m/f   do *do*·moo

Can you call a taxi for me?

Czy może pan/pani   chi *mo*·zhe pan/*pa*·nee
zamówić dla mnie   za·*moo*·veech dla mnye
taksówkę? m/f pol   tak·*soof*·ke
Czy możesz zamówić   chi *mo*·zhesh za·*moo*·veech
dla mnie taksówkę? inf   dla mnye tak·*soof*·ke

I don't think you should drive.

Nie powinien/powinna   nye po·*vee*·nyen/po·*vee*·na
pan/pani kierować. m/f pol   pan/*pa*·nee kye·*ro*·vach
Nie powinieneś/   nye po·vee·*nye*·nesh/
powinnaś kierować. m/f inf   po·*veen*·nash kye·*ro*·vach

---

vodka reader

There can be no doubt that Poles love their *wódka* vood·ka. They even claim to have invented the beverage, much to the disapproval of their Russian neighbours. Polish vodka comes in a number of different colours and flavours. *Żubrówka* zhoo·*broof*·ka (bison vodka) is so called because it's flavoured with grass from the Białowieża Forest on which bison feed.

bimber m	*beem*·ber	moonshine (illegally brewed vodka)
jałowcówka f	ya·wov·*tsoof*·ka	juniper-berry vodka
jarzębiak m	ya·*zhem*·byak	rowanberry vodka
śliwowica f	shlee·vo·*vee*·tsa	plum brandy
wiśniówka f	vish·*nyoof*·ka	cherry vodka
Żubrówka f	zhoo·*broof*·ka	bison vodka

For vodka-drinking etiquette see the box on page 128.

buying food

kupowanie żywności

What's the local speciality?
*Co jest miejscową
specjalnością?*
tso yest myeys·tso·vom
spe·tsyal·nosh·chyom

What's that?
Co to jest?
tso to yest

Can I taste it?
Czy mogę spróbować?
chi mo·ge sproo·bo·vach

Can I have a bag, please?
Czy mogę prosić o torbę?
chi mo·ge pro·sheech o tor·be

I don't need a bag, thanks.
*Dziękuję, ale nie
potrzebuje torby.*
jyen·koo·ye a·le nye
po·tshe·boo·ye tor·bi

How much (is a kilo of cheese)?
*Ile kosztuje
(kilogram sera)?*
ee·le kosh·too·ye
(kee·lo·gram se·ra)

listen for ...

Co podać?
tso po·dach
What would you like?

W czym mogę pomóc?
v chim mo·ge po·moots
Can I help you?

Czy coś jeszcze?
chi tsosh yesh·che
Anything else?

Nie ma.
nye ma
There isn't any.

I'd like ...	Proszę ...	pro·she ...
(20) decagrams/ (200) grams	(20) deko	(dva·jyesh·chya) de·ko
half a dozen	sześć	sheshch
a dozen	dwanaście	dva·nash·chye
half a kilo	pół kilo	poow kee·lo
a kilo	kilo	kee·lo
(two) kilos	(dwa) kilo	(dva) kee·lo
a bottle	butelkę	boo·tel·ke
a jar	słoik	swo·yeek
a packet	paczkę	pach·ke
a piece	kawałek	ka·vow·ek
(three) pieces	(trzy) kawałki	(tshi) ka·vow·kee
(five) pieces	(pięć) kawałków	(pyench) ka·vow·koof
a slice	plasterek	plas·te·rek
(two) slices	(dwa) plasterki	(dva) plas·ter·kee
(six) slices	(sześć) plasterków	(sheshch) plas·ter·koof
a tin	puszkę	poosh·ke
(just) a little	(tylko) trochę	(til·ko) tro·khe
more	więcej	vyen·tsey
some ...	kilka ...	keel·ka ...
that one	tamten	tam·ten
this one	ten	ten

For an explanation of the *deko* de·ko unit of measurement and why nouns change their form with numbers, see **numbers & amounts**, pages 34 and 36.

how would you like that?		
cooked	gotowany m	go·to·va·ni
cured	konserwowany m	kon·ser·vo·va·ni
dried	suszony m	soo·sho·ni
fresh	świeży m	shvye·zhi
frozen	mrożony m	mro·zho·ni
raw	surowy m	soo·ro·vi
smoked	wędzony m	ven·dzo·ni

Less.	Mniej.	mney
A bit more.	Trochę więcej.	tro·khe vyen·tsey
Enough.	Wystarczy.	vis·tar·chi
Please.	Proszę.	pro·she
Please give me …	Proszę …	pro·she …
Thank you.	Dziękuję.	jyen·koo·ye
That's delicious!	To jest pyszne.	to yest pish·ne

Do you have …?	Czy …?	chi …
anything cheaper	jest coś tańszego	yest tsosh tan'·she·go
other kinds	są inne rodzaje	som ee·ne ro·dza·ye

Where can I find the … section?	Gdzie mogę znaleźć dział …?	gjye mo·ge zna·leshch jyow …
dairy	z nabiałem	z na·bya·wem
fish	rybny	rib·ni
frozen goods	z mrożon·kami	z mro·zhon·ka·mee
fruit and vegetable	owocowo-warzywny	o·vo·tso·vo·va·zhiv·ni
meat	z mięsem	z myen·sem
poultry	z drobiem	z dro·byem

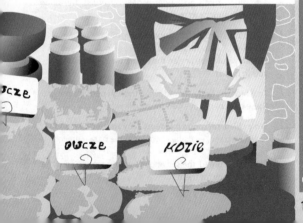

cooking utensils

Could I please borrow a ...?	Czy mogę pożyczyć ...?	chi *mo*·ge po·*zhi*·chich ...
I need a ...	Potrzebuję ...	po·tshe·*boo*·ye ...
chopping board	deskę do krojenia	*des*·ke do kro·*ye*·nya
frying pan	patelnię	pa·*tel*·nye
knife	nóż	noozh
saucepan	garnek	*gar*·nek

For more cooking implements, see the **dictionary**.

some salt with that?

In Polish culture *chleb* khlep (bread) and *sól* sool (salt) have a special symbolic status. They're symbols of fertility and good fortune, but perhaps most importantly, of *gościnność* gosh·*chee*·noshch (hospitality). After a traditional Polish wedding, the bride and groom visit the bride's parents and are welcomed with a gift of bread and salt. According to a tradition that's no longer widely observed, the bride's mother is supposed to say:

Co wolisz: chleb, sól czy pana młodego?
tso *vo*·lesh khlep sool chi *pa*·na mwo·*de*·go
(Which would you prefer: the bread, the salt or your young man?)

To which the bride should reply (though perhaps not in these days of relative gender equality):

Wolę chleb, sól i pana młodego, żeby zarobić na niego.
vo·le khlep sool ee *pa*·na mwo·*de*·go *zhe*·bi za·*ro*·beech na *nye*·go
(I'd like the bread, the salt and my young man to earn the money to pay for them.)

ordering food

Is there a (vegetarian) restaurant near here?

	Czy jest tu gdzieś	chi yest too gjyesh
	restauracja	re·stow·ra·tsya
	(wegetariańska)?	(ve·ge·ta·ryan'·ska)

I don't eat …	*Nie jadam …*	nye ya·dam …
Could you	*Czy można*	chi mo·zhna
prepare a meal	*przygotować*	pshi·go·to·vach
without …?	*jedzenie bez …?*	ye·dze·nye bes …
butter	*masła*	ma·swa
eggs	*jajek*	yai·ek
fish	*ryb*	rib
fish/meat	*wywaru rybnego/*	vi·va·roo rib·ne·go/
stock	*mięsnego*	myens·ne·go
pork	*wieprzowiny*	vye·psho·vee·ni
poultry	*drobiu*	dro·byoo
(red) meat	*(czerwonego)*	(cher·vo·ne·go)
	mięsa	myen·sa

Is this …?	*Czy to jest …?*	chi to yest …
decaffeinated	*bez kofeiny*	bes ko·fe·ee·ni
free-range	*hodowli*	ho·dov·lee
	naturalnej	na·too·ral·ney
genetically	*modyfikowane*	mo·di·fee·ko·va·ne
modified	*genetycznie*	ge·ne·tich·nye
gluten-free	*bezglutenowe*	bes·gloo·te·no·ve
low in fat/sugar	*z niską*	z nees·kom
	zawartością	za·var·tosh·chyom
	tłuszczu/	twoosh·choo/
	cukru	tsoo·kro
organic	*organiczne*	or·ga·neech·ne
salt-free	*bez soli*	bes so·lee

special diets & allergies

I'm on a special diet.
Jestem na specjalnej diecie.
yes·tem na spe·*tsyal*·ney *dye*·chye

I'm vegan/vegetarian.
Jestem weganem/ wegetarianinem.
yes·tem ve·*ga*·nem/ ve·ge·ta·rya·*nee*·nem

I'm allergic to … *Mam uczulenie na …* mam oo·choo·*le*·nye na …

dairy produce	*produkty mleczne*	pro·*dook*·ti *mlech*·ne
eggs	*jajka*	*yai*·ka
gelatine	*żelatynę*	zhe·la·*ti*·ne
gluten	*gluten*	*gloo*·ten
honey	*miód*	myood
MSG	*glutaminian sodu*	gloo·ta·*mee*·nyan *so*·doo
nuts	*orzechy*	o·*zhe*·khi
peanuts	*orzeszki ziemne*	o·*zhesh*·kee *zhyem*·ne
seafood	*owoce morza*	o·*vo*·tse *mo*·zha
shellfish	*małże*	*mow*·zhe

To explain your dietary restrictions with reference to religious beliefs, see **beliefs & cultural differences**, page 139.

This guide to Polish food is in Polish alphabetical order (shown below). It's designed to help you get the most out of your Polish culinary experiences by helping you find your way around menus and markets. Note that adjectives are given in the masculine form only – for more information on how to make the feminine and neuter forms of adjectives, see the **a–z phrasebuilder**, page 17.

A a	Ą ą	B b	C c	Ć ć	D d	E e	Ę ę
F f	G g	H h	I i	J j	K k	L l	Ł ł
M m	N n	Ń ń	O o	Ó ó	P p	R r	S s
Ś ś	T t	U u	W w	Y y	Z z	Ź ź	Ż ż

A

agrest ⑩ a-grest *gooseberry*
alkoholowy ⑩ al-ko-ho-*lo*-vi *alcoholic*
ananas ⑩ a-*na*-nas *pineapple*
arbuz ⑩ *ar*-boos *watermelon*
awokado ⑪ a-vo-*ka*-do *avocado*

B

babka ① *bap*-ka *a sweet spongy yeast cake traditionally baked at Easter*
bakalie ⑩ pl ba-*ka*-lye *dried fruit & nuts*
bakłażan ⑩ ba-*kwa*-zhan *eggplant*
baleron ⑩ ba-*le*-ron *smoked neck of pork (a kind of ham)*
banan ⑩ *ba*-nan *banana*
baranina ① ba-ra-*nee*-na *lamb • mutton*
bar mleczny ⑩ bar *mlech*-ni *'milk bar' – self-service cafeteria-style eatery*
barszcz ⑩ barshch *borshch (beetroot soup) – there are many variations on this theme*
barszcz biały ⑩ barshch *bya*-wi *'white borshch', not actually a beetroot soup but a thick sourish wheat & potato-starch soup flavoured with marjoram*

barszcz czerwony ⑩ barshch cher-*vo*-ni *beetroot soup sometimes served with dumplings, hard-boiled egg slices or beans – a favourite winter food*
barszcz ukraiński ⑩ barshch oo-kra-*yeen*´-skee *beetroot soup with beans & potatoes*
barszcz zabielany ⑩ barshch za-bye-*la*-ni *beetroot soup with sour cream*
barszcz z pasztecikiem ⑩ barshch z pash-te-*chye*-kyem *beetroot soup with a savoury pastry filled with mincemeat*
barszcz z uszkami ⑩ barshch z oosh-*ka*-mee *beetroot soup with small, ravioli-style dumplings stuffed with meat*
bawarka ① ba-*var*-ka *tea with milk*
bazylia ① ba-*zil*-ya *basil*
bażant ⑩ ba-*zhant pheasant*
befsztyk ⑩ *bef*-shtik *beef steak*
— tatarski ta-*tar*-skee *raw minced sirloin served with onion, raw egg yolk & often chopped pickled dill cucumber*
bigos ⑩ *bee*-gos *sauerkraut, cabbage & meat (including game) stew, slow simmered with prunes & mushrooms & flavoured with red wine – generally considered the Polish national dish*

bimber ⓜ *beem*-ber *Polish moonshine, ie home-distilled vodka*

bita śmietana ① *bee*-ta shmye-*ta*-na *whipped cream*

bitki wołowe pl *beet*-kee vo-*wo*-ve *beef cutlets*

bliny pl *blee*-ni *small thick pancakes made from wheat or buckwheat flour & leavened with yeast*

boczek ⓜ *bo*-chek *bacon – served either fried or boiled or baked in a chunk*

botwinka ① bot-*feen*-ka *soup made from the stems & leaves of baby beetroot – often includes a sliced hard-boiled egg*

brokuł ⓜ *bro*-koow *broccoli*

brukselka ① brook-*sel*-ka *Brussels sprouts*

bryndza ① *brin*-dza *ewe's-milk cheese*

bryzol ⓜ *bri*-zol *grilled beef steak*

brzoskwinia ① bzhosk-*fee*-nya *peach*

budyń ⓜ *boo*-din' *milk-based cream dessert – available in commercially prepared packets in a range of flavours including strawberry, chocolate & vanilla*
— **z szynki** z shin-kee *mashed potato, ham & egg pie*

bukiet z jarzyn ⓜ *boo*-kyet z ya-zhin *cooked vegetables served as a side dish*

bulion ⓜ *boo*-lyon *broth*

bułeczka ① boo-*wech*-ka *small bread roll*

bułka ① *boow*-ka *white bread roll*

buraczki ⓜ pl boo-*rach*-kee *chopped or grated braised beetroot & sometimes apple – served as a side dish with meat*

burak ⓜ *boo*-rak *beetroot*

C

cebula ① tse-*boo*-la *onion*

chili ⓝ *chee*-lee *chilli*

chleb ⓜ khlep *bread*
— **razowy** ra-*zo*-vi *dark rye bread*

chłodnik ⓜ khwod-*neek* *baby beetroot soup with yogurt & fresh vegetables – served cold, in summer only*

chrzan ⓜ khshan *horseradish*

ciasto ⓝ *chyas*-to *batter • cake • dough*

ciastko ⓝ *chyast*-ko *biscuit • cookie • pastry • small cake*

cielęcina ① chye-len-*chee*-na *veal*

cocktail ⓝ *kok*-tail *cocktail*

cukier ⓜ *tsoo*-kyer *sugar*

cukierek ⓜ tsoo-*kye*-rek *candy • sweets*

cukinia ① tsoo-*kee*-nya *courgette • zucchini*

ćwikła ① *chfeek*-wa *boiled & grated beetroot with horseradish – a typical accompaniment to roast or smoked meat & sausages*

cykoria ① tsi-*kor*-ya *endive*

cynaderki pl tsi-na-*der*-kee *kidneys*

cynamon ⓜ tsi-*na*-mon *cinnamon*

cytryna ① tsi-*tri*-na *lemon*

czarna kawa ① *char*-na *ka*-va *black coffee*

czarna porzeczka ① *char*-na po-*zhech*-ka *blackcurrant*

czereśnia ① che-*resh*-nya *cherry*

czosnek ⓜ *chos*-nek *garlic*

D

dania jarskie pl *da*-nya *yar*-skye *vegetarian dishes*

dania mięsne pl *da*-nya *myens*-ne *meat dishes*

danie ⓝ *da*-nye *dish*

deser ⓜ *de*-ser *dessert*

desery pl de-*se*-ri *desserts*

dodatki pl do-*dat*-kee *side dishes*

dorsz ⓜ dorsh *cod*

drożdżówka ① drozh-*joof*-ka *brioche (sweet yeast bun)*

drób ⓜ droop *poultry*

drugie danie ⓝ *droo*-gye *da*-nye *main course*

drugie śniadanie ⓝ *droo*-gye shnya-*da*-nye *morning tea*

duszony ⓜ doo-*sho*-ni *stewed*

dynia ① *di*-nya *pumpkin*

dziczyzna ① jyee-*chis*-na *game*

dżem ⓜ jem *jam*

F

farsz ⓜ farsh *stuffing*

fasola ① fa-*so*-la *beans*
— **szparagowa** shpa-ra-*go*-va *green string beans*
— **po bretońsku** po bre-*ton*'-skoo *baked beans in tomato sauce*

faszerowany m fa·she·ro·va·ni *stuffed*

figa ① *fee*·ga *fig*

filet cielęcy m *fee*·let chye·*len*·tsi
veal escalope

flaczki/flaki pl *flach*·kee/*fla*·kee *seasoned
tripe & vegetables cooked in bouillon*

flądra ① *flon*·dra *flounder*

frytki pl *frit*·kee *chips • French fries*

G

galareta/galaretka ① ga·la·*re*·ta/
ga·la·*ret*·ka *meat or fish encased in
aspic – a typical Polish appetiser • sweet
flavoured jelly*

gęś ① gensh *goose*
— **pieczona** pye·*cho*·na *roast goose*

gofry pl *go*·fri *thick rectangular waffles
served with toppings such as whipped
cream, chocolate or jam*

golonka ① go·*lon*·ka *boiled pigs' hocks
often served with sauerkraut or puréed
yellow peas*

gołąbki pl go·*womb*·kee *cabbage leaves
stuffed with minced beef & rice*

gotowany m go·to·*va*·ni *boiled*
— **na parze** na *pa*·zhe *steamed*

goździki pl gozh·*jee*·kee *cloves*

grahamka ① gra·*kham*·ka
small wholemeal roll

grejpfrut m *greyp*·froot *grapefruit*

groch m grokh *lentils*
— **włoski** *vwos*·kee *chickpea*

grochówka ① gro·*khoof*·ka *lentil soup*

groszek m *gro*·shek *green peas*

gruszka ① *groosh*·ka *pear*

grzaniec z piwa m *gzha*·nyets z *pee*·va
mulled beer

grzaniec z wina m *gzha*·nyets z *vee*·na
mulled wine

grzanka ① *gzhan*·ka *toast*

grzyby (marynowane) pl
gzhi·bi (ma·ri·no·*va*·ne)
(marinated) wild mushrooms

gulasz m *goo*·lash *goulash*

H

herbata ① her·*ba*·ta *tea*
— **bez cukru** bes *tsoo*·kroo
tea without sugar
— **z cukrem** z *tsoo*·krem
tea with sugar
— **z cytryną** z tsi·*tri*·nom *tea with a slice
of lemon*
— **ziołowa** zhyo·*wo*·va *herbal tea*

herbatniki pl her·bat·*nee*·kee *biscuits*

homar m *ho*·mar *lobster*

I

imbir m *eem*·beer *ginger*

indyk m *een*·dik *turkey*

J

jabłecznik m ya·*bwech*·neek
apple strudel

jabłko ① *yabw*·ko *apple*

jadłodajnia ① ya·dwo·*dai*·nya *restaurant*

jadłospis m ya·*dwo*·spees *menu*

jagnię m *yag*·nye *lamb*

jagoda ① ya·*go*·da *blueberry*

jajecznica ① ya·yech·*nee*·tsa
scrambled eggs

jajka pl *yai*·ka *eggs*
— **na boczku** na *boch*·koo
bacon & eggs
— **na szynce** na *shin*·tse *ham & eggs*
— **sadzone** sa·*dzo*·ne *fried eggs*

jajko ① *yai*·ko *egg*
— **na miękko** na *myen*·ko
soft-boiled egg
— **na twardo** na *tfar*·do
hard-boiled egg
— **w majonezie** v ma·yo·*ne*·zhye
hard-boiled egg in mayonnaise

jarski m *yar*·skee *vegetarian*

jarzębiak m ya·*zhem*·byak *vodka
flavoured with rowanberry*

jarzyny pl ya·*zhi*·ni *vegetables*

jogurt m *yo*·goort *yogurt*

K

kabanos m ka·ba·nos *thin dry smoked pork sausage*

kaczka ① kach·ka *duck*
— **pieczona** pye·cho·na *roast duck*
— **z jabłkami** z yabw·ka·mee *roast duck stuffed with apples*

kajzerka ① kai·zer·ka *small white round roll*

kalafior m ka·la·fyor *cauliflower*

kanapka ① ka·nap·ka *sandwich*

kapusta ① ka·poos·ta *cabbage*
— **kiszona/kwaszona** kee·sho·na/kfa·sho·na *sauerkraut*

kapuśniak m ka·poosh·nyak *sauerkraut soup*

karp m karp *carp*
— **po grecku** po grets·koo *carp served cold in an onion & tomato sauce*
— **w galarecie** v ga·la·re·chye *carp in aspic*
— **z wody** z vo·di *boiled carp*

karta dań ① kar·ta dan' *menu*

karta win ① kar·ta veen *wine list*

kartofel m kar·to·fel *potato*

kartoflanka ① kar·to·flan·ka *potato & vegetable soup*
— **z grzybami** z gzhi·ba·mee *potato & vegetable soup with mushrooms*

kasza ① ka·sha *cereals • gruel • porridge*
— **gryczana** gri·cha·na *buckwheat served as a cereal*
— **jęczmienna** yench·myen·na *pearl barley*
— **manna** ma·na *semolina served as a cereal*

kawa ① ka·va *coffee*
— **neska** nes·ka *instant coffee*
— **z ekspresu** z eks·pre·soo *espresso coffee*
— **ze śmietanką** ze shmye·tan·kom *coffee with cream*
— **z mlekiem** z mle·kyem *coffee with milk*

kawiarnia ① ka·vyar·nya *café*

kawior m ka·vyor *caviar*

keks m keks *fruit cake*

kieliszek m kye·lee·shek *glass (for wine & spirits)*

kiełbasa ① kyew·ba·sa *sausage*
— **z rożna** z rozh·na *spit-roasted sausage*
— **z rusztu** z roosh·too *grilled or barbecued sausage*

kisiel m kee·shyel *jelly-type dessert made with potato starch*

klopsiki/klopsy pl klop·shee·kee/ klop·si *meatballs made with ground beef, pork or veal or a combination of these*

kluski pl kloos·kee *dumplings • noodles*

kminek m kmee·nek *caraway seeds*

knedle pl kned·le *dumplings stuffed with plums, cherries or apples*

koktajl m kok·tail *milkshake*

kolacja ① ko·lats·ya *evening meal*

kołduny pl kow·doo·ni *savoury dumplings*

kompot m kom·pot *fruit compote*

konfitury pl kon·fee·too·ri *preserves*

koniak m ko·nyak *brandy*

koper/koperek m ko·per/ko·pe·rek *dill*

kopytka pl ko·pit·ka *potato dumplings similar to gnocchi*

korniszony pl kor·nee·sho·ni *small pickled gherkins*

kotlet m kot·let *chop*
— **cielęcy** chye·len·tsi *veal cutlet or chop*
— **de volaille** de vo·lail *chicken breast fillet fried in breadcrumbs*
— **mielony** mye·lo·ni *mincemeat patty fried in breadcrumbs*
— **schabowy** skha·bo·vi *pork chop fried in breadcrumbs*

krewetki pl kre·vet·kee *prawns • shrimps*

krokiet m kro·kyet *croquette*

królik m kroo·leek *rabbit*

krupnik m kroop·neek *barley, meat & vegetable soup • honey liqueur*

kukurydza ① koo·koo·ri·dza *corn • maize*

kurczak m koor·chak *chicken*
— **pieczony** pye·cho·ni *roast chicken*
— **z rożna** z rozh·na *spit-roasted chicken*

L

leszcz ⓜ leshch *bream*
likier ⓜ lee·kyer *liqueur*
lody pl lo·di *ice cream*

Ł

łosoś ⓜ wo·sosh *salmon*
— **wędzony** ven·dzo·ni *smoked salmon*

M

majeranek ⓜ ma·ye·ra·nek *marjoram*
mak ⓜ mak *poppy seeds*
makaron ⓜ ma·ka·ron *macaroni • pasta*
makowiec ⓜ ma·ko·vyets *poppy-seed strudel*
makrela ⓕ ma·kre·la *mackerel*
malina ⓕ ma·lee·na *raspberry*
małże pl mow·zhe *mussels*
mandarynka ⓕ man·da·rin·ka *mandarin*
marchew ⓕ mar·khef *carrot*
marchewka z groszkiem ⓕ
mar·khef·ka z grosh·kyem
boiled carrots with green peas
margaryna ⓕ mar·ga·ri·na *margarine*
marynowany ⓜ ma·ri·no·va·ni *marinated*
masło ⓝ mas·wo *butter*
mąka ⓕ mon·ka *flour*
melba ⓕ mel·ba *ice cream with fruit & whipped cream*
mielony ⓜ mye·lo·ni *minced*
mięso ⓝ myen·so *meat*
— **mielone** mye·lo·ne *mincemeat*
migdał ⓜ meeg·dow *almond*
miód ⓜ myood *honey*
— **pitny** peet·ni *mead*
mizeria ⓕ mee·zer·ya
sliced fresh cucumber in sour cream
mleko ⓝ mle·ko *milk*
morela ⓕ mo·re·la *apricot*

N

nabiał ⓜ na·byow *dairy produce*
nadzienie ⓝ na·jye·nye *stuffing*
nadziewany ⓜ na·jye·va·ni *stuffed*
naleśniki pl na·lesh·nee·kee
crêpes • pancakes
— **z dżemem** z je·mem *pancakes with jam*
— **z serem** z se·rem *pancakes stuffed with sweetened white soft cheese*
nalewka ⓕ na·lef·ka *homemade spirit made from vodka flavoured with herbs & berries*
napiwek ⓜ na·pee·vek *tip*
napój ⓜ na·pooy *nonalcoholic drink*
nóżki w galarecie pl noosh·kee v ga·la·re·chye *jellied pigs' knuckles*

O

obiad firmowy ⓜ o·byad feer·mo·vi
set menu
obiady domowe pl o·bya·di do·mo·ve
home-cooked set meals
obwarzanek ⓜ ob·va·zha·nek
ring-shaped pretzel
ogórek ⓜ o·goo·rek *cucumber*
— **kiszony/kwaszony** kee·sho·ni/
kfa·sho·ni *dill cucumber*
oliwki pl o·leef·kee *olives*
omlet ⓜ om·let *omelette*
— **z dżemem** z je·mem *omelette with jam*
— **z pieczarkami** z pye·char·ka·mee
omelette with mushrooms
orzech ⓜ o·zhekh *nut • walnut*
— **kokosowy** ko·ko·so·vi *coconut*
— **laskowy** las·ko·vi *hazelnut*
— **włoski** vwos·kee *walnut*
orzeszek ziemny ⓜ o·zhe·shek zhyem·ni
peanut
oscypek/oszczypek ⓜ os·tsi·pek/
osh·chi·pek *ewe's-milk cheese*
ostrygi pl os·tri·gee *oysters*
owoc ⓜ o·vots *fruit*

owoce i orzechy pl o-*vo*-tse ee o-*zhe*-khi
fruit & nuts

owoce morza pl o-*vo*-tse *mo*-zha seafood

ozór ⓜ *o*-zoor tongue

P

panierowany ⓜ pa-nye-ro-*va*-ni crumbed

papryka ⓕ pap-*ri*-ka bell pepper •
capsicum

parówka ⓕ pa-*roof*-ka frankfurter

parówki z musztardą pl pa-*roof*-kee z
moosh-*tar*-dom boiled frankfurters
served with mustard

pasztecik ⓜ pash-*te*-cheek savoury pastry
stuffed with minced meat

pasztet z drobiu ⓜ *pash*-tet z *drob*-yoo
chicken pâté

pączek ⓜ *pon*-chek doughnut

pieczarka pl pye-*char*-ka mushroom

pieczarki z patelni pl pye-*char*-kee z
pa-*tel*-nee fried button mushrooms

pieczeń ⓕ pye-chen' roasted
— **cielęca** chye-*len*-tsa roast veal
— **wieprzowa** vye-*psho*-va roast pork
— **wołowa** vo-*wo*-va roast beef

pieczony ⓜ pye-*cho*-ni baked • roasted

pieprz ⓜ pyepsh pepper (condiment)

piernik ⓜ *pyer*-neek gingerbread –
traditionally made in Toruń & Gdańsk

pierogi pl pye-*ro*-gee ravioli-like dumplings
made from noodle dough, commonly
stuffed with mincemeat, sauerkraut,
mushroom, cheese & potato
— **leniwe** le-*nee*-ve dumplings filled
with curd cheese
— **ruskie** *roos*-kye dumplings filled with
soft, white cheese & potatoes
— **z jagodami** z ya-go-*da*-mee
dumplings filled with blueberries
— **z kapustą i grzybami** z ka-*poos*-tom
ee gzhi-*ba*-mee dumplings filled with
sauerkraut & wild mushrooms
— **z mięsem** z myen-sem dumplings
filled with mincemeat
— **z serem** z se-rem dumplings filled
with soft, white cheese

pierożki pl pye-*rozh*-kee a smaller version
of **pierogi**

pietruszka ⓕ pyet-*roosh*-ka parsley

pikantny ⓜ pee-*kant*-ni spicy

piwo ⓝ *pee*-vo beer
— **beczkowe** bech-*ko*-ve draught beer
— **butelkowe** boo-*tel*-ko-ve
bottled beer

placki kartoflane/ziemniaczane pl
plats-kee kar-to-*fla*-ne/zhyem-na-*cha*-ne
fried potato pancakes

polędwica ⓕ po-len-*dvee*-tsa sirloin
— **pieczona** pye-*cho*-na roasted
sirloin steak

pomarańcza ⓕ po-ma-*ran*'-cha orange

pomidor ⓜ po-*mee*-dor tomato

por ⓜ por leek

porzeczka ⓕ po-*zhech*-ka currant

posiłek ⓜ po-*shee*-wek meal

potrawa ⓕ po-*tra*-va course • dish

potrawy jarskie pl po-*tra*-vi *yar*-skye
vegetarian dishes

poziomka ⓕ po-*zhyom*-ka
wild stawberry

przekąska ⓕ pshe-*kons*-ka snack

przekąski pl pshe-*kons*-kee
appetisers • hors d'oeuvres

przyprawy pl pshi-*pra*-vi spices

przystawki pl pshis-*taf*-kee
accompaniments • side dishes

pstrąg ⓜ pstrong trout

pyzy pl *pi*-zi steamed potato dumplings

R

rachunek ⓝ ra-*khoo*-nek bill

rak ⓜ rak crayfish

restauracja ⓕ res-tow-*ra*-tsya
restaurant

rodzynka ⓕ ro-*jin*-ka raisin

rolmops ⓜ *rol*-mops marinated herring

rosół ⓝ *ro*-soow beef or chicken soup
— **z makaronem** z ma-ka-*ro*-nem
bouillon with noodles

rum ⓜ room rum

rumsztyk ⓜ *room*-shtik rump steak

ryba ① *ri-*ba *fish*
— **w galarecie** v ga-la-*re*-chye *in aspic*
ryż ⋒ rizh *rice*
rzodkiewka ① zhod-*kyef*-ka *radish*

S

sałata ① sa-*wa*-ta *lettuce*
sałatka ① sa-*wat*-ka *salad*
— **jarzynowa** ya-zhi-*no*-va *salad made with potato, vegetables & mayonnaise*
— **owocowa** o-vo-*tso*-va *fruit salad*
— **z pomidorów** z po-mee-*do*-roof *tomato salad*
sardynka ① sar-*din*-ka *sardine*
schab ⋒ skhab *loin of pork*
— **pieczony** pye-*cho*-ni *roasted pork flavoured with prunes*
seler ⋒ *se*-ler *celery*
ser ⋒ ser *cheese*
— **biały** *bya*-wi *white medium-soft cheese*
— **topiony** to-*pyo*-ni *cheese spread*
— **żółty** *zhoow*-ti *hard cheese*
serdelki pl ser-*del*-kee *sausages similar to frankfurters but thicker*
sernik ⋒ *ser*-neek *cheesecake*
serwetka ① ser-*vet*-ka *napkin*
siekany ⋒ shye-*ka*-ni *chopped*
słodki ⋒ *swod*-kee *sweet*
smażony ⋒ sma-*zho*-ni *fried*
sok ⋒ sok *juice*
— **owocowy** o-vo-*tso*-vi *fruit juice*
— **pomidorowy** po-mee-do-*ro*-vi *tomato juice*
sól ① sool *salt*
sos ⋒ sos *gravy • sauce*
— **chrzanowy** khsha-*no*-vi *horseradish sauce*
— **grzybowy** gzhi-*bo*-vi *mushroom sauce*
— **pomidorowy** po-mee-do-*ro*-vi *sauce made from tomatoes*
specjalność zakładu ① spe-*tsyal*-noshch za-*kwa*-doo *speciality of the house*
spis potraw ① spees *po*-traf *menu*

stek ⋒ stek *steak*
surowy ⋒ soo-*ro*-vi *raw • uncooked*
surówka ① soo-*roof*-ka *vegetable salad*
— **z kiszonej kapusty** z kee-*sho*-ney ka-*poos*-ti *sauerkraut, sometimes served with chopped apple & onion*
szampan ⋒ *sham*-pan *champagne*
szarlotka ① shar-*lot*-ka *apple cake*
szaszłyk ⋒ *shash*-wik *shish kebab*
szczupak ⋒ *shchoo*-pak *pike*
szklanka ① *shklan*-ka *glass (for tea, water, soft drinks)*
sznycel ⋒ *shni*-tsel *escalope • schnitzel*
szparagi pl shpa-*ra*-gee *asparagus*
szpinak ⋒ *shpee*-nak *spinach*
szprotki pl *shprot*-kee *sprats (small herrings)*
sztuka mięsa ① *shtoo*-ka *myen*-sa *boiled beef served with horseradish*
szynka ① *shin*-ka *ham*

Ś

śledź ⋒ shlej *herring*
— **w oleju** v o-*le*-yoo *herring in oil with onion*
— **w śmietanie** v shmye-*ta*-nye *herring in sour cream*
śliwka ① *shleef*-ka *plum*
śliwowica ① shlee-vo-*vee*-tsa *plum brandy*
śmietana ① shmye-*ta*-na *sour cream*
śmietanka ① shmye-*tan*-ka *cream*

T

talerz ⋒ *ta*-lesh *plate*
tatar ⋒ *ta*-tar *minced sirloin served raw with onion, raw egg yolk & often chopped dill cucumber*
tort ⋒ tort *cream cake*
truskawka ① troos-*kaf*-ka *strawberry*
truskawkowy ① troos-kaf-*ko*-vi *strawberry*
tuńczyk ⋒ *toon* '-chik *tuna*
twaróg ⋒ *tfa*-roog *cottage cheese*
tymianek ⋒ ti-*mya*-nek *thyme*

W

wafle pl *vaf*·le sweet wafer biscuits
warzywa pl va·*zhi*·va vegetables
wątróbka ① von·*troop*·ka liver
wędzony ven·*dzo*·ni smoked
węgorz ⓜ *ven*·gosh eel
— **wędzony** ven·*dzo*·ni smoked eel
w galarecie v ga·la·*re*·chye in aspic • jellied
widelec ⓜ vee·de·lets fork
wieprzowina ① vye·psho·*vee*·na pork
winiak ⓜ *vee*·nyak grape brandy
wino ⓝ *vee*·no wine
— **białe** *bya*·we white wine
— **czerwone** cher·*vo*·ne red wine
— **słodkie** *swod*·kye sweet wine
— **wytrawne** vi·*trav*·ne dry wine
winogrono ⓝ vee·no·*gro*·no grape
wiśnia ① *veesh*·nya cherry
wiśniówka ① veesh·*nyoof*·ka cherry-flavoured vodka
woda ① *vo*·da water
— **mineralna** mee·ne·*ral*·na mineral water
wołowina ① vo·wo·*vee*·na beef
wódka ① *vood*·ka vodka
— **myśliwska** mish·*leef*·ska vodka flavoured with juniper berries

Z

zając ⓜ *za*·yonts hare
zakąski ① pl za·*kons*·kee appetisers • hors d'oeuvres • starters
zapiekanka ① za·pye·*kan*·ka half a bread roll filled with cheese & mushrooms, baked & served hot
ziemniak ⓜ *zhyem*·nyak potato
ziemniaki pl zhyem·*nya*·kee potatoes
zioła pl *zhyo*·wa herbs
zioło ⓝ *zhyo*·wo herb

zrazy zawijane pl *zra*·zi za·vee·*ya*·ne beef rolls in a sour-cream sauce stuffed with mushrooms and/or bacon
z rożna z *rozh*·na spit-roasted
z rusztu z *roosh*·too grilled
zsiadłe mleko ⓝ *zshyad*·we *mle*·ko sour milk (similar in taste to buttermilk & drunk with vegetable dishes)
zupa ① *zoo*·pa soup
— **cebulowa** tse·boo·*lo*·va onion soup
— **fasolowa** fa·so·*lo*·va bean soup
— **grochowa** gro·*kho*·va lentil soup
— **grzybowa** gzhi·*bo*·va mushroom soup
— **jarzynowa** ya·zhi·*no*·va vegetable soup
— **mleczna** *mlech*·na semolina, rice or spaghetti cooked in milk & sweetened as a breakfast food
— **ogórkowa** o·goor·*ko*·va pickled dill cucumber soup
— **owocowa** o·vo·*tso*·va sweet chilled fruit soup
— **pomidorowa** po·mee·do·*ro*·va tomato soup
— **rybna** *rib*·na fish soup
— **szczawiowa** shcha·*vyo*·va sorrel soup
— **ziemniaczana** zhyem·nya·*cha*·na potato soup

Ż

żeberka pl zhe·*ber*·ka ribs
żubrówka ① zhoo·*broof*·ka 'bison vodka' – vodka flavoured with grass from the Białowieża forest on which bison feed
żurek ⓜ *zhoo*·rek sour rye-flour soup with smoked pork sausage
żytnia (wódka) ① *zhit*·nya (*vood*·ka) dry vodka

emergencies

Help!	*Na pomoc!*	na *po*·mots
Stop!	*Stój!*	stooy
Go away!	*Odejdź!*	o·deyj
Thief!	*Złodziej!*	zwo·jyey
Fire!	*Pożar!*	po·zhar
Watch out!	*Uważaj!*	oo·*va*·zhai

Call the police!
Zadzwoń po policję!   zad·zvon' po po·*lee*·tsye

Call a doctor!
Zadzwoń po lekarza!   zad·zvon' po le·*ka*·zha

Call an ambulance!
Zadzwoń po karetkę!   zad·zvon' po ka·*ret*·ke

It's an emergency.
To nagły wypadek.   to *nag*·wi vi·*pa*·dek

There's been an accident.
Tam był wypadek.   tam biw vi·*pa*·dek

I've been injured.
Jestem ranny/a. m/f   *yes*·tem *ra*·ni/na

Could you please help?
Czy może pan/pani   chi *mo*·zhe pan/*pa*·nee
mi pomóc? m/f   mee *po*·moots

signs

Szpital	shpee·tal	**Hospital**
Policja	po·*lee*·tsya	**Police**
Komisariat	ko·mee·*sar*·yat	**Police Station**
Policji	po·*lee*·tsyee	
Oddział Nagłych	od·jyow *na*·gwikh	**Emergency**
Wypadków	vi·*pad*·koof	**Department**

Can I use your phone?
Czy mogę użyć telefon?   chi *mo*·ge *oo*·zhich te·*le*·fon

I'm going to call the police.
Wezwę policję.   *vez*·ve po·*lee*·tsye

I'm lost.
Zgubiłem/am się. m/f   zgoo·*bee*·wem/wam shye

Where are the toilets?
Gdzie są toalety?   gjye som to·a·*le*·ti

She's having a baby.
Ona rodzi dziecko.   o·na ro·jee *jyet*·sko

He/She is having a/an …	*On/Ona ma …*	on/o·na ma …
allergic reaction	*reakcje alergiczną*	re·*ak*·tsye a·ler·*geech*·nom
asthma attack	*atak astmy*	a·tak *ast*·mi
epileptic fit	*atak epilepsji*	a·tak e·pee·*lep*·syee
heart attack	*atak serca*	a·tak *ser*·tsa

Is it safe …?	*Czy jest bezpiecznie …?*	chi yest bes·*pyech*·nye …
at night	*w nocy*	v *no*·tsi
for gay men/ lesbians	*dla gejów/ lesbijek*	dla *ge*·yoof/ les·*bee*·yek
for travellers	*dla podróżnych*	dla po·*droozh*·nikh
for women	*dla kobiet*	dla *ko*·byet
on your own	*w pojedynkę*	v po·ye·*din*·ke

police

policja

Where's the police station?
Gdzie jest posterunek policji?   gje yest pos·te·*roo*·nek po·*lee*·tsyee

I want to report an offence.
Chciałem/am zgłosić przestępstwo. m/f   khchow·em/am zgwo·sheech pshe·*stempst*·fo

I've been ...	Zostałem/am ... m/f	zo·*stow*·em/am ...
He's been ...	On został ...	on zos·tow ...
She's been ...	Ona została ...	o·na zos·*tow*·a ...
assaulted	napadnięty/a m/f	na·pad·*nyen*·ti/ta
attacked by	zaatakowany/a	za·a·ta·ko·*va*·ni/na
a dog	przez psa m/f	pshes psa
raped	zgwałcony/a m/f	zgvow·*tso*·ni/na
robbed	okradziony/a m/f	o·kra·*jyo*·ni/na
He tried to	On próbował	on proo·*bo*·vow
... me.	... mnie.	... mnye
She tried to	Ona próbowała	o·na proo·bo·*va*·wa
... me.	... mnie.	... mnye
assault	napaść na	*na*·pashch na
rape	zgwałcić	zgvow·cheech
rob	okraść	*o*·krashch

It was him.
To był on.   to biw on

It was her.
To była ona.   to *bi*·wa *o*·na

I have insurance.
Mam ubezpieczenie.   mam oo·bes·pye·*che*·nye

My ... was stolen.
Mój ... został skradziony. m   mooy ... zos·tow skra·*jyo*·ni
Moja ... została skradziona. f   mo·ya ... zos·*tow*·a skra·*jyo*·na
Moje zostało ... skradzione. n   mo·ye ... zos·*tow*·o skra·*jyo*·ne

My ... were stolen.
Moje ... zostały   mo·ye ... zos·*tow*·i
skradzione.   skra·*jyo*·ne

mind your p's

When a Pole has turned over a new leaf and has decided to eschew bad habits in favour of a clean and healthy lifestyle, he or she might say *Nie robię nic na 'p'!* nye *ro*·bye neets na pe. This literally translates as 'I'm not doing anything beginning with a "p".' What they have in mind is the following trinity: *nie piję, nie palę, nie pierdolę* nye *pee*·ye nye *pa*·le nye pyer·*do*·le, which means 'no smoking, no drinking and no bonking'.

I've lost my ...	*Zgubiłem/am ...* m/f	zgoo·*bee*·wem/wam ...
backpack	*plecak*	*ple*·tsak
bag	*torbę*	*tor*·be
credit card	*kartę*	*kar*·te
	kredytową	kre·di·*to*·vom
handbag	*torebkę*	to·*rep*·ke
jewellery	*biżuterię*	bee·zhoo·*ter*·ye
money	*pieniądze*	pye·*nyon*·dze
papers	*dokumenty*	do·koo·*men*·ti
travellers	*czeki*	*che*·kee
cheques	*podróżne*	po·*droozh*·ne
passport	*paszport*	*pash*·port
wallet	*portfel*	*port*·fel

I (don't) understand.
(Nie) Rozumiem.   (nye) ro·*zoo*·myem

Could I please have a/an (English) interpreter?
Czy mogę prosić o   chi *mo*·ge pro·sheech o
(angielskiego)   (an·gyel·*skye*·go)
tłumacza?   twoo·*ma*·cha

What am I accused of?
O co jestem oskarżony/a? m/f   o tso *yes*·tem os·kar·*zho*·ni/na

I'm sorry.
Przepraszam.   pshe·*pra*·sham

I didn't realise I was doing anything wrong.
Nie zdawałem/am sobie   nye zda·*vow*·em/am *so*·bye
sprawy, że robię   *spra*·vi zhe *ro*·bye
coś złego. m/f   tsosh *zwe*·go

I didn't do it.
Ja tego nie ya *te*·go nye
zrobiłem/am. m/f zro·*bee*·wem/wam

Can I pay an on-the-spot fine?
Czy mogę zapłacić chi *mo*·ge za·*pwa*·cheech
karę miejscu? *ka*·re na *myeys*·tsoo

Can I make a phone call?
Czy mogę zadzwonić? chi *mo*·ge za·*dzvo*·neech

the police may say ...

Jest pan/pani	yest pan/*pa*·nee	**You're charged**
oskarżony/a	os·kar·*zho*·ni/na	**with ...**
o ... m/f	o ...	
On/Ona jest	on/*o*·na yest	**He/She is**
oskarżony/a	os·kar·*zho*·ni/na	**charged with ...**
o ... m/f	o ...	
brak wizy	brak *vee*·zi	**not having a visa**
kradzież	*kra*·jyesh	**theft**
kradzież	*kra*·jyesh	**shoplifting**
sklepową	skle·*po*·vom	
napad	*na*·pad	**assault**
posiadanie	po·shya·*da*·nye	**possession**
(nielegalnych	(nye·le·*gal*·nikh	**(of illegal**
substancji)	soob·*stan*·tsyee)	**substances)**
przekroczenie	pshe·kro·*che*·nye	**overstaying**
okresu pobytu	o·*kre*·soo po·*bi*·too	**a visa**
poza termin	*po*·za *ter*·meen	
ważności wizy	vazh·*nosh*·chee *vee*·zi	
zakłócenie	za·kwoo·*tse*·nye	**disturbing**
spokoju	spo·*ko*·yoo	**the peace**
To jest mandat	to yest *man*·dat	**It's a ... fine.**
za ...	za ...	
nadmierną	nad·*myer*·nom	**speeding**
prędkość	*prend*·koshch	
parkowanie	par·ko·*va*·nye	**parking**

I want to contact my consulate.
*Chcę się skontaktować z
moim konsulatem.*
khtse shye skon·tak·*to*·vach z
mo·yeem kon·soo·*la*·tem

Can I have a lawyer (who speaks English)?
*Czy mogę prosić o
prawnika (który mówi
po angielsku).*
chi mo·ge pro·sheech o
prav·*nee*·ka (ktoo·ri moo·vee
po an·*gyel*·skoo)

I want to contact my embassy.
*Chcę się skontaktować
z moją ambasadą.*
khtse shye skon·tak·*to*·vach
z mo·yom am·ba·*sa*·dom

This drug is for personal use.
*To lekarstwo jest do
użytku osobistego.*
to le·*karst*·fo yest do
oo·*zhit*·koo o·so·bees·*te*·go

I have a prescription for this drug.
*Mam receptę na to
lekarstwo.*
mam re·*tsep*·te na to
le·*karst*·fo

doctor

lekarz

Where's the nearest ...?	Gdzie jest najbliższy/a/e ...? m/f	gjye yest nai·bleezh·shi/sha/she ...
dentist	dentysta m	den·tis·ta
doctor	lekarz m	le·kash
emergency department	pogotowie ratunkowe n	po·go·to·vye ra·toon·ko·ve
hospital	szpital m	shpee·tal
medical centre	ośrodek zdrowia m	o·shro·dek zdro·vya
optometrist	okulista m	o·koo·lees·ta
outpatient clinic	ambulatorium n	am·boo·la·tor·yoom
(night) pharmacist	apteka (nocna) f	ap·te·ka (nots·na)

I need a doctor (who speaks English).
Szukam lekarza (który mówi po angielsku).
shoo·kam le·ka·zha (ktoo·ri moo·vee po an·gyel·skoo)

Could I see a female doctor?
Czy mogę się widzieć z lekarzem kobietą?
chi mo·ge shye vee·jyech z le·ka·zhem ko·bye·tom

Could the doctor come here?
Czy lekarz może tutaj przyjść?
chi le·kash mo·zhe too·tai pshiyshch

Is there an after-hours emergency number?
Czy jest numer do nagłych wypadków po godzinach pracy?
chi yest noo·mer do nag·wikh vi·pad·koof po go·jee·nakh pra·tsi

I've run out of my medication.
Skończyły mi się lekarstwa.
skon·chi·wi mee shye le·karst·fa

the doctor may say ...

Co panu/pani dolega? m/f
    tso *pa*·noo/*pa*·nee do·*le*·ga **What's the problem?**

Gdzie boli?
    gjye *bo*·lee   **Where does it hurt?**

Czy ma pan/pani temperaturę? m/f
    chi ma pan/*pa*·nee   **Do you have a temperature?**
    tem·pe·ra·*too*·re

Jak długo jest pan/pani w tym stanie? m/f
    yak *dwoo*·go yest   **How long have you been**
    pan/*pa*·nee v tim *sta*·nye **like this?**

Czy już kiedyś pan/pani to miał/miała? m/f
    chi yoosh *kye*·dish   **Have you had this before?**
    pan/*pa*·nee to
    myow/*myow*·a

Jak długo pan/pani podróżuje? m/f
    yak *dwoo*·go pan/*pa*·nee **How long are you**
    po·droo·*zhoo*·ye   **travelling for?**

Czy jest pan/pani aktywny/a seksualnie? m/f
    chi yest pan/*pa*·nee   **Are you sexually active?**
    ak·*tiv*·ni/na sek·soo·*al*·nye

Czy miał/miała pan/pani seks bez zabezpieczenia? m/f
    chi myow/*myow*·a   **Have you had unprotected**
    pan/*pa*·nee seks bes   **sex?**
    za·bes·pye·*che*·nya

Czy pan/pani ...? m/f	chi pan/*pa*·nee ...	**Do you ...?**
pije	*pee*·ye	**drink**
pali	*pa*·lee	**smoke**
zażywa	za·*zhi*·va	**take drugs**
narkotyki	nar·ko·*ti*·kee	

Czy ...?	chi ...	**Are you ...?**
ma pan/pani	ma pan/*pa*·nee	**allergic to**
na coś alergię m/f	na tsosh a·*ler*·gye	**anything**
zażywa pan/	za·*zhi*·va pan/	**on medication**
pani leki m/f	*pa*·nee *le*·kee	

Musi pan/pani iść do szpitala. m/f
  moo·shee pan/*pa*·nee
  eeshch do shpe·*ta*·la
    You need to be admitted to
    hospital.

Powinien/Powinna pan/pani iść do kontroli po powrocie
do domu. m/f
  po·*vee*·nyen/po·*vee*·na
  pan/*pa*·nee eeshch do
  kon·*tro*·lee po pov·*ro*·chye
  do *do*·moo
    You should have it checked
    when you go home.

Powinien/Powinna pan/pani wrócić do domu na leczenie. m/f
  po·*vee*·nyen/po·*vee*·na
  pan/*pa*·nee *vroo*·cheech
  do *do*·moo na le·*che*·nye
    You should return home for
    treatment.

This is my usual medicine.
To jest lekarstwo które
zazwyczaj zażywam.
  to yest le·*karst*·fo *ktoo*·re
  zaz·*vi*·chai za·*zhi*·vam

What's the correct dosage?
Jaka jest prawidłowa
dawka?
  ya·ka yest pra·vee·*dwo*·va
  daf·ka

My child weighs (20 kilos).
Moje dziecko waży
(dwadzieścia kilogramów).
  mo·ye *jyets*·ko *va*·zhi
  (dva·*jyesh*·chya kee·lo·*gra*·moof)

Please use a new syringe.
Proszę użyć nową
strzykawkę.
  pro·she *oo*·zhich *no*·vom
  stshi·*kaf*·ke

I have my own syringe.
Mam własną strzykawkę.
  mam *vwas*·nom stshi·*kaf*·ke

I don't want a blood transfusion.
Nie chcę transfuzji krwi.
  nye khtse trans·*foo*·zyee krfee

health

195

I've been	Byłem/am	bi·wem/wam
vaccinated	szczepiony/a	shche·pyo·ni/na
against ...	na ... m/f	na ...
hepatitis A/B/C	żółtaczkę	zhoow·tach·ke
	typu A/B/C	ti·poo a/be/tse
tetanus	tężec	ten·zhets
typhoid	tyfus	ti·foos
I need new ...	Potrzebuję	po·tshe·boo·ye
	nowe ...	no·ve ...
contact lenses	soczewki	so·chef·kee
	kontaktowe	kon·tak·to·ve
glasses	okulary	o·koo·la·ri

My prescription is ...
Moja recepta jest ...   mo·ya re·tsep·ta yest ...

How much will it cost?
Ile to będzie kosztowało?   ee·le to ben·jye kosh·to·va·wo

Can I have a receipt for my insurance?
Czy mogę prosić o   chi mo·ge pro·sheech o
rachunek dla mojego   ra·khoo·nek dla mo·ye·go
ubezpieczenia?   oo·bes·pye·che·nya

---

doctor, doctor!

The correct way of addressing a male doctor or dentist is *panie doktorze* pa·nye dok·to·zhe. The female equivalent is *pani doktor* pa·nee dok·tor.

---

symptoms & conditions

objawy chorób i stan zdrowia

I'm sick.
Jestem chory/a. m/f   yes·tem kho·ri/ra

My friend is (very) sick.
Mój kolega jest (bardzo)   mooy ko·le·ga yest (bar·dzo)
chory. m   kho·ri
Moja koleżanka jest   mo·ya ko·le·zhan·ka yest
(bardzo) chora. f   (bar·dzo) kho·ra

My child is (very) sick.
Moje dziecko jest (bardzo) chore. mo·ye jyets·ko yest (bar·dzo) kho·re

I've been injured.
Jestem ranny/a. m/f yes·tem ra·ni/na

I've been vomiting.
Miałem/am wymioty. m/f myow·em/am vi·myo·ti

He/She has been injured.
On/Ona jest ranny/a. m/f on/o·na yest ra·ni/na

He/She has been vomiting.
On/Ona miała wymioty. on/o·na myow/myow·a vi·myo·ti

It hurts here.
Tutaj boli. too·tai bo·lee

I'm dehydrated.
Jestem odwodniony/a. m/f yes·tem od·vod·nyo·ni/na

I can't sleep.
Nie mogę spać. nye mo·ge spach

I can't eat.
Nie mogę jeść. nye mo·ge yeshch

I feel depressed.
Jestem w depresji. yes·tem v de·pres·yee

I feel dizzy.
Kręci mi się w głowie. kren·chee mee shye v gwo·vye

I feel shivery.
Mam dreszcze. mam dresh·che

I feel nauseous.
Mam mdłości. mam mdwosh·chee

I feel hot and cold.
Mam dreszcze. mam dresh·che

I feel …	Czuję się …	choo·ye shye …
anxious	zaniepokojony/a m/f	za·nye·po·ko·yo·ni/na
better	lepiej	le·pyey
strange	dziwnie	jeev·nye
weak	słaby/a m/f	swa·bi/ba
worse	gorzej	go·zhey

arms & legs

Poles generally say *ręka* ren·ka for both 'hand' and 'arm'. The word *ramię* ra·mye can be used specifically to refer to the hand though. Similarly, the word *noga* no·ga refers to both the leg and foot, but you can you use the word *stopa* sto·pa to single out the part below the ankle.

I think it's the medication I'm on.
Myślę, że to z powodu   mish·le zhe to s po·vo·doo
lekarstw, które zażywam.   le·karstf ktoo·re za·zhi·vam

I'm on medication for …
Biorę leki na …   byo·re le·kee na …

He/She is on medication for …
On/Ona bierze leki na …   on/o·na bye·zhe le·kee na …

I have (a/an) …
Mam …   mam …

He/She has (a/an) …
On/Ona ma …   on/o·na ma …

I've recently had (a/an) …
Niedawno   nye·dav·no
miałem/am … m/f   myow·em/am …

He/She has recently had (a/an) …
On/Ona niedawno   on/o·na nye·dav·no
miał/miała …   myow/myow·a …

asthma	*astma* f	ast·ma
cold n	*przeziębienie* n	pshe·zhyem·bye·nye
constipation	*zatwardzenie* n	zat·far·dze·nye
cough	*kaszel* m	ka·shel
diabetes	*cukrzyca* f	tsook·shi·tsa
diarrhoea	*rozwolnienie* n	roz·vol·nye·nye
fever	*gorączka* f	go·ronch·ka
headache	*ból głowy* m	bool gwo·vi
nausea	*mdłości* f pl	mdwosh·chee
pain n	*ból* m	bool
sore throat	*ból gardła* m	bool gar·dwa

women's health

(I think) I'm pregnant.
(Myślę, że) Jestem w ciąży. (mish·le zhe) yes·tem f chyon·zhi

I'm on the pill.
Jestem na środkach yes·tem na shrod·kakh
antykoncepcyjnych. an·ti·kon·tsep·tsiy·nikh

I haven't had my period for (six) weeks.
Nie miałam okresu nye myow·am o·kre·soo
przez (sześć) tygodni. pshes (sheshch) ti·god·nee

I've noticed a lump here.
Zauważyłam tutaj guz. za·oo·va·zhi·wam too·tai goos

Do you have something for (period pain)?
Czy jest coś na chi yest tsosh na
(bóle okresowe)? (boo·le o·kre·so·ve)

the doctor may say ...

Czy używa pani środki antykoncepcyjne?
  chi oo·zhi·va pa·nee **Are you using**
  shrod·kee **contraception?**
  an·ti·kon·tsep·tsiy·ne

Czy ma pani menstruację?
  chi ma pa·nee **Are you**
  men·stroo·a·tsye **menstruating?**

Czy jest pani w ciąży?
  chi yest pa·nee v chyon·zhi **Are you pregnant?**

Kiedy ostatni raz miała pani okres?
  kye·di os·tat·nee ras myow·a **When did you last have**
  pa·nee o·kres **your period?**

Jest pani w ciąży.
  yest pa·nee v chyon·zhi **You're pregnant.**

I have a ...	*Mam ...*	mam ...
urinary tract	*zapalenie dróg*	za·pa·*le*·nye droog
infection	*moczowych*	mo·*cho*·vikh
yeast infection	*infekcję*	een·*fek*·tsye
	grzybiczą	gzhi·*bee*·chom
I need (a/the) ...	*Chciałem/am ...* m/f	khchow·em/am ...
contraception	*środki anty-*	*shrod*·kee an·ti·
	koncepcyjne	kon·tsep·*tsiy*·ne
morning-after	*pigułkę*	pee·*goow*·ke
pill	*aborcyjną*	a·bor·*tsiy*·nom
pregnancy test	*test ciążowy*	test chyon·*zho*·vi

allergies

alergie

I have a skin allergy.
   Mam alergię skórną.   mam a·*ler*·gye *skoor*·nom

I'm allergic to ...	*Mam alergię na ...*	mam a·ler·*gye* na ...
He/She is	*On/Ona ma*	on/*o*·na ma
allergic to ...	*alergię na ...*	a·ler·*gye* na ...
antibiotics	*antybiotyki*	an·ti·byo·*ti*·kee
anti-	*leki przeciw-*	*le*·kee pshe·cheef·
inflammatories	*zapalne*	za·*pal*·ne
aspirin	*aspirynę*	as·pee·*ri*·ne
bees	*pszczoły*	*pshcho*·wi
codeine	*kodeinę*	ko·de·*ee*·ne
penicillin	*penicylinę*	pe·nee·tsi·*lee*·ne
pollen	*pyłek*	*pi*·wek
sulphur-based	*leki na*	*le*·kee na
drugs	*bazie siarki*	ba·zhye *shyar*·kee
inhaler	*inhalator* m	een·kha·*la*·tor
injection	*zastrzyk* m	*zast*·shik
antihistamines	*antyhistaminy* pl	an·ti·hees·ta·*mee*·ni

For a list of food-related allergies, see **special diets & allergies**, page 178.

alternative treatments

I don't use (Western medicine).
Nie stosuję   nye sto·*soo*·ye
(medycyny zachodniej).   (me·di·*tsi*·ni za·*khod*·nyey)

Can I see	*Czy mogę się*	chi *mo*·ge shye
someone who	*skonsultować z*	skon·*sool*·to·vach z
practises …?	*kimś kto*	keemsh kto
	praktykuje …?	prak·ti·*koo*·ye …
acupuncture	*akupunkturę*	a·koo·poonk·*too*·re
naturopathy	*naturopatię*	na·too·ro·*pa*·tye
reflexology	*refleksologię*	re·fle·kso·*lo*·gye

take the plunge

Look closely at a map of Poland and you'll see a number of towns with the word *Zdrój* zdrooy (mineral spa) tacked onto them, eg *Krynica-Zdrój* kri·*nee*·tsa·zdrooy. Poland has a long tradition of *uzdrowisko* ooz·dro·*vees*·ko (mineral spa towns), which draw visitors from all over Europe.

Polish spas are not merely places for a spot of R&R or pampering, however. They're celebrated for the curative powers of their *woda mineralna* vo·da mee·ne·*ral*·na (mineral water). The health-conscious flock to them to undertake *leczenie* le·*che*·nye (treatment) for a wide spectrum of ailments – anything from obesity to orthopaedic disorders. The varying composition of the waters means that spa towns specialise in the treatment of particular *choroba* kho·*ro*·ba (diseases).

Polish mineral spas offer an elaborate range of treaments. You can 'take the waters' at a *pijalnia* pee·*yal*·nya (pump room), selecting from a 'menu' of waters, or you can opt for a *błoto lecznicze* bwo·to lech·*nee*·che (therapeutic mud wrap) or a *masaż* ma·sash (massage). More adventurous souls can choose from a smorgasbord of new-age treatments including electrotherapy, light therapy, magnetotherapy, fonotherapy, inhalation therapy, cryotherapy, kinesitherapy and mechanotherapy.

parts of the body

My ... hurts.
Boli mnie ...   *bo·lee mnye ...*

I can't move my ...
Nie mogę ruszać ...   *nye mo·ge roo·shach ...*

I have a cramp in my ...
Mam skurcz w ...   *mam skoorch v ...*

My ... is/are swollen.
Mam spuchnięty/ą/e ... m/f/n&pl   *mam spookh·nyen·ti/tom/te ...*

For other parts of the body, see the **dictionary**.

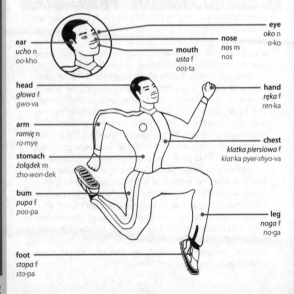

ear
ucho n
oo·kho

eye
oko n
o·ko

nose
nos m
nos

mouth
usta f
oos·ta

head
głowa f
gwo·va

hand
ręka f
ren·ka

arm
ramię n
ra·mye

chest
klatka piersiowa f
klat·ka pyer·shyo·va

stomach
żołądek m
zho·won·dek

bum
pupa f
poo·pa

leg
noga f
no·ga

foot
stopa f
sto·pa

pharmacist

aptekarz

I need something for (a headache).
Chciałem/am coś na
(ból głowy). m/f
khchow·em/am tsosh na
(bool gwo·vi)

Do I need a prescription for (antihistamines)?
Czy potrzebuję receptę
na (środek
antyhistaminowy)?
chi po·tshe·boo·ye re·tsep·te
na (shro·dek
an·ti·hees·ta·mee·no·vi)

I have a prescription.
Mam receptę.
mam re·tsep·te

How many times a day?
Ile razy dziennie?
ee·le ra·zi jye·nye

Will it make me drowsy?
Czy będę po tym
ospały/a? m/f
chi ben·de po tim
os·pa·wi/wa

the pharmacist may say ...

Dwa/Trzy razy dziennie. dva/tshi ra·zi jye·nye	**Twice/Three times a day.**
Przed jedzeniem. pshet ye·dze·nyem	**Before eating.**
W czasie jedzenia. v cha·shye ye·dze·nya	**With food.**
Po jedzeniu. po ye·dze·nyoo	**After eating.**
Czy pan/pani zażywał/zażywała to już kiedyś? m/f chi pan/pa·nee za·zhi·vow/ za·zhi·va·wa to yoosh kye·dish	**Have you taken this before?**
Musi pan/pani dokończyć tę serię. moo·shee pan/pa·nee do·kon'·chich te ser·ye	**You must complete the course.**

antiseptic	środki	shrod·kee
	odkażające pl	od·ka·zha·*yon*·tse
contraceptives	środki	shrod·kee
	antykoncepcyjne pl	an·ti·kon·tsep·*tsiy*·ne
painkillers	środki	shrod·kee
	przeciwbólowe pl	pshe·cheef·boo·*lo*·ve
rehydration salts	sóle fizjologiczne pl	so·le fee·zyo·lo·*geech*·ne

For more pharmaceutical items, see the **dictionary**.

dentist

dentysta

I have a ...	Mam ...	mam ...
broken tooth	złamany ząb	zwa·*ma*·ni zomb
cavity	dziurę w zębie	*jyoo*·re v *zem*·bye
toothache	ból zęba	bool *zem*·ba
I need (a/an) ...	Chciałem/am... m/f	khchow·em/am...
anaesthetic	znieczulenie	znye·choo·*le*·nye
filling	plombę	*plom*·be

I've lost a filling.
Wypadła mi plomba.   vi·*pad*·wa mee *plom*·ba

My dentures are broken.
Moja proteza zębowa   *mo*·ya pro·*te*·za zem·*bo*·va
jest pęknięta.   yest penk·*nyen*·ta

My gums hurt.
Bolą mnie dziąsła.   *bo*·lom mnye *jyon*·swa

I don't want it extracted.
Nie chcę go wyrywać.   nye khtse go vi·*ri*·vach

the dentist may say ...

Proszę otworzyć szeroko.	
pro·she ot·*vo*·zhich she·*ro*·ko	**Open wide.**
Proszę popłukać.	
pro·she pop·*woo*·kach	**Rinse.**

A

Polish nouns in the **dictionary** have their gender indicated by ⓜ (masculine), ⓕ (feminine) or ⓝ (neuter). If it's a plural noun, you'll also see pl, but you won't see a gender marker as all plural nouns in this dictionary belong to the general (genderless) plural category (refer to the **a–z phrasebuilder** for more on this). When a word that could be either a noun or a verb has no gender indicated, it's a verb. For added clarity, certain words are marked as adjectives a or verbs v. Adjectives, however, are given in the masculine form only. Both nouns and adjectives are provided in the nominative case only. For information on case and gender, refer to the **a–z phrasebuilder**.

A

aboard *na pokładzie* na po·*kwa*·jye
abortion *aborcja* ⓕ a·*bor*·tsya
abroad *za granicą* za gra·*nee*·tsom
accident *wypadek* ⓜ vi·*pa*·dek
accommodation *nocleg* ⓜ *nots*·leg
account (bill) *konto* ⓝ *kon*·to
acid (drug) *LSD* ⓜ el·es·de
acid rain *kwaśny deszcz* ⓜ *kfash*·ni deshch
activist *aktywista* ⓜ ak·ti·*vees*·ta
actor *aktor/aktorka* ⓜ/ⓕ *ak*·tor/ak·*tor*·ka
adaptor *zasilacz* ⓜ za·*shee*·lach
addiction *nałóg* ⓜ *na*·woog
address *adres* ⓜ *a*·dres
administration *administracja* ⓕ a·dmee·nee·*stra*·tsya
admission (price) *wstęp* ⓜ fstemp
admit (let in) v *wpuszczać* fpoosh·chach
adult *dorosły* ⓜ do·*ro*·swi
advertisement *reklama* ⓕ re·*kla*·ma
advice *rada* ⓕ *ra*·da
aeroplane *samolot* ⓜ sa·*mo*·lot
Africa *Afryka* ⓕ a·*fri*·ka
after *po* · za po · za
afternoon *popołudnie* ⓝ po·po·*wood*·nye
aftershave *woda po goleniu* ⓕ *vo*·da po go·*le*·nyoo
again *znowu* *zno*·voo
age *wiek* ⓜ vyek
(three days) ago *(trzy dni) temu* (tshi dnee) *te*·moo
agree *zgodzić się* *zgo*·jeech shye
agriculture *rolnictwo* ⓝ rol·*neetst*·fo

agritourist farm *gospodarstwo agroturystyczne* ⓝ gos·po·*darst*·fo a·gro·too·ris·*tich*·ne
AIDS *AIDS* ⓜ ayds
air *powietrze* ⓝ po·*vye*·tshe
air conditioning *klimatyzacja* ⓕ klee·ma·ti·*za*·tsya
airline *linia lotnicza* ⓕ *lee*·nya lot·*nee*·cha
airmail *poczta lotnicza* ⓕ *poch*·ta lot·*nee*·cha
airplane *samolot* ⓜ sa·*mo*·lot
airport *lotnisko* ⓝ lot·*nees*·ko
airport tax *opłata lotniskowa* ⓕ o·*pwa*·ta lot·nees·*ko*·va
aisle (on plane) *przejście (w samolocie)* ⓝ *psheysh*·chye (v sa·mo·*lo*·chye)
alarm clock *budzik* ⓜ *boo*·jeek
alcohol *alkohol* ⓜ al·*ko*·khol
allergy *alergia* ⓕ a·*ler*·gya
almond *migdał* ⓜ *meeg*·dow
almost *prawie* *pra*·vye
alone *samotny* sa·*mot*·ni
already *już* yoosh
altar *ołtarz* ⓜ *ow*·tazh
altitude *wysokość* ⓕ vi·*so*·koshch
always *zawsze* *zaf*·she
ambassador *ambasador* ⓜ am·ba·*sa*·dor
amber *bursztyn* ⓜ *boorsh*·tin
ambulance *karetka pogotowia* ⓕ ka·*ret*·ka po·go·*to*·vya
anaemia *anemia* ⓕ a·*ne*·mya
anarchist *anarchista* ⓜ a·nar·*khees*·ta
ancient *starożytny* sta·ro·*zhit*·ni
and *i* ee
angry *zły* zwi

animal *zwierzę* ⑩ *zvye*·zhe
ankle *kostka* ① *kos*·tka
another (a different one) *inny* ee·ni
another (one more) *jeszcze jeden*
  yesh·che ye·den
answer n *odpowiedź* ① od·*po*·vyej
answer *odpowiadać* od·po·*vya*·dach
ant *mrówka* ① *mroof*·ka
antibiotics *antybiotyki* pl an·ti·byo·*ti*·kee
antique *antyk* ⑩ *an*·tik
antiseptic *środek odkażający* ⑩
  shro·dek od·ka·zha·*yon*·tsi
any (some) *jakiś* ya·keesh
any (whichever) *dowolny* do·*vol*·ni
apartment *mieszkanie* ⑩ myesh·*ka*·nye
apple *jabłko* ⑩ *yabw*·ko
appointment *spotkanie* ⑩ spot·*ka*·nye
apricot *morela* ① mo·*re*·la
April *kwiecień* ⑩ *kfye*·chen'
Aquarius *Wodnik* ⑩ *vod*·neek
architect *architekt* ⑩ ar·*khee*·tekt
architecture *architektura* ①
  ar·khee·tek·*too*·ra
Aries *Baran* ⑩ *ba*·ran
arm (body) *ręka* ① *ren*·ka
arrest *aresztować* a·resh·*to*·vach
arrivals (general) *przyjazdy* pl pshi·*yaz*·di
arrivals (plane) *przyloty* pl pshi·*lo*·ti
arrive *przyjechać* pshi·*ye*·khach
art *sztuka* ① *shtoo*·ka
art gallery *galeria sztuki* ①
  ga·*ler*·ya *shtoo*·kee
artist *artysta/artystka* ⑩/①
  ar·*tis*·ta/ar·*tis*·tka
Art nouveau *sztuka secesyjna* ①
  shtoo·ka se·tse·*siy*·na
ashtray *popielniczka* ① po·pyel·*neech*·ka
Asia *Azja* ① *az*·ya
ask (a question) *pytać* *pi*·tach
ask (for something) *prosić* pro·sheech
aspirin *aspiryna* ① as·pee·*ri*·na
asthma *astma* ① *ast*·ma
at *przy* • *w* pshi • v
athletics *lekkoatletyka* ① lek·ko·at·le·*ti*·ka
August *sierpień* ⑩ *shyer*·pyen'
aunt *ciotka* ① *chyot*·ka
Australia *Australia* ⑩ ows·*tra*·lya
automated teller machine (ATM)
  bankomat ⑩ ban·*ko*·mat
autumn *jesień* ① *ye*·shyen'
avenue *aleja* ① a·*le*·ya
avocado *awokado* ⑩ a·vo·*ka*·do
awful *okropny* o·*krop*·ni

B

B&W (film) *panchromatyczny*
  pan·khro·ma·*tich*·ni
baby *niemowlę* ⑩ nye·*mov*·le
baby food *odżywka dla niemowląt* ①
  od·*zhif*·ka dla nye·*mov*·lont
baby powder *zasypka dla niemowląt* ①
  za·*sip*·ka dla nye·*mov*·lont
babysitter *opiekunka do dziecka* ①
  o·pye·*koon*·ka do *jye*·tska
back (body) *plecy* pl *ple*·tsi
back (position) *tył* ⑩ tiw
backpack *plecak* ⑩ *ple*·tsak
bacon *boczek* ⑩ *bo*·chek
bad *zły* zwi
bag *torba* ① *tor*·ba
baggage *bagaż* ⑩ *ba*·gash
baggage allowance *dopuszczalna ilość*
  bagażu ① do·poosh·*chal*·na ee·loshch
  ba·*ga*·zhoo
baggage claim *odbiór bagażu* ⑩
  od·byoor ba·*ga*·zhoo
bakery *piekarnia* ① pye·*kar*·nya
balance (account) *stan konta* ⑩
  stan *kon*·ta
balcony *balkon* ⑩ *bal*·kon
ball (sport) *piłka* ① *peew*·ka
ballet *balet* ⑩ *ba*·let
Baltic Sea *Morze Bałtyckie* ⑩
  mo·zhe bow·*tits*·kye
banana *banan* ⑩ *ba*·nan
band (music) *zespół* ⑩ *zes*·poow
bandage *bandaż* ⑩ *ban*·dash
Band-Aid *plaster* ⑩ *plas*·ter
bank (money) *bank* ⑩ bank
bank account *konto bankowe* ⑩
  kon·to ban·*ko*·ve
banknote *banknot* ⑩ *bank*·not
baptism *chrzest* ⑩ khshest
bar *bar* ⑩ bar
barber *fryzjer* ⑩ *friz*·yer
baseball *baseball* ⑩ *beys*·bol
basketball *koszykówka* ① ko·shi·*koof*·ka
bath *kąpiel* ① *kom*·pyel
bathing suit *strój kąpielowy* ⑩
  strooy kom·pye·*lo*·vi
bathroom *łazienka* ① wa·*zhyen*·ka
battery (general) *bateria* ① ba·*te*·rya
battery (car) *akumulator* ⑩
  a·koo·moo·*la*·tor
be *być* bich
beach *plaża* ① *pla*·zha

beach volleyball *siatkówka plażowa* ①
shyat·*koof*·ka pla·*zho*·va

bean *fasola* ① fa·*so*·la

beautician *kosmetyczka* ① kos·me·*tich*·ka

beautiful *piękny* pyenk·ni

beauty salon *salon kosmetyczny* ⓜ
sa·lon kos·me·*tich*·ni

because *ponieważ* po·*nye*·vash

bed *łóżko* ⓝ *woozh*·ko

bed linen *pościel* ① *posh*·chyel

bedroom *sypialnia* ① si·*pyal*·nya

bee *pszczoła* ① *pshcho*·wa

beef *wołowina* ① vo·wo·*vee*·na

beer *piwo* ⓝ *pee*·vo

before *przed* pshet

beggar *żebrak/żebraczka* ⓜ/①
zhe·brak/zhe·*brach*·ka

behind *za* za

Belarus *Białoruś* ① bya·*wo*·roosh

Belgium *Belgia* ① *bel*·gya

Berlin *Berlin* ⓜ *ber*·leen

beside *obok* o·bok

best *najlepszy* nai·*lep*·shi

bet *zakład* ⓜ *za*·kwad

bet *zakładać się* za·*kwa*·dach shye

better *lepszy* *lep*·shi

between *między* *myen*·dzi

Bible *biblia* ① *bee*·blya

bicycle *rower* ⓜ *ro*·ver

big *duży* *doo*·zhi

bigger *większy* *vyenk*·shi

biggest *największy* nai·*vyenk*·shi

bike *rower* ⓜ *ro*·ver

bike chain *łańcuch rowerowy* ⓜ
wan'·tsookh ro·ve·*ro*·vi

bike path *ścieżka rowerowa* ①
shchyezh·ka ro·ve·ro·va

bill (restaurant) *rachunek* ⓜ ra·*khoo*·nek

binoculars *lornetka* ① lor·*net*·ka

bird *ptak* ⓜ ptak

birth certificate *akt urodzenia* ⓜ
akt oo·ro·*je*·nya

birthday *urodziny* pl oo·ro·*jee*·ni

biscuit *herbatnik* ⓜ her·*bat*·neek

bison *żubr* ⓜ zhoobr

bite (dog etc) n *ugryzienie* ⓝ
oo·gri·*zhye*·nye

bite (insect) n *ukąszenie* ⓝ
oo·kon·*she*·nye

bitter *gorzki* *gosh*·kee

black *czarny* *char*·ni

bladder *pęcherz* ⓜ *pen*·khesh

blanket *koc* ⓜ kots

blind a *ślepy* ⓜ *shle*·pi

blister *odcisk* ⓜ *od*·cheesk

blood *krew* ① kref

blood group *grupa krwi* ① *groo*·pa krfee

blue *niebieski* nye·*byes*·kee

board (plane, ship) v *wchodzić na
pokład* ⓜ *fkho*·jeech *na po*·kwad

boat *łódź* ① wooj

body *ciało* ⓝ *chya*·wo

boiled *gotowany* go·to·*va*·ni

bone *kość* ① koshch

book *książka* ① *ksyonzh*·ka

book (make a booking) *rezerwować*
re·zer·*vo*·vach

booked out *wyprzedany* vi·pshe·*da*·ni

book shop *księgarnia* ① kshyen·*gar*·nya

boots (footwear) *buty* pl *boo*·ti

border *granica* ① gra·*nee*·tsa

bored *znudzony* znoo·*dzo*·ni

boring *nudny* *noo*·dni

borrow *pożyczać* po·*zhi*·chach

bottle *butelka* ① boo·*tel*·ka

bottle opener *otwieracz do butelek* ⓜ
ot·*fye*·rach do boo·*te*·lek

bottle shop *sklep monopolowy* ⓜ
sklep mo·no·po·*lo*·vi

bottom (body) *tyłek* ⓜ *ti*·wek

bottom (position) *dno* ⓝ dno

bowl (plate) *miska* ① *mee*·ska

box *pudełko* ⓝ poo·*dew*·ko

boy *chłopiec* ⓜ *khwo*·pyets

boyfriend *chłopak* ⓜ *khwo*·pak

bra *biustonosz* ⓜ byoo·*sto*·nosh

brakes *hamulce* pl ha·*mool*·tse

brandy *winiak* ⓜ *vee*·nyak

Bratislava *Bratysława* ① bra·ti·*swa*·va

brave *odważny* od·*vazh*·ni

bread *chleb* ⓜ khlep

break *złamać* *zwa*·mach

break down *psuć się* psooch shye

breakfast *śniadanie* ⓝ shnya·*da*·nye

breast *pierś* ① pyersh

breathe *oddychać* ot·*di*·khach

bribe *łapówka* ① wa·*poof*·ka

bribe *przekupywać* pshe·koo·*pi*·vach

bridge (structure) *most* ⓜ most

briefcase *teczka* ① *tech*·ka

bring *przynosić* pshi·no·*sheech*

broccoli *brokuł* ⓜ *bro*·koow

brochure *broszura* ① bro·*shoo*·ra

broken *połamany* po·wa·*ma*·ni

broken down *zepsuty* zep·*soo*·ti

brother *brat* ⓜ brat

brown brązowy ⓜ bron-zo-vi
bruise siniak ⓜ shee-nyak
brush szczotka ⓕ shchot-ka
bucket wiadro ⓝ vya-dro
Buddhist buddysta ⓜ bood-dis-ta
budget budżet ⓜ boo-jet
buffet bufet ⓜ boo-fet
bug pluskwa ⓕ ploosk-fa
build budować boo-do-vach
builder budowniczy ⓜ boo-dov-nee-chi
building budynek ⓜ boo-di-nek
burn poparzenie ⓝ po-pa-zhe-nye
burnt spalony spa-lo-ni
bus (city) autobus ⓜ ow-to-boos
bus (intercity) autokar ⓜ ow-to-kar
business firma ⓕ feer-ma
business class klasa biznesowa ⓕ
  kla-sa beez-ne-so-va
businessperson biznesmen ⓜ
  beez-nes-men
business trip podróż służbowa ⓕ
  pod-roosh swoozh-bo-va
busker grajek uliczny ⓜ
  gra-yek oo-leech-ni
bus station dworzec autobusowy ⓜ
  dvo-zhets ow-to-boo-so-vi
bus stop przystanek ⓜ pshi-sta-nek
busy (of person) zajęty za-yen-ti
busy (street, etc) ruchliwy rookh-lee-vi
but ale a-le
butcher rzeźnik ⓜ zhezh-neek
butcher's shop sklep mięsny ⓜ
  sklep myens-ni
butter masło ⓝ mas-wo
butterfly motyl ⓜ mo-til
button guzik ⓜ goo-zheek
buy kupować koo-po-vach

cabbage kapusta ⓕ ka-poos-ta
café kawiarnia ⓕ ka-vyar-nya
cafeteria stołówka ⓕ sto-woof-ka
cake ciasto ⓝ chyas-to
cake shop cukiernia ⓕ tsoo-kyer-nya
calculator kalkulator ⓜ kal-koo-la-tor
calendar kalendarz ⓜ ka-len-dash
call (phone) v dzwonić dzvo-neech
camera aparat ⓜ a-pa-rat
camera shop sklep fotograficzny ⓜ
  sklep fo-to-gra-feech-ni
camp obozować o-bo-zo-vach

camping ground kamping ⓜ kam-peeng
camping store sklep turystyczno-
  sportowy ⓜ sklep too-ris-tich-no-
  spor-to-vi
can puszka ⓕ poosh-ka
can (have permission) móc moots
can (know how to) umieć oo-myech
can (manage to do something) potrafić
  po-tra-feech
Canada Kanada ⓕ ka-na-da
cancel unieważniać oo-nye-vazh-nyach
cancer rak ⓜ rak
Cancer Rak ⓜ rak
candle świeca ⓕ shvye-tsa
candy cukierek ⓜ tsoo-kye-rek
canoeing kajakarstwo ⓝ ka-ya-karst-fo
can opener otwieracz do konserw ⓜ
  ot-fye-rach do kon-serf
Capricorn Koziorożec ⓜ ko-zhyo-ro-zhets
capsicum papryka ⓕ pa-pri-ka
car samochód ⓜ sa-mo-khoot
caravan przyczepa kampingowa ⓕ
  pshi-che-pa kam-peen-go-va
cards (playing) karty kar-ti
car hire wypożyczalnia samochodów ⓕ
  vi-po-zhi-chal-nya sa-mo-kho-doof
car park parking ⓜ par-keeng
Carpathian mountains Karpaty kar-pa-ti
car registration rejestrowanie
  samochodu ⓝ re-ye-stro-va-nye
  sa-mo-kho-doo
carrot marchewka ⓕ mar-khef-ka
carry nosić no-sheech
carton karton ⓜ kar-ton
cash gotówka ⓕ go-toof-ka
cash (a cheque) zrealizować czek
  zre-a-lee-zo-vach chek
cashier kasjer/kasjerka ⓜ/ⓕ
  kas-yer/kas-yer-ka
cash register kasa fiskalna ⓕ
  ka-sa fees-kal-na
casino kasyno ⓝ ka-si-no
cassette kaseta ⓕ ka-se-ta
castle zamek ⓜ za-mek
cat kot ⓜ kot
cathedral katedra ⓕ ka-te-dra
Catholic katolik ⓜ ka-to-leek
cauliflower kalafior ⓜ ka-la-fyor
cave jaskinia ⓕ yas-kee-nya
CD CD ⓝ tse-de
cell phone telefon komórkowy ⓜ
  te-le-fon ko-moor-ko-vi
cemetery cmentarz ⓜ tsmen-tash

cent cent ⓜ tsent
centimetre centymetr ⓜ tsen·ti·metr
centre środek ⓜ shro·dek
ceramics ceramika ⓕ tse·ra·mee·ka
cereal (breakfast) płatki śniadaniowe pl pwat·kee shnya·da·nyo·ve
certificate (education) dyplom ⓜ dip·lom
certificate (general) zaświadczenie ⓝ za·shvyad·che·nye
chain łańcuch ⓜ wan'·tsookh
chair krzesło ⓝ kshes·wo
chairlift (skiing) wyciąg krzesełkowy ⓜ vi·chyonk kshe·sew·ko·vi
champagne szampan ⓜ sham·pan
chance (opportunity) szansa ⓕ shan·sa
change zmiana ⓕ zmya·na
change (coins) reszta ⓕ resh·ta
change (money) rozmieniać roz·mye·nyach
changing room szatnia ⓕ shat·nya
charming uroczy oo·ro·chi
chat up pogadać po·ga·dach
cheap tani ta·nee
cheat oszust ⓜ o·shoost
check (banking) czek ⓜ chek
check (bill) sprawdzenie ⓝ sprav·dze·nye
check (money) sprawdzać sprav·dzach
check-in (desk) zameldowanie ⓝ za·mel·do·va·nye
cheese ser ⓜ ser
chef szef kuchni ⓜ shef kookh·nee
chemist (pharmacist) farmaceuta ⓜ far·ma·tsew·ta
chemist (pharmacy) apteka ⓕ ap·te·ka
cheque (banking) czek ⓜ chek
cherry czereśnia ⓕ che·resh·nya
chess szachy pl sha·khi
chessboard szachownica ⓕ sha·khov·nee·tsa
chest (body) klatka piersiowa ⓕ klat·ka pyer·shyo·va
chestnut kasztanowiec ⓜ kash·ta·no·vyets
chewing gum guma do żucia ⓕ goo·ma do zhoo·chya
chicken kurczak ⓜ koor·chak
child dziecko ⓝ jye·tsko
child-minding service usługi opieki nad dzieckiem pl oos·woo·gee o·pye·kee nad jyets·kyem
children dzieci pl jye·chee

child seat siedzenie dla dziecka ⓝ shye·dze·nye dla jyets·ka
China Chiny pl khee·ni
chiropractor kręgarz ⓜ kren·gash
chocolate czekolada ⓕ che·ko·la·da
choose wybierać vi·bye·rach
chopsticks pałeczki pa·wech·kee
Christian chrześcijanin ⓜ khsheh·chee·ya·neen
Christian name imię ⓝ ee·mye
Christmas Boże Narodzenie ⓝ bo·zhe na·ro·dze·nye
Christmas Day Dzień Bożego Narodzenia ⓜ jyen' bo·zhe·go na·ro·dze·nya
Christmas Eve Wigilia ⓕ vee·gee·lya
church kościół ⓜ kosh·chyoow
cider napój jabłkowy ⓜ na·pooy yabw·ko·vi
cigar cygaro ⓝ tsi·ga·ro
cigarette papieros ⓜ pa·pye·ros
cigarette lighter zapalniczka ⓕ za·pal·neech·ka
cinema kino ⓝ kee·no
circus cyrk ⓜ tsirk
citizenship obywatelstwo ⓝ o·bi·va·telst·fo
city miasto ⓝ myas·to
city centre centrum ⓝ tsen·troom
classical klasyczny ⓜ kla·sich·ni
clean a czysty chi·sti
clean v sprzątać spshon·tach
cleaning sprzątanie ⓝ spshon·ta·nye
client klient ⓜ klee·yent
cliff urwisko ⓝ oor·vee·sko
climb wspinać się vspee·nach shye
cloakroom szatnia ⓕ sha·tnya
clock zegar ⓜ ze·gar
close a bliski blees·kee
close v zamykać za·mi·kach
closed zamknięty zam·knyen·ti
clothing ubranie ⓝ oo·bra·nye
clothing store sklep odzieżowy ⓜ sklep o·jye·zho·vi
cloud chmura ⓕ khmoo·ra
clutch (car) sprzęgło ⓝ spshen·gwo
coach (bus) autokar ⓜ ow·to·kar
coach (trainer) trener ⓜ tre·ner
coach trenować tre·no·vach
coast wybrzeże ⓝ vi·bzhe·zhe
coat płaszcz ⓜ pwashch
cocaine kokaina ⓕ ko·ka·ee·na
cockroach karaluch ⓜ ka·ra·lookh

cocktail *koktail* ⓜ *kok*-tail
cocoa *kakao* ⓝ ka-*ka*-o
coconut *kokos* ⓜ *ko*-kos
coffee *kawa* ⓕ *ka*-va
coins *monety* pl mo-*ne*-ti
cold (illness) *katar* ⓜ *ka*-tar
cold *zimno* ⓝ *zhee*-mno
cold *zimny* *zheem*-ni
(have a) cold *być przeziębionym*
  bich pshe-zhyem-*byo*-nim
colleague *współpracownik/*
  współpracowniczka ⓜ/ⓕ
  fspoow-pra-*tsov*-neek/
  fspoow-pra-tsov-*neech*-ka
collect call *rozmowa opłacona*
  przez odbierającego ⓕ roz-*mo*-va
  o-pwa-*tso*-na pshes od-bye-ra-yon-*tse*-go
college *uniwersytet* ⓜ oo-nee-ver-*si*-tet
colour *kolor* ⓜ *ko*-lor
comb *grzebień* ⓜ *gzhe*-byen´
come (by mechanised means)
  przyjść pshiyshch
come (on foot) *przychodzić* pshi-*kho*-jeech
comedy *komedia* ⓕ ko-*me*-dya
comfortable *wygodny* vi-*god*-ni
commission *prowizja* ⓕ pro-*vee*-zya
communion *komunia* ⓕ ko-*moo*-nya
communist *komunista* ⓜ ko-moo-*nee*-ta
company (firm) *firma* ⓕ *feer*-ma
compass *kompas* ⓜ *kom*-pas
complain *skarżyć się* skar-zhich shye
complaint *skarga* ⓕ *skar*-ga
complimentary (free) *bezpłatny*
  bes-*pwa*-tni
computer *komputer* ⓜ kom-*poo*-ter
computer game *gra komputerowa* ⓕ
  gra kom-poo-te-*ro*-va
concert *koncert* ⓜ *kon*-tsert
concussion *wstrząs mózgu* ⓜ
  vstshons *mooz*-goo
conditioner (hair) *odżywka*
  (do włosów) ⓕ od-*zhif*-ka (do *vwo*-soof)
condom *kondom* ⓜ *kon*-dom
conference (big) *konferencja* ⓕ
  kon-fe-*ren*-tsya
conference (small) *narada* ⓕ na-*ra*-da
confession (religious) *spowiedź* ⓕ
  spo-vyej
confirm (a booking) *potwierdzać*
  pot-*fyer*-dzach
conjunctivitis *zapalenie spojówek* ⓜ
  za-pa-*le*-nye spo-*yoo*-vek

connection (transport) *połączenie* ⓝ
  po-won-*che*-nye
conservative *konserwatywny*
  kon-ser-va-*tiv*-ni
constipation *zatwardzenie* ⓝ
  zat-far-*dze*-nye
consulate *konsulat* ⓜ kon-*soo*-lat
contact lenses *soczewki kontaktowe* pl
  so-*chef*-kee kon-tak-*to*-ve
contraceptives *środki antykoncepcyjne* pl
  shrod-kee an-ti-kon-tsep-*tsiy*-ne
contract *kontrakt* ⓜ *kon*-trakt
convenience store
  sklep wielobranżowy ⓜ
  sklep vye-lo-bran-*zho*-vi
convent *klasztor* ⓜ *klash*-tor
cook *kucharz* ⓜ *koo*-khash
cook *gotować* go-*to*-vach
cookie *herbatnik* ⓜ her-*ba*-tneek
cooking *gotowanie* ⓝ go-to-*va*-nye
cool (groovy) *fajny* *fai*-ni
cool (temperature) *chłodny* *khwo*-dni
corkscrew *korkociąg* ⓜ kor-*ko*-chyong
corn *kukurydza* ⓕ koo-koo-*ri*-dza
corner *róg* ⓜ roog
corrupt *a zepsuty* ze-*psoo*-ti
corruption *korupcja* ⓕ ko-*roop*-tsya
cost *koszt* ⓜ kosht
cost *kosztować* ⓜ kosh-*to*-vach
cotton *bawełna* ⓕ ba-*vew*-na
cotton balls *waciki* pl va-*chee*-kee
cotton buds *pałeczki higieniczne* pl
  pa-*wech*-kee hee-gye-*neech*-ne
couchette *kuszetka* ⓕ koo-*shet*-ka
cough *kaszel* ⓜ *ka*-shel
cough *kaszleć* kash-lech
cough medicine *lekarstwo na kaszel* ⓝ
  le-*karst*-fo na *ka*-shel
count *liczyć* lee-*chich*
counter (at bar) *lada* ⓕ *la*-da
country *kraj* ⓜ krai
countryside *okolica* ⓕ o-ko-*lee*-tsa
coupon *kupon* ⓜ *koo*-pon
courgette *cukinia* ⓕ tsoo-*kee*-nya
court (legal) *sąd* ⓜ sond
court (tennis) *kort* ⓜ kort
couscous *kuskus* ⓜ *koos*-koos
cover charge *opłata za wejście do baru* ⓕ
  o-*pwa*-ta za veysh-chye do *ba*-roo
cow *krowa* ⓕ *kro*-va
cracker *krakers* ⓜ *kra*-kers
crafts *rękodzieła* pl ren-ko-*jye*-wa
crash *wypadek* ⓜ vi-*pa*-dek
crazy *szalony* sha-*lo*-ni

cream (food) *śmietana* ① shmye-*ta*-na
cream (lotion) *krem* ⓜ krem
crèche *przedszkole* ⓝ pshet-*shko*-le
credit *kredyt* ⓜ *kre*-dit
credit card *karta kredytowa* ①
 kar-ta kre-di-*to*-va
cricket (sport) *krykiet* ⓜ *kri*-kyet
crop (riding) *bicz* ⓜ beech
cross (religious) *krzyż* ⓜ kshish
crowded *zatłoczony* za-two-*cho*-ni
crystal *kryształ* ⓜ *krish*-tow
cucumber *ogórek* ⓜ o-*goo*-rek
cup *filiżanka* ① fee-lee-*zhan*-ka
cupboard *szafka kuchenna* ①
 shaf-ka koo-*khe*-na
currency exchange *kantor* ⓜ *kan*-tor
current (electricity) *prąd* ⓜ pront
current affairs *sprawy bieżące* pl
 spra-vi bye-*zhon*-tse
curry *curry* ⓝ *ka*-ri
custom *zwyczaj* ⓜ *zvi*-chai
customs *urząd celny* ⓜ oo-zhont *tsel*-ni
cut *skaleczenie* ⓝ ska-le-*che*-nye
cut *ciąć* chyonch
cutlery *sztućce* pl shtooch-tse
CV *życiorys* ⓜ zhi-*chyo*-ris
cycle (ride) v *jeździć na rowerze*
 yezh-jeech na ro-*ve*-zhe
cycling *jazda na rowerze* ①
 yaz-da na ro-*ve*-zhe
cyclist *rowerzysta* ⓜ ro-ve-*zhi*-sta
cystitis *zapalenie pęcherza* ⓝ
 za-pa-*le*-nye pen-*khe*-zha
Czech (language) (*język*) *czeski* ⓜ
 (*yen*-zik) *che*-skee
Czech Republic *Czechy* pl *che*-khi

D

dad *tata* ⓜ *ta*-ta
daily *codzienny* tso-*jye*-ni
dance *taniec* ⓜ *ta*-nyets
dance *tańczyć* tan'-chich
dancing *tańce* pl tan'-tse
dangerous *niebezpieczny*
 nye-bes-*pyech*-ni
dark *ciemny* *chyem*-ni
date (appointment) *randka* ① *rand*-ka
date (day) *data* ① *da*-ta
date (fruit) *daktyl* ⓜ *dak*-til
date (go out with) *chodzić (z kimś)*
 kho-jeech (z keemsh)

date of birth *data urodzenia* ①
 da-ta oo-ro-*dze*-nya
daughter *córka* ① *tsoor*-ka
dawn *świt* ⓜ shveet
day *dzień* ⓜ jyen'
day after tomorrow *pojutrze* ⓝ
 po-*yoo*-tshe
day before yesterday *przedwczoraj* ⓜ
 pshet-*fcho*-rai
dead *martwy* *mart*-fi
deaf *głuchy* *gwoo*-khi
deal (cards) *rozdawać* roz-*da*-vach
December *grudzień* ⓜ *groo*-jyen'
decide *decydować* de-tsi-*do*-vach
deep (water) *głęboki* gwem-*bo*-kee
deforestation *ogołocenie z lasów* ⓝ
 o-go-wo-*tse*-nye z la-soof
degrees (temperature) *stopnie* pl
 sto-pnye
delay *opóźnienie* ⓝ o-poozh-*nye*-nye
delicatessen *delikatesy* pl de-lee-ka-*te*-si
deliver *dostarczyć* dos-*tar*-chich
democracy *demokracja* ① de-mo-*kra*-tsya
demonstration (rally) *demonstracja* ①
 de-mon-*stra*-tsya
Denmark *Dania* ① *da*-nya
dental dam (safe sex) *lateksowe gumy
 do koferdamu* pl la-tek-*so*-ve *goo*-mi do
 ko-fer-*da*-moo
dental floss *nić dentystyczna* ①
 neech den-*tis*-*ti*-chna
dentist *dentysta* ⓜ den-*tis*-ta
deodorant *dezodorant* ⓜ de-zo-*do*-rant
depart *odjeżdżać od-yezh*-jach
department store *dom towarowy* ⓜ
 dom to-va-*ro*-vi
departure (by air) *odlot* ⓜ *od*-lot
departure (by land) *odjazd* ⓜ *od*-yazd
departure gate *brama odlotów* ①
 bra-ma od-*lo*-toof
deposit *depozyt* ⓜ de-*po*-zit
derailleur *przerzutka* ① pshe-*zhoot*-ka
descendant *potomek* ⓜ po-*to*-mek
design *projekt* ⓜ *pro*-yekt
dessert *deser* ⓜ *de*-ser
destination *miejsce przeznaczenia* ⓝ
 myeys-tse pshez-na-*che*-nya
details *detale* pl de-*ta*-le
diabetes *cukrzyca* ① tsook-*shi*-tsa
diaper *pieluszka* ① pye-*loosh*-ka
diaphragm (contraceptive)
 spirala antykoncepcyjna ①
 spee-*ra*-la an-ti-kon-tsep-*tsiy*-na

diarrhoea *rozwolnienie* ⓝ roz·vol·*nye*·nye
diary *notatnik* ⓜ no·*tat*·neek
dice *kostki do gry* pl *kos*·tkee do gri
dictionary *słownik* ⓜ *swov*·neek
die *umierać* oo·*mye*·rach
diet *dieta* ⓕ *dye*·ta
different *różny* *roozh*·ni
difficult *trudny* *trood*·ni
digital *cyfrowy* tsi·*fro*·vi
dining car *wagon restauracyjny* ⓜ
  va·gon res·tow·ra·*tsiy*·ni
dinner *kolacja* ⓕ ko·*la*·tsya
direct *bezpośredni* bes·po·*shred*·nee
direct-dial *rozmowa bezpośrednia* ⓕ
  roz·*mo*·va bes·po·*shred*·nya
direction *kierunek* ⓜ kye·*roo*·nek
director *dyrektor* ⓜ di·*re*·ktor
dirty *brudny* *brood*·ni
disabled *niepełnosprawny*
  nye·pew·no·*sprav*·ni
disco *dyskoteka* ⓕ dis·ko·*te*·ka
discount *zniżka* ⓕ *zneesh*·ka
discrimination *dyskryminacja* ⓕ
  dis·kree·mee·*na*·tsya
disease *choroba* ⓕ kho·*ro*·ba
dish (food) *potrawa* ⓕ po·*tra*·va
dish (plate) *talerz* ⓜ *ta*·lesh
disk (CD-ROM) *dysk kompaktowy* ⓜ
  disk kom·pak·*to*·vi
disk (floppy) *dyskietka* ⓕ dis·*kyet*·ka
diving *nurkowanie* ⓝ noor·ko·*va*·nye
diving equipment *sprzęt do
  nurkowania* ⓜ spshent do
  noor·ko·*va*·nya
divorced *rozwiedziony* roz·vye·*jyo*·ni
dizzy *zawrotny* za·*vrot*·ni
do *robić* *ro*·beech
doctor *lekarz* ⓜ *le*·kash
dog *pies* ⓜ pyes
dole *zasiłek* ⓜ za·*shee*·wek
doll *lalka* ⓕ *lal*·ka
dollar *dolar* ⓜ *do*·lar
door *drzwi* jvee
double *podwójny* pod·*vooy*·ni
double bed *łóżko małżeńskie* ⓝ
  woozh·ko mow·*zhen*'·skye
double room *pokój dwuosobowy* ⓜ
  po·kooy dvoo·o·so·*bo*·vi
down *na dół* na doow
downhill *zjazd* ⓜ zyazd
dozen *tuzin* ⓜ *too*·zheen
drama *dramat* ⓜ *dra*·mat

dream *sen* ⓜ sen
dress *sukienka* ⓕ soo·*kyen*·ka
dried *suszony* soo·*sho*·ni
dried fruit *suszony owoc* ⓜ
  soo·*sho*·ni o·vots
drink *napój* ⓜ *na*·pooy
drink *pić* peech
drink (alcoholic) *drink* ⓜ dreenk
drive *kierować* kye·*ro*·vach
drivers licence *prawo jazdy* ⓝ
  pra·vo yaz·di
drug (illicit) *narkotyk* ⓜ nar·*ko*·tik
drug (medicinal) *lek* ⓜ lek
drug dealer *handlarz narkotyków* ⓜ
  hand·lash nar·ko·*ti*·koof
drugs (illicit) *narkotyki* nar·ko·*ti*·kee
drug trafficking *przemyt narkotyków* ⓜ
  pshe·mit nar·ko·*ti*·koof
drug user *narkoman* ⓜ nar·*ko*·man
drum *bęben* ⓜ *bem*·ben
drums (kit) *perkusja* ⓕ per·*koo*·sya
drunk *pijany* pee·*ya*·ni
dry *suchy* soo·khi
dry (clothes) *suszyć* soo·shich
dry (oneself) *wycierać* vi·*chye*·rach
duck *kaczka* ⓕ *kach*·ka
dummy (pacifier) *smoczek* ⓜ *smo*·chek
duty-free *bezcłowy* bes·*tswo*·vi
DVD *DVD* ⓜ dee·vee·*dee*

E

each *każdy* *kazh*·di
ear *ucho* ⓝ *oo*·kho
early *wcześnie* *vchesh*·nye
earn *zarabiać* za·*ra*·byach
earplugs *zatyczki do uszu* pl
  za·*tich*·kee do oo·shoo
earrings *kolczyki* pl kol·*chi*·kee
earth *ziemia* ⓕ *zhye*·mya
earthquake *trzęsienie ziemi* ⓝ
  tshen·*shye*·nye *zhye*·mee
east *wschód* ⓜ vskhood
Easter *Wielkanoc* ⓕ vyel·*ka*·nots
easy *łatwy* *wa*·tfi
eat *jeść* yeshch
economy class *klasa oszczędnościowa* ⓕ
  kla·sa osh·chend·nosh·*chyo*·va
ecstasy (drug) *ekstaza* ⓕ eks·*ta*·za
eczema *egzema* ⓕ eg·*ze*·ma
editor *redaktor* ⓜ re·*dak*·tor
education *oświata* ⓕ osh·*vya*·ta
egg *jajko* ⓝ *yai*·ko

election *wybory* pl vi·*bo*·ri
electrician *elektryk* ⓜ e·*lek*·trik
electricity *elektryczność* ⓕ
   e·lek·*trich*·noshch
elevator *winda* ⓕ *veen*·da
email *email* ⓔ e·*mail*
embarrassed *zakłopotany*
   za·kwo·po·*ta*·ni
embassy *ambasada* ⓕ am·ba·*sa*·da
emergency *nagły przypadek* ⓜ
   na·gwi pshi·*pa*·dek
employee *pracownik* ⓜ pra·*tsov*·neek
employer *pracodawca* ⓜ pra·tso·*daf*·tsa
empty *pusty* poos·ti
end *koniec* ⓜ *ko*·nyets
endangered species *zagrożone gatunki*
   za·gro·*zho*·ne ga·*toon*·kee
engaged (phone) *zajęty* za·*yen*·ti
engaged (to be married)
   zaręczony za·ren·*cho*·ni
engagement (to marry)
   zaręczyny za·ren·*chi*·ni
engine *silnik* ⓜ *sheel*·neek
engineer *inżynier* ⓜ een·*zhi*·nyer
engineering *inżynieria* ⓕ een·zhi·*nyer*·ya
England *Anglia* ⓕ *an*·glya
English (language/nationality)
   angielski an·*gyel*·skee
enjoy (oneself) *cieszyć się* *chye*·shich shye
enough *dosyć* *do*·sich
enter *wejść* veyshch
entertainment guide
   informator rozrywkowy ⓜ
   een·for·*ma*·tor roz·rif·*ko*·vi
entry *wejście* ⓝ *veysh*·chye
envelope *koperta* ⓕ ko·*per*·ta
environment *środowisko* ⓝ
   shro·do·*vees*·ko
epilepsy *padaczka* ⓕ pa·*dach*·ka
equality *równość* ⓕ *roov*·noshch
equipment *sprzęt* ⓜ spshent
estate agency *agencja handlu*
   nieruchomościami ⓕ a·*gen*·tsya
   han·dloo nye·roo·kho·mosh·*chya*·mee
euro *euro* ⓝ *ew*·ro
Europe *Europa* ⓕ ew·*ro*·pa
European Union *Unia Europejska* ⓕ
   oo·nya ew·ro·*pey*·ska
euthanasia *eutanazja* ⓕ ew·ta·*na*·zya
evening *wieczór* ⓜ *vye*·choor
every *każdy* *kazh*·di
everyone *każdy* *kazh*·di
everything *wszystko* *fshist*·ko

exactly *dokładnie* do·*kwa*·dnye
example *przykład* ⓜ *pshi*·kwad
excellent *doskonały* dos·ko·*na*·wi
excess baggage *nadbagaż* ⓜ
   nad·*ba*·gash
exchange *wymiana* ⓕ vi·*mya*·na
exchange *wymieniać* vi·*mye*·nyach
exchange rate *kurs wymiany* ⓜ
   koors vi·*mya*·ni
excluded *wyłączony* vi·won·*cho*·ni
exhaust (car) *wydech* ⓜ *vi*·dekh
exhibition *wystawa* ⓕ vis·*ta*·va
exit *wyjście* ⓝ *viysh*·chye
expensive *drogi* *dro*·gee
experience *doświadczenie* ⓝ
   dosh·vyad·*che*·nye
exploitation *wyzysk* ⓜ *vi*·zisk
export permit *zezwolenie eksportowe* ⓝ
   zez·vo·*le*·nye eks·por·*to*·ve
express *ekspresowy* eks·pre·*so*·vi
express mail *list ekspresowy* ⓜ
   leest eks·pre·*so*·vi
extension (visa) *przedłużenie* ⓝ
   pshe·dwoo·*zhe*·nye
eye *oko* ⓝ *o*·ko

F

fabric *materiał* ⓜ ma·*ter*·yow
face *twarz* ⓕ tfash
face cloth *myjka* ⓕ *miy*·ka
factory *fabryka* ⓕ fa·*bri*·ka
factory worker *robotnik* ⓜ ro·*bot*·neek
fall (autumn) *jesień* ⓕ *ye*·shyen′
fall (down) *upadać* oo·*pa*·dach
family *rodzina* ⓕ ro·*jee*·na
family name *nazwisko* ⓝ naz·*vees*·ko
famous *sławny* *swav*·ni
fan (machine) *wentylator* ⓜ ven·ti·*la*·tor
fan (sport, politics) *kibic* ⓜ *kee*·beets
far *daleki* da·*le*·kee
fare *taryfa* ⓕ ta·*ri*·fa
farm *gospodarstwo rolne* ⓝ
   gos·po·*darst*·fo *rol*·ne
farmer *rolnik* ⓜ *rol*·neek
fashion *moda* ⓕ *mo*·da
fast *szybki* *shib*·kee
fat *tłusty* *twoos*·ti
father *ojciec* ⓜ *oy*·chyets
father-in-law *teść* ⓜ teshch
faucet *kran* ⓜ kran
fault (someone's) *wina* ⓕ *vee*·na
faulty *wadliwy* vad·*lee*·vi

fax machine *faks* Ⓜ faks
February *luty* Ⓜ loo·ti
feed *karmić* kar·meech
feel (touch) *czuć* chooch
feeling (physical) *uczucie* Ⓝ oo·choo·chye
feelings *uczucia* pl oo·choo·chya
female *żeński* zhen'·skee
fence *płot* Ⓜ pwot
fencing (sport) *szermierka* Ⓕ sher·myer·ka
ferry n *prom* Ⓜ prom
festival *festiwal* Ⓜ fes·tee·val
fever *gorączka* Ⓕ go·ronch·ka
few *kilka* keel·ka
fiancé *narzeczony* Ⓜ na·zhe·cho·ni
fiancée *narzeczona* Ⓕ na·zhe·cho·na
fig *figa* Ⓕ fee·ga
fight *walka* Ⓕ val·ka
fill *wypełnić* vi·pew·neech
fillet *filet* Ⓜ fee·let
film (camera/cinema) *film* Ⓜ feelm
film speed *czułość filmu* Ⓕ choo·woshch feel·moo
find *znaleźć* zna·lezhch
fine *ładny* wad·ni
fine n *kara* Ⓕ ka·ra
finger *palec* Ⓜ pa·lets
finish (end) *koniec* Ⓜ ko·nyets
finish (in sport) *meta* Ⓕ me·ta
finish *kończyć* kon'·chich
Finland *Finlandia* Ⓕ feen·lan·dya
fire (general) *ogień* Ⓜ o·gyen'
fire (inferno) *pożar* Ⓜ po·zhar
firewood *drewno opałowe* Ⓝ drev·no o·pa·wo·ve
first *pierwszy* pyerf·shi
first-aid kit *apteczka pierwszej pomocy* Ⓕ ap·tech·ka pyerf·shey po·mo·tsi
first class *pierwsza klasa* Ⓕ pyerf·sha kla·sa
first name *imię* Ⓝ ee·mye
fish *ryba* Ⓕ ri·ba
fishing *rybołówstwo* Ⓝ ri·bo·woos·tfo
fishmonger *handlarz ryb* Ⓜ han·dlash rib
flag *flaga* Ⓕ fla·ga
flash (camera) *flesz* Ⓜ flesh
flashlight *latarka* Ⓕ la·tar·ka
flat (apartment) *mieszkanie* Ⓝ myesh·ka·nye
flat *płaski* pwas·kee
flea *pchła* Ⓕ pkhwa
flight *lot* Ⓜ lot

flood *powódź* Ⓕ po·vooj
floor *podłoga* Ⓕ pod·wo·ga
floor (storey) *piętro* Ⓝ pyen·tro
florist *kwiaciarnia* Ⓕ kvya·chyar·nya
flour *mąka* Ⓕ mon·ka
flower *kwiat* Ⓜ kvyat
flu *grypa* Ⓕ gri·pa
flute *flet* Ⓜ flet
fly *mucha* Ⓕ moo·kha
fly *latać* la·tach
foggy *mglisty* mglees·ti
follow *iść za* eeshch za
food *żywność* Ⓕ zhiv·noshch
foot (body) *stopa* Ⓕ sto·pa
football (soccer) *piłka nożna* Ⓕ peew·ka nozh·na
footpath *ścieżka* Ⓕ shchyesh·ka
foreign *zagraniczny* za·gra·nee·chni
forest *las* Ⓜ las
forever *na zawsze* na zaf·she
forget *zapomnieć* za·pom·nyech
forgive *przebaczyć* pshe·ba·chich
fork *widelec* Ⓜ vee·de·lets
fortnight *dwa tygodnie* dva ti·go·dnye
foul (soccer) n *faul* Ⓜ fa·ool
foyer *foyer* Ⓜ foo·a·ye
fragile *kruchy* Ⓜ kroo·khi
France *Francja* Ⓕ fran·tsya
free (available) *wolny* vol·ni
free (gratis) *bezpłatny* bes·pwat·ni
free (not bound) *wolny* vol·ni
freeze *zamrażać* za·mra·zhach
fresh *świeży* Ⓜ shfye·zhi
Friday *piątek* Ⓜ pyon·tek
fridge *lodówka* Ⓕ lo·doof·ka
fried *smażony* sma·zho·ni
friend *przyjaciel/przyjaciółka* Ⓜ/Ⓕ pshi·ya·chyel/pshi·ya·choow·ka
from *od* • z *od* • z
frost *mróz* Ⓜ mrooz
frozen *mrożony* mro·zho·ni
fruit *owoc* Ⓜ o·vots
fry *smażyć* sma·zhich
frying pan *patelnia* Ⓕ pa·tel·nya
full *pełny* pew·ni
full-time *w pełnym wymiarze godzin* v pew·nim vi·mya·zhe go·jeen
fun *zabawa* Ⓕ za·ba·va
(have) fun *mieć frajdę* myech frai·de
funeral *pogrzeb* Ⓜ pog·zheb
funny *zabawny* za·bav·ni
furniture *meble* pl me·ble
future *przyszłość* Ⓕ pshish·woshch

G

game *gra* ① gra
garage *garaż* ⑩ ga·razh
garbage *śmieci* pl shmye·chee
garbage can *pojemnik na śmieci* ⑩
po·*yem*·neek na *shmye*·chee
garden *ogród* ⑩ o·grood
gardener *ogrodnik* ⑩ o·*grod*·neek
gardening *ogrodnictwo* ⑥
o·grod·*neets*·fo
garlic *czosnek* ⑩ *chos*·nek
garnet *granat* ⑩ gra·nat
gas (for cooking) *gaz* ⑩ gaz
gas (petrol) *benzyna* ① ben·*zi*·na
gastroenteritis
choroba przewodu pokarmowego ①
kho·ro·ba pshe·*vo*·doo po·kar·mo·*ve*·go
gate (airport, etc) *wejście* ⑥ *veysh*·chye
gauze *gaza* ① ga·za
gay (homosexual) *gej* gey
gearbox *skrzynia biegów* ①
skshi·nya bye·goof
Gemini *Bliźnięta* pl bleezh·*nyen*·ta
Germany *Niemcy* pl *nyem*·tsi
get *dostać* dos·tach
get off (bus, train) *wysiadać* vi·*shya*·dach
gift *prezent* ⑩ *pre*·zent
gig *koncert* ⑩ *kon*·tsert
gin *dżin* ⑩ jeen
girl *dziewczyna* ① jyev·*chi*·na
girlfriend *dziewczyna* ① jyev·*chi*·na
give *dać* dach
given name *imię* ⑥ ee·mye
glandular fever *mononukleoza*
zakaźna ① mo·no·noo·kle·*o*·za
za·*kazh*·na
glass (drinking) *szklanka* ① *shklan*·ka
glasses (spectacles) *okulary* pl o·koo·*la*·ri
glassware *wyroby szklane* pl
vi·*ro*·bi *shkla*·ne
gloves *rękawiczki* pl ren·ka·*veech*·kee
glue *klej* ⑩ kley
go (by mechanised means) *jechać*
ye·khach
goal (sport) *gol* ⑩ gol
goalkeeper *bramkarz* ⑩ *bram*·kash
goat *koza* ① *ko*·za
god (general) *bóg* ⑩ boog
goggles (skiing) *gogle* pl *go*·gle

goggles (swimming) *okulary do*
pływania pl o·koo·*la*·ri do pwi·*va*·nya
gold *złoto* ⑥ *zwo*·to
golf ball *piłeczka golfowa* ①
pee·*wech*·ka gol·*fo*·va
golf course *pole golfowe* ⑥
po·le gol·*fo*·ve
good *dobry* *do*·bri
goodbye *do widzenia* do vee·*dze*·nya
go out *wychodzić* vi·*kho*·jeech
go out with (date) *mieć randkę z*
myech *rand*·ke z
go shopping *chodzić po sklepach*
kho·jeech po *skle*·pakh
government *rząd* ⑩ zhond
gram *gram* ⑩ gram
grandchild *wnuk/wnuczka* ⑩/①
vnook/*vnooch*·ka
grandfather *dziadek* ⑩ *jya*·dek
grandmother *babcia* ① *bab*·chya
grapes *winogrona* pl vee·no·*gro*·na
grass (lawn) *trawa* ① *tra*·va
grateful *wdzięczny* ① *vjyench*·ni
grave *grób* ⑩ groob
great (fantastic) *wspaniały* vspa·*nya*·wi
green *zielony* zhye·*lo*·ni
greengrocer *sklep warzywny* ⑩
sklep va·*zhiv*·ni
grey *szary* *sha*·ri
grocery *sklep spożywczy* ⑩
sklep spo·*zhiv*·chi
groundnut *orzeszek ziemny* ⑩
o·*zhe*·shek *zhyem*·ni
grow *rosnąć* *ros*·nonch
guarantee *gwarancja* ① gva·*ran*·tsya
guess *zgadywać* zga·*di*·vach
guesthouse *pensjonat* ⑩ pen·*syo*·nat
guide (person) *przewodnik* ⑩
pshe·*vod*·neek
guidebook *przewodnik* ⑩ pshe·*vod*·neek
guide dog *pies przewodnik* ⑩
pyes pshe·*vod*·neek
guided tour *wycieczka z*
przewodnikiem ① vi·*chyech*·ka z
pshe·vod·*nee*·kyem
guilty *winny* *vee*·ni
guitar *gitara* ① gee·*ta*·ra
gum *guma* ① *goo*·ma
gun *pistolet* ⑩ pees·*to*·let
gym (place) *siłownia* ① shee·*wov*·nya
gymnastics *gimnastyka* ① geem·nas·*ti*·ka
gynaecologist *ginekolog* ⑩ gee·ne·*ko*·log

H

hair *włosy* pl vwo·si
hairbrush *szczotka do włosów* ①
  shchot·ka do vwo·soof
haircut *strzyżenie* ① stshi·zhe·nye
hairdresser *fryzjer* ⓜ fri·zyer
halal *halal* ⓝ ha·lal
half *połówka* ① po·woof·ka
hallucination *halucynacja* ①
  ha·loo·tsi·na·tsya
ham *szynka* ① shin·ka
hammer *młotek* ⓜ mwo·tek
hammock *hamak* ⓜ ha·mak
hand *ręka* ① ren·ka
handbag *torebka* ① to·rep·ka
handball *piłka ręczna* ①
  peew·ka rench·na
handicraft *rękodzielnictwo* ⓝ
  ren·ko·jyel·neetst·fo
handkerchief *chusteczka* ①
  khoos·tech·ka
handmade *ręcznie robiony*
  rench·nye ro·byo·ni
handsome *przystojny* pshi·stoy·ni
happy *szczęśliwy* shchen·shlee·vi
harassment *napastowanie* ⓝ
  na·pas·to·va·nye
harbour *port* ⓜ port
hard (not soft) *twardy* tfar·di
hard-boiled *ugotowany na twardo*
  oo·go·to·va·ni na tfar·do
hardware store *sklep metalowy* ⓜ
  sklep me·ta·lo·vi
hashish *haszysz* ⓜ ha·shish
hat *kapelusz* ⓜ ka·pe·loosh
have *mieć* myech
hay fever *katar sienny* ⓜ ka·tar shye·ni
hazelnut *orzech laskowy* ⓜ
  o·zhekh las·ko·vi
he *on* on
head *głowa* ① gwo·va
headache *ból głowy* ⓜ bool gwo·vi
headlights *reflektory* pl re·fle·kto·ri
health *zdrowie* ⓝ zdro·vye
hear *słyszeć* swi·shech
hearing aid *aparat słuchowy* ⓜ
  a·pa·rat swoo·kho·vi
heart *serce* ⓝ ser·tse
heart attack *atak serca* ⓜ a·tak ser·tsa
heart condition *stan serca* ⓜ stan ser·tsa
heat *upał* ⓜ oo·pow

heated *podgrzewany* pod·gzhe·va·ni
heater *grzejnik* ⓜ gzhey·neek
heating *ogrzewanie* ⓝ o·gzhe·va·nye
heavy (weight) *ciężki* ⓜ chyensh·kee
helmet *kask* ⓜ kask
help *pomoc* ① po·mots
help *pomagać* po·ma·gach
hepatitis *żółtaczka* ① zhoow·tach·ka
her (possessive) *jej* yey
herb *zioło* ⓝ zhyo·wo
herbalist *zielarz* ⓜ zhye·lash
here *tutaj* too·tai
heroin *heroina* ① he·ro·ee·na
herring *śledź* ⓜ shlej
high (height) *wysoki* vi·so·kee
highchair *wysokie krzesełko dla dziecka* ⓝ
  vi·so·kye kshe·sew·ko dla jye·tska
high school *gimnazjum* ⓝ
  geem·na·zyoom
highway *szosa* ① sho·sa
hike *wędrować* ven·dro·vach
hiking *wędrówka* ① ven·droof·ka
hiking boots *buty turystyczne* pl
  boo·ti too·ris·tich·ne
hill *wzgórze* ⓝ vzgoo·zhe
Hindu *Hindus/Hinduska* ⓜ/①
  heen·doos/heen·doos·ka
hire *wynajmować* vi·nai·mo·vach
his *jego* ye·go
historical *historyczny* khees·to·rich·ni
history *historia* ① khees·to·rya
hitchhike *autostop* ⓜ ow·to·stop
HIV *HIV* ⓜ heev
hockey *hokej na trawie* ⓜ
  ho·key na tra·vye
holiday *święto* ⓝ shvyen·to
holidays *wakacje* pl va·ka·tsye
home *dom* ⓜ dom
homeless *bezdomny* bes·dom·ni
homemaker *gospodyni domowa* ①
  gos·po·di·nee do·mo·va
homeopathy *homeopatia* ①
  ho·me·o·pa·tya
homesick *tęsknota za domem* ①
  tensk·no·ta za do·mem
homosexual *homoseksualista* ⓜ
  ho·mo·sek·soo·a·lees·ta
honey *miód* ⓜ myood
honeymoon *miesiąc miodowy* ⓜ
  mye·shonts myo·do·vi
horoscope *horoskop* ⓜ ho·ros·kop
horse *koń* ⓜ koń

horse racing *wyścigi konne* pl
vish·*chee*·gee ko·ne
horse riding *jazda konna* ① *yaz*·da ko·na
hospital *szpital* ⑩ *shpee*·tal
hospitality *gościnność* ①
gosh·*chee*·noshch
hot *gorący* go·*ron*·tsi
hotel *hotel* ⑩ *ho*·tel
hot water *ciepła woda* ① *chyep*·wa vo·da
hot water bottle *termofor* ⑩ ter·*mo*·for
hour *godzina* ① go·*jee*·na
house *dom* ⑩ dom
how *jak* yak
how much *ile* ee·le
hug *przytulić* pshi·*too*·leech
huge *olbrzymi* ol·*bzhi*·mee
humanities *nauki humanistyczne* pl
na·oo·kee khoo·ma·nees·*tich*·ne
human resources *dział kadr* ⑩ jyow kadr
human rights *prawa człowieka* pl
pra·va chwo·*vye*·ka
hundred *sto* ⑩ sto
hungry *głodny* gwo·dni
hunting *polowanie* ⑩ po·lo·*va*·nye
(in a) hurry *w pośpiechu* v posh·*pye*·khoo
hurt *zranić* zra·neech
husband *mąż* ⑩ monzh

I

I *Ja* ya
ice *lód* ⑩ lood
ice axe *czekan* ⑩ che·kan
ice cream *lody* pl *lo*·di
ice-cream parlour *lodziarnia* ①
lo·*jyar*·nya
ice hockey *hokej na lodzie* ⑩
ho·key na *lo*·jye
identification *identyfikacja* ①
ee·den·ti·fee·*ka*·tsya
identification card (ID) *dowód tożsamości* ①
do·vood tozh·sa·*mosh*·chee
idiot *idiota/idiotka* ⑩/①
ee·*dyo*·ta/ee·*dyot*·ka
if *jeśli* yesh·lee
ill *chory* kho·ri
immigration *imigracja* ①
ee·mee·*gra*·tsya
important *ważny* vazh·ni
impossible *niemożliwy* nye·mozh·*lee*·vi
in *w* v

included *wliczony* vlee·*cho*·ni
income tax *podatek dochodowy* ⑩
po·*da*·tek do·kho·*do*·vi
India *Indie* pl een·dye
indicator *wkaźnik* ⑩ *vskazh*·neek
indigestion *niestrawność* ①
nye·*strav*·noshch
indoor *w pomieszczeniu* ⑩
v po·myesh·*che*·nyoo
industry *przemysł* ⑩ *pshe*·misw
infection *infekcja* ① een·*fek*·tsya
inflammation *zapalenie* ⑩ za·pa·*le*·nye
influenza *grypa* ① gri·pa
information *informacja* ①
een·for·*mats*·ya
in front of *przed* pshet
ingredient *składnik* ⑩ *skwad*·neek
inject *wstrzykiwać* vstshi·*kee*·vach
injection *zastrzyk* ⑩ *zast*·shik
injured *ranny* ra·ni
injury *rana* ① ra·na
inner tube *dętka* ① *dent*·ka
innocent *niewinny* nye·*vee*·ni
insect *owad* ⑩ o·vad
insect repellent *środek na owady* ⑩
shro·dek na o·*va*·di
inside *wewnątrz* vev·*nontsh*
instructor *instruktor* ⑩ een·*strook*·tor
insurance *ubezpieczenie* ⑩
oo·bes·pye·*che*·nye
interesting *interesujący*
een·te·re·soo·*yon*·tsi
intermission *przerwa* ① *psher*·va
international *międzynarodowy*
myen·dzi·na·ro·*do*·vi
internet *internet* ⑩ een·*ter*·net
internet café *kawiarnia internetowa* ①
ka·*vyar*·nya een·ter·ne·*to*·va
interpreter *tłumacz/tłumaczka* ⑩/①
twoo·mach/twoo·*mach*·ka
invite *zapraszać* za·*pra*·shach
Ireland *Irlandia* ① eer·*lan*·dya
iron (for clothes) *żelazko* ⑩ zhe·*las*·ko
island *wyspa* ① *vis*·pa
Israel *Izrael* ⑩ eez·*ra*·el
it *to* • *ono* ⑩ to/o·no
IT *informatyka* ① een·for·ma·*ti*·ka
Italy *Włochy* pl *vwo*·khi
itch *swędzenie* ⑩ sven·*dze*·nye
itinerary *trasa podróży* ①
tra·sa po·*droo*·zhi
IUD *spirala* ① spee·*ra*·la

english–polish

J

jacket *kurtka* ① koort·ka
jail *więzienie* ⑩ vyen·zhye·nye
jam *dżem* ⑩ jem
January *styczeń* ⑩ sti·chen´
Japan *Japonia* ① ya·po·nya
jar *słoik* ⑩ swo·yeek
jealous *zazdrosny* zaz·dros·ni
jeans *dżinsy* pl jeen·si
jet lag *jetlag* ⑩ jet·lag
jewellery *biżuteria* ① bee·zhoo·ter·ya
Jewish *żydowski* ⑩ zhi·dof·skee
job *praca* ① pra·tsa
jogging *bieganie* ⑩ bye·ga·nye
joke *żart* ⑩ zhart
journalist *dziennikarz* ⑩ jye·nee·kash
journey *podróż* ① po·droosh
judge *sędzia* ⑩ sen·jya
juice *sok* ⑩ sok
July *lipiec* ⑩ lee·pyets
jump *skakać* ska·kach
jumper (sweater) *sweter* ⑩ sve·ter
June *czerwiec* ⑩ cher·vyets

K

kayaking *kajakarstwo* ⑩ ka·ya·karst·fo
ketchup *keczup* ⑩ ke·choop
key (door etc) *klucz* ⑩ klooch
keyboard *klawiatura* ① kla·vya·too·ra
kick *kopać* ko·pach
kidney *nerka* ① ner·ka
kill *zabić* za·beech
kilogram *kilogram* ⑩ kee·lo·gram
kilometre *kilometr* ⑩ kee·lo·metr
kind (nice) *miły* mee·wi
kindergarten *przedszkole* ⑩ pshet·shko·le
king *król* ⑩ krool
kiosk *kiosk* ⑩ kyosk
kiss *pocałunek* ⑩ po·tsa·woo·nek
kiss *całować* tsa·wo·vach
kitchen *kuchnia* ① kookh·nya
Kiyev *Kijów* ⑩ kee·yoof
knee *kolano* ⑩ ko·la·no
knife *nóż* ⑩ noosh
know (be acquainted with) *znać* znach
know (be aware of) *wiedzieć* vye·jyech
kosher *koszerny* ko·sher·ni

L

labourer *robotnik* ⑩ ro·bot·neek
lace (fabric) *koronka* ① ko·ron·ka
lake *jezioro* ⑩ ye·zhyo·ro
lamb (meat) *jagnięcina* ①
  yag·nyen·chee·na
land *ziemia* ① zhye·mya
landlady *właścicielka* ①
  vwash·chee·chyel·ka
landlord *właściciel* ⑩ vwash·chee·chyel
language *język* ⑩ yen·zik
large *duży* doo·zhi
last (final) *ostatni* os·tat·nee
last (previous) *poprzedni* po·pshed·nee
late *późno* poozh·no
later *później* poozh·nyey
laugh *śmiać się* shmyach shye
laundrette *pralnia samoobsługowa* ①
  pral·nya sa·mo·ob·swoo·go·va
laundry (clothes) *bielizna do prania* ①
  bye·leez·na do pra·nya
laundry (place) *pralnia* ① pral·nya
laundry (room) *pralnia* ① pral·nya
law *prawo* ⑩ pra·vo
lawyer *prawnik* ⑩ prav·neek
laxative *środek przeczyszczający* ⑩
  shro·dek pshe·chish·cha·yon·tsi
lazy *leniwy* le·nee·vi
leaf *liść* ⑩ leeshch
learn *uczyć się* oo·chich shye
leather *skóra* ① skoo·ra
lecturer *wykładowca* ⑩ vik·wa·dof·tsa
ledge *występ* ⑩ vis·temp
left (direction) *lewy* ⑩ le·vi
left-luggage office
  przechowalnia bagażu ①
  pshe·kho·val·nya ba·ga·zhoo
leg (body) *noga* ① no·ga
legal *prawny* prav·ni
lemon *cytryna* ① tsi·tri·na
lemonade *lemoniada* ① le·mo·nya·da
lens (camera) *obiektyw* ⑩ o·byek·tif
lentil *soczewica* ① so·che·vee·tsa
Leo *Lew* ⑩ lev
lesbian *lesbijka* ① les·beey·ka
less *mniej* mnyey
letter (mail) *list* ⑩ leest
liar *kłamca* ⑩ kwam·tsa
Libra *Waga* ① va·ga
librarian *bibliotekarz* ⑩ beeb·lyo·te·kash
library *biblioteka* ① beeb·lyo·te·ka
lice *wszy* pl vshi

licence *licencja* ① lee-*tsen*-tsya
lie (not stand) *leżeć le*-zhech
lie (not tell the truth) *kłamać kwa*-mach
life *życie* ⓝ *zhi*-chye
life jacket *kamizelka ratunkowa* ①
 ka-mee-*zel*-ka ra-toon-*ko*-va
lift (elevator) *winda* ① *veen*-da
light *światło* ⓝ *shvyat*-wo
light (colour) *jasny yas*-ni
light (weight) *lekki le*-kee
light bulb *żarówka* ① zha-*roof*-ka
light meter *światłomierz* ⓜ
 shvya-*two*-myesh
like *lubić loo*-beech
lime (fuit) *limona* ① lee-*mo*-na
linen (material) *len* ⓜ len
linen (sheets) *pościel* ① *posh*-chyel
linguist *lingwista* ⓜ leen-*gvees*-ta
lip balm *szminka ochronna* ①
 shmeen-ka o-*khro*-na
lips *wargi* pl *var*-gee
lipstick *szminka* ① *shmeen*-ka
liquor store *sklep monopolowy* ⓜ
 sklep mo-no-po-*lo*-vi
listen *słuchać swoo*-khach
Lithuania *Litwa* ① *lee*-tfa
little (quantity) *trochę tro*-khe
little (size) *mały ma*-wi
live (life) *żyć* zhich
live (somewhere) *mieszkać myesh*-kach
liver *wątroba* ① von-*tro*-ba
local *miejscowy* myeys-*tso*-vi
lock *zamek* ⓜ *za*-mek
lock *zamykać na klucz*
 za-*mi*-kach na klooch
locked *zamknięty* zam-*knyen*-ti
lollies *cukierki* pl tsoo-*kyer*-kee
long *długi dwoo*-gee
look *patrzeć pat*-shech
look after *opiekować się*
 o-pye-*ko*-vach shye
look for *szukać shoo*-kach
lookout *punkt widokowy* ⓜ
 poonkt vee-do-*ko*-vi
loose *luźny loozh*-ni
lose *tracić tra*-cheech
lost *zgubiony* zgoo-*byo*-ni
lost-property office *biuro rzeczy*
 znalezionych ⓜ *byoo*-ro *zhe*-chi
 zna-le-*zhyo*-nikh
(a) lot *dużo doo*-zho
loud *głośny gwosh*-ni
love *miłość* ① *mee*-woshch

love *kochać ko*-khach
lover *kochanek* ⓜ ko-*kha*-nek
low *niski nees*-kee
lubricant *smar* ⓜ smar
luck *szczęście shchen*-shchye
lucky *szczęśliwy* shchen-*shlee*-vi
luggage *bagaż* ⓜ *ba*-gash
luggage locker *schowek na bagaż* ⓜ
 skho-vek na *ba*-gash
lump *guz* ⓜ goos
lunch *lunch* ⓜ lanch
lung *płuco* ⓝ *pwoo*-tso
luxury *luksusowy* look-soo-*so*-vi

M

machine *maszyna* ① ma-*shi*-na
magazine *magazyn* ⓜ ma-*ga*-zin
mail (letters) *list* ⓜ leest
mail (postal system) *poczta* ① *poch*-ta
mail *przysyłać pshis*-wach
mailbox *skrzynka pocztowa* ①
 skshin-ka poch-*to*-va
main *główny gwoov*-ni
main road *główna ulica* ①
 gwoov-na oo-*lee*-tsa
make *robić ro*-beech
make-up *makijaż* ⓜ ma-*kee*-yash
man *mężczyzna* ⓜ menzh-*chiz*-na
manager (business) *kierownik* ⓜ
 kye-*rov*-neek
manager (sport) *menedżer* ⓜ me-*ne*-jer
mandarin *mandarynka* ① man-da-*rin*-ka
mango *mango* ⓝ *man*-go
manual worker *robotnik* ⓜ ro-*bo*-tneek
many *dużo doo*-zho
map (of country) *mapa* ① *ma*-pa
map (of town) *plan* ⓜ plan
March *marzec* ⓜ *ma*-zhets
margarine *margaryna* ① mar-ga-*ri*-na
marijuana *marihuana* ①
 ma-ree-khoo-*a*-na
marital status *stan cywilny* ⓜ
 stan tsi-*veel*-ni
market *rynek* ⓜ *ri*-nek
marriage *małżeństwo* ⓝ mow-*zhen'*-stfo
married (of man) *żonaty* zho-*na*-ti
married (of woman) *zamężna*
 za-*men*-zhna
marry *poślubić* po-*shloo*-beech
mass (Catholic) *msza* ① msha
massage *masaż* ⓜ *ma*-sash

masseur/masseuse
  masażysta/masażystka ⓜ/①
  ma·sa·zhi·sta/ma·sa·zhis·tka

mat *mata* ① ma·ta

match (sports) *mecz* ⓜ mech

matches (for lighting) *zapałki* pl
  za·pow·kee

mattress *materac* ⓜ ma·te·rats

May *maj* ⓜ mai

maybe *być może* bich mo·zhe

mayor *burmistrz* ⓜ boor·meestsh

me *mi* mee

meal *posiłek* ⓜ po·shee·wek

measles *odra* ① od·ra

meat *mięso* ⓝ myen·so

mechanic *mechanik* ⓜ me·kha·neek

medicine (medication) *lekarstwo* ⓝ
  le·karst·fo

medicine (study/profession)
  medycyna ① me·di·tsi·na

meditation *medytacja* ① me·di·ta·tsya

meet (first time) *zapoznać za·poz·*nach

meet (get together) *spotkać spot·*kach

melon *melon* ⓜ me·lon

member *członek* ⓜ chwo·nek

memory card/stick *karta pamięci* ①
  kar·ta pa·myen·chee

menstruation *menstruacja* ①
  men·stroo·a·tsya

menu *jadłospis* ⓜ ya·dwo·spees

message *wiadomość* ① vya·do·moshch

metal *metal* ⓜ me·tal

metre *metr* ⓜ metr

metro (train) *metro* ⓝ me·tro

metro station *stacja metra* ①
  sta·tsya me·tra

microwave oven *kuchenka
  mikrofalowa* ① koo·khen·ka
  mee·kro·fa·lo·va

midday *południe* ⓝ po·wood·nye

midnight *północ* ① poow·nots

migraine *migrena* ① mee·gre·na

military *wojsko* ⓝ voy·sko

milk *mleko* ⓝ mle·ko

milk bar *bar mleczny* ⓜ bar mlech·ni

millimetre *milimetr* ⓜ mee·lee·metr

million *milion* ⓜ meel·yon

mineral water *woda mineralna* ①
  vo·da mee·ne·ral·na

minibus *minibus* ⓜ mee·nee·boos

Minsk *Mińsk* ⓜ meen'sk

minute *minuta* ① mee·noo·ta

mirror *lustro* ⓝ loos·tro

miscarriage *poronienie* ⓝ po·ro·nye·nye

Miss *panna* ① pa·na

miss (feel absence of) *odczuwać brak*
  od·choo·vach brak

miss (not catch train etc) *spóźnić się*
  spoozh·neech shye

mistake *pomyłka* ① po·miw·ka

mix *mieszać* mye·shach

mobile phone *telefon komórkowy* ⓜ
  te·le·fon ko·moor·ko·vi

modem *modem* ⓜ mo·dem

modern *nowoczesny* no·vo·ches·ni

moisturiser *krem nawilżający* ⓜ
  krem na·veel·zha·yon·tsi

monastery *klasztor* ⓜ klash·tor

Monday *poniedziałek* ⓜ po·nye·jya·wek

money *pieniądze* pl pye·nyon·dze

monk *mnich* ⓜ mneekh

month *miesiąc* ⓜ mye·shonts

monument *pomnik* ⓜ pom·neek

moon *księżyc* ⓜ kshyen·zhits

more *więcej* vyen·tsey

morning *rano* ⓝ ra·no

Moscow *Moskwa* ① mosk·fa

mosque *meczet* ⓜ me·chet

mosquito *komar* ⓜ ko·mar

mosquito coil *spirala na komary* ①
  spee·ra·la na ko·ma·ri

mosquito net *moskitiera* ①
  mos·kee·tye·ra

motel *motel* ⓜ mo·tel

mother *matka* ① mat·ka

mother-in-law (wife's mother)
  teściowa ① tesh·chyo·va

mother-in-law (husband's mother)
  świekra ① shwyek·ra

motorbike *motor* ⓜ mo·tor

motorboat *motorówka* ① mo·to·roof·ka

motorway *autostrada* ① ow·to·stra·da

mountain *góra* ① goo·ra

mountain bike *rower górski* ⓜ
  ro·ver goor·skee

mountaineering *wycieczka
  wysokogórska* ① vi·chyech·ka
  vi·so·ko·goor·ska

mountain lodge *schronisko górskie* ⓝ
  skhro·nees·ko goor·skye

mouse *mysz* ① mish

mouth *usta* pl oos·ta

movie *film* ⓜ feelm

Mr *pan* ⓜ pan

Mrs *pani* ① pa·nee

Ms *pani* ① pa·nee

mud *błoto* ⓝ bwo·to
muesli *muesli* ⓝ moos·lee
mum *mama* ⓕ ma·ma
mumps *świnka* ⓕ shfeen·ka
murder *morderca* ⓜ mor·der·tsa
murder *mordować* mor·do·vach
muscle *mięsień* ⓜ myen·shyen'
museum *muzeum* ⓝ moo·ze·oom
mushroom *grzyb* ⓜ gzhib
music *muzyka* ⓕ moo·zi·ka
musician *muzyk* ⓜ moo·zik
Muslim *muzułmanin* ⓜ
  moo·zoow·ma·neen
mussel *małż* ⓜ mowzh
mustard *musztarda* ⓕ moosh·tar·da
mute *niemy* nye·mi
my *mój/moja/moje* ⓜ/ⓕ/ⓝ
  mooy/mo·ya/mo·ye

N

nail clippers *obcążki do paznokci* pl
  ob·tsonzh·kee do paz·nok·chee
name *imię* ⓝ ee·mye
napkin *serwetka* ⓕ ser·vet·ka
nappy *pieluszka* ⓕ pye·loosh·ka
nappy rash *pieluszkowe zapalenie
  skóry* ⓝ pye·loosh·ko·ve za·pa·le·nye
  skoo·ri
nationality *narodowość* ⓕ
  na·ro·do·voshch
national park *park narodowy* ⓜ
  park na·ro·do·vi
nature *natura* ⓕ na·too·ra
naturopathy *naturopatia* ⓕ
  na·too·ro·pa·tya
nausea *mdłości* pl mdwosh·chee
near *bliski* blees·kee
nearby *w pobliżu* v po·blee·zhoo
nearest *najbliższy* nai·bleezh·shi
necessary *konieczny* ko·nyech·ni
neck *szyja* ⓕ shi·ya
necklace *naszyjnik* ⓜ na·shiy·neek
need *potrzebować* po·tshe·bo·vach
needle (sewing) *igła* ⓕ ee·gwa
needle (syringe) *igła* ⓕ ee·gwa
negative *negatywny* ne·ga·tiv·ni
negatives (photos) *negatyw* ⓜ ne·ga·tif
neither *żaden* zha·den
net *siatka* ⓕ shyat·ka
Netherlands *Holandia* ⓕ ho·lan·dya
network (phone) *sieć* ⓕ shyech
never *nigdy* neeg·di
new *nowy* no·vi

news *wiadomości* pl vya·do·mosh·chee
newsagency *kiosk z prasą* ⓜ
  kyosk z pra·som
newspaper *gazeta* ⓕ ga·ze·ta
newsstand *kiosk z gazetami* ⓜ
  kyosk z ga·ze·ta·mee
New Year's Day *Nowy Rok* ⓜ no·vi rok
New Year's Eve *Sylwester* ⓜ sil·ves·ter
New Zealand *Nowa Zelandia* ⓕ
  no·va ze·lan·dya
next (following) *następny* nas·temp·ni
next to *obok* o·bok
nice *miły* mee·wi
nickname *przydomek* ⓜ pshi·do·mek
night *noc* ⓕ nots
nightclub *klub nocny* ⓜ kloob nots·ni
no *nie* nye
noisy *hałaśliwy* ha·wa·shlee·vi
none *żaden* zha·den
nonsmoking *niepalący* nye·pa·lon·tsi
noodles *makaron* ⓜ ma·ka·ron
noon *południe* ⓝ po·wood·nye
north *północ* ⓕ poow·nots
Norway *Norwegia* ⓕ nor·ve·gya
nose *nos* ⓜ nos
not *nie* nye
notebook *notes* ⓜ no·tes
nothing *nic* neets
November *listopad* ⓜ lees·to·pat
now *teraz* te·ras
nuclear energy *energia nuklearna* ⓕ
  e·ner·gya noo·kle·ar·na
nuclear waste *odpady nuklearne* pl
  od·pa·di noo·kle·ar·ne
number *numer* ⓜ noo·mer
numberplate *tablica rejestracyjna* ⓕ
  ta·blee·tsa re·ye·stra·tsiy·na
nun *zakonnica* ⓕ za·ko·nee·tsa
nurse *pielęgniarz/pielęgniarka* ⓜ/ⓕ
  pye·leng·nyash/pye·leng·nyar·ka
nut (food) *orzech* ⓜ o·zhekh

O

oak (tree) *dąb* ⓜ domb
oats *płatki owsiane* pl
  pwat·kee ov·shya·ne
ocean *ocean* ⓜ o·tse·an
October *październik* ⓜ pazh·jyer·neek
off (power) *wyłączone* vi·won·cho·ne
off (spoiled) *niezdatny* nyez·dat·ni
office *biuro* byoo·ro
office worker *pracownik biurowy* ⓜ
  pra·tsov·neek byoo·ro·vi

often *często* chen·sto
oil (cooking) *olej* ⓜ o·ley
oil (petrol) *ropa naftowa* ⓕ
ro·pa naf·to·va
old *stary* sta·ri
olive *oliwka* ⓕ o·leef·ka
olive oil *olej z oliwek* ⓜ o·ley z o·lee·vek
Olympic Games *olimpiada* ⓕ
o·leem·pya·da
on *na* na
on (power) *włączone* vwon·cho·ne
once *raz* ras
one *jeden* ye·den
one-way ticket *bilet w jedną stronę* ⓜ
bee·let v yed·nom stro·ne
onion *cebula* ⓕ tse·boo·la
only *tylko* til·ko
on time *na czas* na chas
open (business) a *otwarty* ot·far·ti
open v *otwierać* ot·fye·rach
opening hours *godziny otwarcia* pl
go·jee·ni ot·far·chya
opera *opera* ⓕ o·pe·ra
opera house *opera* ⓕ o·pe·ra
operation (medical) *operacja* ⓕ
o·pe·ra·tsya
opinion *opinia* ⓕ o·pee·nya
opposite *naprzeciwko* na·pshe·cheef·ko
optometrist *okulista* ⓜ o·koo·lees·ta
or *lub • albo* loob • al·bo
orange (fruit) *pomarańcza* ⓕ
po·ma·ran′·cha
orange (colour) *pomarańczowy* ⓜ
po·ma·ran′·cho·vi
orange juice *sok pomarańczowy* ⓜ
sok po·ma·ran′·cho·vi
orchestra *orkiestra* ⓕ or·kyes·tra
order (command) *zamówienie* ⓝ
za·moo·vye·nye
order (tidiness) *porządek* ⓜ po·zhon·dek
order *zamawiać* za·ma·vyach
ordinary *zwyczajny* zvi·chai·ni
orgasm *orgazm* ⓜ or·gazm
original *oryginalny* o·ri·gee·nal·ni
Orthodox Church *kościół prawosławny* ⓜ
kosh·chyoow pra·vo·swav·ni
other *inny* ee·ni
our *nasz* nash
out of order *zepsuty* zep·soo·ti
outpatient clinic *ambulatorium* ⓝ
am·boo·la·tor·yoom
outside *na zewnątrz* na zev·nontsh

ovarian cyst *zapalenie jajników* ⓝ
za·pa·le·nye yai·nee·koof
ovary *jajnik* ⓜ yai·neek
oven *piekarnik* ⓜ pye·kar·neek
overcoat *płaszcz* ⓜ pwashch
overdose *przedawkowanie* ⓝ
pshe·daf·ko·va·nye
overnight *nocny* nots·ni
overseas *zagranica* ⓕ za·gra·nee·tsa
owe *być winnym* bich vee·nim
owner *właściciel/właścicielka* ⓜ/ⓕ
vwash·chee·chyel/vwash·chee·chyel·ka
oyster *ostryga* ⓕ os·tri·ga
ozone layer *warstwa ozonowa* ⓕ
varst·fa o·zo·no·va

P

pacemaker *rozrusznik* ⓜ roz·roosh·neek
pacifier (dummy) *smoczek* ⓜ smo·chek
package *paczka* ⓕ pach·ka
packet (general) *paczka* ⓕ pach·ka
padlock *kłódka* ⓕ kwood·ka
page *strona* ⓕ stro·na
pain *ból* ⓜ bool
painful *bolesny* bo·les·ni
painkiller *środek przeciwbólowy* ⓜ
shro·dek pshe·cheef·boo·lo·vi
painter (artist) *malarz* ⓜ ma·lash
painting (a work) *malarstwo* ⓝ
ma·lars·tfo
painting (the art) *obraz* ⓜ o·bras
pair (couple) *para* ⓕ pa·ra
Pakistan *Pakistan* ⓜ pa·kees·tan
palace *pałac* ⓜ pa·wats
pan *rondel* ⓜ ron·del
pants (trousers) *spodnie* pl spod·nye
pantyhose *rajstopy* pl rai·sto·pi
paper *papier* ⓜ pa·pyer
paperwork *praca biurowa* ⓕ
pra·tsa byoo·ro·va
pap smear *wymaz z szyki macicy* ⓜ
vi·mas z shiy·kee ma·chee·tsi
paraplegic *osoba z niedowładem nóg* ⓕ
o·so·ba z nye·do·vwa·dem noog
parcel *paczka* ⓕ pach·ka
parents *rodzice* pl ro·jee·tse
park *park* ⓜ park
park (a car) *parkować* par·ko·vach
parliament *parlament* ⓜ par·la·ment
part (component) *część* ⓕ chenshch
part-time *na pół etatu* na poow e·ta·too
party (night out) *impreza* ⓕ eem·pre·za

party (politics) *partia* ① *par*-tya
pass (go by) *mijać* mee-yach
pass (kick/throw) *podać* po-dach
passenger *pasażer* ⓜ pa-*sa*-zher
passport *paszport* ⓜ *pash*-port
past *przeszłość* ① pshesh-woshch
pasta *makaron* ⓜ ma-*ka*-ron
pastry *ciasta* pl *chyas*-ta
path *ścieżka* ① *shchyesh*-ka
pay *płacić* pwa-cheech
payment *zapłata* ① za-*pwa*-ta
peace *pokój* ⓜ *po*-kooy
peach *brzoskwinia* ① bzhosk-*fee*-nya
peak (mountain) *szczyt* ⓜ shchit
peanut *orzeszek ziemny* ⓜ
o-*zhe*-shek *zhyem*-ni
pear *gruszka* ① *groosh*-ka
pedal *pedał* ⓜ *pe*-dow
pedestrian *pieszy* ⓜ *pye*-shi
pen (ballpoint) *długopis* ⓜ dwoo-*go*-pees
pencil *ołówek* ⓜ o-*woo*-vek
penis *członek* ⓜ *chwo*-nek
penknife *scyzoryk* ⓜ stsi-*zo*-rik
pensioner *emeryt/emerytka* ⓜ/①
e-*me*-rit/e-*me*-rit-ka
people *ludzie* pl *loo*-jye
pepper (bell) *papryka* ① pa-*pri*-ka
pepper (condiment) *pieprz* ⓜ pyepsh
per (day) *od • przez* od • pshes
per cent *procent* ⓜ *pro*-tsent
perfect a *doskonały* dos-ko-*na*-wi
performance *przedstawienie* ⓝ
pshet-sta-*vye*-nye
perfume *perfumy* pl per-*foo*-mi
permit *zezwolenie* ⓝ ze-zvo-*le*-nye
person *osoba* ① o-*so*-ba
petrol *benzyna* ① ben-*zi*-na
petrol station *stacja benzynowa* ①
sta-tsya ben-zi-*no*-va
pharmacist *aptekarz* ⓜ ap-*te*-kash
pharmacy *apteka* ① ap-*te*-ka
phone book *książka telefoniczna* ①
kshyonsh-ka te-le-fo-*neech*-na
phone box *budka telefoniczna* ①
bood-ka te-le-fo-*neech*-na
phonecard *karta telefoniczna* ①
kar-ta te-le-fo-*neech*-na
photo *zdjęcie* ⓝ *zdyen*-chye
photograph *fotografować*
fo-to-gra-*fo*-vach
photographer *fotograf* ⓜ fo-*to*-graf
photography *fotografika* ①
fo-to-gra-*fee*-ka

phrasebook *minirozmówki* pl
mee-nee-roz-*moof*-kee
piano *pianino* ⓝ pya-*nee*-no
pickaxe *kilof* ⓜ *kee*-lof
picnic *piknik* ⓜ *peek*-neek
piece *kawałek* ⓜ ka-*va*-wek
pig *świnia* ① *shfee*-nya
pill *pastylka* ① pas-*til*-ka
(the) pill *pigułka antykoncepcyjna* ①
pee-*goow*-ka an-ti-kon-tsep-*tsiy*-na
pillow *poduszka* ① po-*doosh*-ka
pillowcase *poszewka* ① po-*shef*-ka
pine (tree) *sosna* ① *sos*-na
pink *różowy* roo-*zho*-vi
Pisces *Ryby* pl *ri*-bi
place *miejsce* ⓝ *myeys*-tse
place of birth *miejsce urodzenia* ⓝ
myeys-tse oo-ro-*dze*-nya
plane *samolot* ⓜ sa-*mo*-lot
planet *planeta* ① pla-*ne*-ta
plant *roślina* ① rosh-*lee*-na
plastic a *plastykowy* plas-ti-*ko*-vi
plate *talerz* ⓜ *ta*-lesh
plateau *płaskowyż* ⓜ pwas-*ko*-vish
platform *peron* ⓜ *pe*-ron
play v *grać* grach
play (theatre) n *sztuka* *shtoo*-ka
plug (bath) n *korek* ⓜ *ko*-rek
plug (electricity) n *wtyczka* ① *ftich*-ka
plum *śliwka* ① *shleef*-ka
plumber *hydraulik* ⓜ hi-dra-oo-leek
pocket *kieszeń* ① *kye*-shen'
pocket knife *scyzoryk* ⓜ stsi-*zo*-rik
poetry *poezja* ① po-*ez*-ya
point *wskazywać* vska-*zi*-vach
poisonous *trujący* troo-*yon*-tsi
Poland *Polska* ① *pol*-ska
police *policja* ① po-*leets*-ya
police officer (in city) *policjant* ⓜ
po-*leets*-tsyant
police officer (in country)
posterunkowy ⓜ pos-te-roon-*ko*-vi
police station *komisariat policji* ⓜ
ko-mee-*sar*-yat po-*leets*-yee
policy *polisa* ① po-*lee*-sa
politician *polityk* ⓜ po-*lee*-tik
politics *polityka* ① po-lee-*ti*-ka
pollution *zanieczyszczenie* ⓝ
za-nye-chish-*che*-nye
pool (game) *bilard* ⓜ *bee*-lard
pool (swimming) *basen* ⓜ *ba*-sen
poor (wealth) *biedny* byed-ni
popular *popularny* po-poo-*lar*-ni

pork *wieprzowina* ① vyep·sho·vee·na
pork sausage *kiełbasa wieprzowa* ①
 kyew·ba·sa vyep·sho·va
port (river/sea) *port* ⑩ port
positive *pozytywny* po·zi·tiv·ni
possible *możliwy* ⑩ mozh·lee·vi
post *poczta* ① poch·ta
post *posłać* po·si·wach
postcard *pocztówka* ① poch·toof·ka
postcode *kod pocztowy* ⑩ kod poch·to·vi
poster *plakat* ⑩ pla·kat
post office *urząd pocztowy* ⑩
 oo·zhond poch·to·vi
pot (cooking) *garnek* ⑩ gar·nek
potato *ziemniak* ⑩ zhyem·nyak
pottery *ceramika* ① tse·ra·mee·ka
pound (money/weight) *funt* ⑩ foont
poverty *ubóstwo* ⑩ oo·boost·fo
powder *proszek* ⑩ pro·shek
power *władza* ① vwa·dza
Prague *Praga* ① pra·ga
prawn *krewetka* ① kre·vet·ka
prayer *modlitwa* ① mod·leet·fa
prayer book *modlitewnik* ⑩
 mod·lee·tev·neek
prefer *woleć* vo·lech
pregnant *w ciąży* v chyon·zhi
premenstrual tension *napięcie*
 przedmiesiączkowe ⑩ na·pyen·chye
 pshet·mye·shonch·ko·ve
prepare *przygotować* pshi·go·to·vach
prescription *recepta* ① re·tse·pta
present (gift) *prezent* ⑩ pre·zent
present (time) *teraźniejszość* ①
 te·razh·nyey·shoshch
president *prezydent* ⑩ pre·zi·dent
pretty *ładny* wad·ni
price *cena* ① tse·na
priest *kapłan* ⑩ kap·wan
prime minister *premier* ⑩ prem·yer
printer (computer) *drukarka* ①
 droo·kar·ka
prison *więzienie* ⑩ vyen·zhye·nye
prisoner *więzień* ⑩ vyen·zhyen'
private *prywatny* pri·vat·ni
produce *produkować* pro·doo·ko·vach
profit *zysk* ⑩ zisk
program *program* ⑩ pro·gram
projector *rzutnik* ⑩ zhoot·neek
promise *obiecywać* o·bye·tsi·vach
prostitute n *prostytutka* ① pros·ti·toot·ka
protect *chronić* khro·neech

protected *chroniony* khro·nyo·ni
protest *protest* ⑩ pro·test
protest *protestować* pro·tes·to·vach
provisions *zapasy* pl za·pa·si
pub (bar) *pub* ⑩ pab
public phone *telefon publiczny* ⑩
 te·le·fon poob·leech·ni
public toilet *toaleta publiczna* ①
 to·a·le·ta poob·leech·na
publishing *wydawnictwo* ⑩
 vi·dav·neetst·fo
pull *ciągnąć* chyong·nonch
pump *pompa* ① pom·pa
puncture *przebicie* ⑩ pshe·bee·chye
puppet *marionetka* ① ma·ryo·net·ka
puppet show *przedstawienie*
 kukiełkowe ⑩ pshet·sta·vye·nye
 koo·kyew·ko·ve
pure *czysty* chis·ti
purple *fioletowy* fyo·le·to·vi
purse *portmonetka* ① port·mo·net·ka
push *pchać* pkhach
put *kłaść* kwashch

quadriplegic *osoba sparaliżowana* ①
 o·so·ba spa·ra·lee·zho·va·na
qualifications *kwalifikacje* pl
 kva·lee·fee·ka·tsye
quality *jakość* ① ya·koshch
quarantine *kwarantanna* ① kfa·ran·ta·na
quarter *ćwierć* ① chfyerch
queen *królowa* ① kroo·lo·va
question *pytanie* ⑩ pi·ta·nye
queue *kolejka* ① ko·ley·ka
quick *szybki* shib·kee
quiet *cichy* chee·khi

rabbit *królik* ⑩ kroo·leek
rabies *wścieklizna* ① fshchyek·leez·na
race (sport) *wyścigi* pl vish·chee·gee
racism *rasizm* ⑩ ra·sheezm
racquet *rakieta* ① ra·kye·ta
radiator *grzejnik* ⑩ gzhey·neek
radio *radio* ⑩ ra·dyo
radish *rzodkiewka* ① zhod·kyef·ka
railway station *stacja kolejowa* ①
 sta·tsya ko·le·yo·va

rain *deszcz* ⓜ deshch
raincoat *płaszcz nieprzemakalny* ⓜ pwashch nye-pshe-ma-*kal*-ni
rally (protest) *wiec* ⓜ viets
rape *gwałt* ⓜ gvowt
rape *gwałcić* gvow-cheech
rare (steak) *na pół surowy* na poow soo-*ro*-vi
rare (uncommon) *rzadki* zhad-kee
rash *wysypka* ① vi-*sip*-ka
raspberry *malina* ① ma-*lee*-na
rat *szczur* ⓜ shchoor
rave (party) *impreza* ① eem-*pre*-za
raw *surowy* soo-*ro*-vi
razor *brzytwa* ① *bzhit*-fa
razor blade *żyletka* ① zhi-*let*-ka
read *czytać* chi-tach
reading *czytanie* ⓝ chi-*ta*-nye
ready *gotowy* go-*to*-vi
real-estate agent *agent nieruchomości* ⓜ *a*-gent nye-roo-kho-*mosh*-chee
realistic *realistyczny* re-a-lees-*tich*-ni
rear (location) *a tylny* ⓜ *til*-ni
reason *powód* ⓜ *po*-vood
receipt *rachunek* ⓜ ra-*khoo*-nek
recently *ostatnio* os-*tat*-nyo
recommend *polecać* po-*le*-tsach
recyclable *do wtórnego przerobu* do vtoor-*ne*-go pshe-*re*-boo
recycle *przetwarzać* pshet-*fa*-zhach
red *czerwony* cher-*vo*-ni
red wine *wino czerwone* ⓝ *vee*-no cher-*vo*-ne
referee *sędzia* ① *sen*-jya
reference *wzmianka* ① *vzmyan*-ka
refrigerator *lodówka* ① lo-*doof*-ka
refugee *uchodźca* ⓜ oo-*khoj*-tsa
refund *zwrot pieniędzy* ⓜ zvrot pye-*nyen*-dzi
refuse *odmawiać* od-*ma*-vyach
regional *regionalny* re-gyo-*nal*-ni
registered mail *list polecony* ⓜ leest po-le-*tso*-ni
reiki *reiki* ⓝ *rey*-kee
relax *odpoczywać* od-po-*chi*-vach
religion *religia* ① re-*lee*-gya
religious *religijny* re-lee-*geey*-ni
remote *daleki* da-*le*-kee
remote control *pilot* ⓜ *pee*-lot
rent *czynsz* ⓜ chinsh
rent *wynająć* vi-*na*-yonch
repair *naprawić* na-*pra*-veech

reservation (booking) *rezerwacja* ① re-zer-*va*-tsya
rest *odpoczywać* od-po-*chi*-vach
restaurant *restauracja* ① res-tow-*ra*-tsya
retired *emerytowany* e-me-ri-to-*va*-ni
return *wracać* *vra*-tsach
return ticket *bilet powrotny* ⓜ *bee*-let po-*vro*-tni
rhythm *rytm* ⓜ ritm
rib (body) *żebro* ⓝ *zhe*-bro
rice *ryż* ⓜ rizh
rich (wealthy) *bogaty* bo-*ga*-ti
ride *jazda* ① *yaz*-da
ride (bike, horse) v *jeździć* yezh-jeech
right (correct) *prawidłowy* pra-vee-*dwo*-vi
right (direction) *prawoskrętny* pra-vo-*skrent*-ni
ring (jewellery) *pierścionek* ⓜ pyersh-*chyo*-nek
ring (phone) *dzwonić* dzvo-neech
rip-off *zdzierstwo* ⓝ *zjyerst*-fo
river *rzeka* ① *zhe*-ka
road *droga* ① *dro*-ga
road map *mapa drogowa* ① *ma*-pa dro-*go*-va
rob *okraść* o-krashch
rock *skała* ① *ska*-wa
rock (music) *rock* ⓜ rok
rock climbing *wspinaczka skałkowa* ① fspee-*nach*-ka skow-*ko*-va
roll (bread) *bułka* ① *boow*-ka
romantic *romantyczny* ro-man-*tich*-ni
room *pokój* ① po-kooy
room number *numer pokoju* ⓜ *noo*-mer po-*ko*-yoo
rope *lina* ① *lee*-na
round (drinks) *kolejka* ① ko-*ley*-ka
round a *okrągły* o-krong-wi
route *trasa* ① *tra*-sa
rowing *wioślarstwo* ⓝ vyo-*shlarst*-fo
rubbish *śmieci* pl *shmye*-chee
rubella *różyczka* ① roo-*zhich*-ka
rug *dywan* ⓜ *di*-van
rugby *rugby* ⓝ *rag*-bi
ruins *ruiny* pl roo-ee-ni
rule *reguła* ① re-*goo*-wa
rum *rum* ⓜ room
run *biegać* bye-gach
running *bieganie* ⓝ bye-*ga*-nye
Russia *Rosja* ① *ro*-sya

S

sad *smutny* smoo·tni
saddle *siodło* ⓝ shyo·dwo
safe *sejf* ⓜ seyf
safe *bezpieczny* bes·pyech·ni
safe sex *bezpieczny seks* ⓜ
  bes·pyech·ni seks
Sagittarius *Strzelec* ⓜ stshe·lets
saint *święty* ⓜ shvyen·ti
salad *sałatka* ① sa·wat·ka
salary *pensja* ① pen·sya
sale *sprzedaż* ① spshe·dash
sales assistant
  sprzedawca/sprzedawczyni ⓜ/①
  spshe·daf·tsa/spshe·daf·chi·nee
sales tax *podatek obrotowy* ⓜ
  po·da·tek o·bro·to·vi
salt *sól* ① sool
same *taki sam* ⓜ ta·kee sam
sand *piasek* ⓜ pya·sek
sandals *sandały* pl san·da·wi
sandwich *kanapka* ① ka·nap·ka
sanitary napkin *podpaski higieniczne* pl
  pod·pas·kee hee·gye·neech·ne
Saturday *sobota* ① so·bo·ta
sauce *sos* ⓜ sos
saucepan *rondel* ⓜ ron·del
sausage *kiełbasa* ① kyew·ba·sa
say *mówić* moo·veech
scalp *skóra głowy* ① skoo·ra gwo·vi
scarf *szal* ⓜ shal
school *szkoła* ① shko·wa
science *nauka* ① na·oo·ka
scientist *naukowiec* ⓜ now·ko·vyets
scissors *nożyczki* pl no·zhich·kee
score *zdobyć* zdo·bich
scoreboard *tablica wyników* ①
  ta·blee·tsa vi·nee·koof
Scorpio *Skorpion* ⓜ skor·pyon
Scotland *Szkocja* ① shko·tsya
sculpture *rzeźba* ① zhezh·ba
sea *morze* ⓝ mo·zhe
seasick *choroba morska* ①
  kho·ro·ba mor·ska
seaside *wybrzeże* ⓝ vib·zhe·zhe
season *sezon* ⓜ se·zon
seat (place) *miejsce* ⓝ myeys·tse
seatbelt *pasy bezpieczeństwa* pl
  pa·si bes·pye·chen´st·fa
second *sekunda* ① se·koon·da
second *drugi* droo·gee

second class *druga klasa* ①
  droo·ga kla·sa
secondhand *używany* oo·zhi·va·ni
secretary *sekretarz/sekretarka* ⓜ/①
  se·kre·tash/se·kre·tar·ka
see *widzieć* vee·jyech
selfish *samolubny* sa·mo·loob·ni
self-service *samoobsługowy*
  sa·mo·ob·swoo·go·vi
sell *sprzedawać* spshe·da·vach
send *wysyłać* vi·si·wach
sensible *sensowny* sen·sov·ni
separate *osobny* o·so·bni
September *wrzesień* ⓜ vzhe·shyen´
serious *poważny* po·vazh·ni
service *obsługa* ① ob·swoo·ga
service charge *dodatek za obsługę* ⓜ
  do·da·tek za ob·swoo·ge
service station *stacja obsługi* ①
  sta·tsya ob·swoo·gee
serviette *serwetka* ① ser·vet·ka
several *kilka* keel·ka
sew *szyć* shich
sex *seks* ⓜ seks
sexism *seksizm* ⓜ sek·sheezm
sexy *seksowny* sek·sov·ni
shade *cień* ⓜ chyen´
shadow *cień* ⓜ chyen´
shampoo *szampon* ⓜ sham·pon
shape *kształt* ⓜ kshtowt
share (accommodation) v *mieszkać z kimś*
  myesh·kach z keemsh
share (with) *dzielić się* jye·leech shye
shave *golić się* go·leech shye
shaving cream *krem do golenia* ⓜ
  krem do go·le·nya
she *ona* o·na
sheep *owca* ① ov·tsa
sheet (bed) *prześcieradło* ⓝ
  pshesh·chye·ra·dwo
shelf *półka* ① poow·ka
shiatsu *shiatsu* ⓝ shya·tsoo
shingles (illness) *półpasiec* ⓜ
  poow·pa·shyets
ship *statek* ⓜ sta·tek
shirt *koszula* ① ko·shoo·la
shoes *buty* pl boo·ti
shoe shop *sklep obuwniczy* ⓜ
  sklep o·boov·nee·chi
shoot *strzelać* stshe·lach
shop *sklep* ⓜ sklep
shop *robić zakupy* ro·beech za·koo·pi
shopping *zakupy* pl za·koo·pi

shopping centre *centrum zakupowe* ⓜ *tsen·troom za·koo·po·ve*
short (height) *niski nees·*kee
short (length) *krótki kroot·*kee
shorts *szorty* pl *shor·*ti
shoulder *ramię* ⓝ *ra·*mye
shout *krzyczeć kshi·*chech
show *pokaz* ⓜ *po·*kas
show *pokazać po·ka·*zach
shower *prysznic* ⓜ *prish·*neets
shut *zamknięty* zam·*knyen·*ti
shy *nieśmiały* ⓜ nyesh·*mya·*vi
sick *chory kho·*ri
side *strona* ⓕ *stro·*na
sign *znak* ⓜ znak
sign *podpisać się* pod·*pee·*sach shye
signature *podpis* ⓜ *pod·*pees
silk *jedwab* ⓜ *yed·*vab
silver *srebro* ⓝ *sre·*bro
SIM card *karta SIM* ⓕ *kar·*ta seem
simple *prosty pros·*ti
since (time) *od* od
sing *śpiewać* shpye·*vach*
Singapore *Singapur* ⓜ seen·*ga·*poor
singer *śpiewak* ⓜ *shpye·*vak
single (person) *nieżonaty/ niezamężna* ⓜ/ⓕ nye·zho·*na·*ti/ nye·za·*menzh·*na
single room *pokój jednoosobowy* ⓜ *po·*kooy ye·dno·o·so·*bo·*vi
sister *siostra* ⓕ *shyos·*tra
sit *siedzieć shye·*jech
size (general) *rozmiar* ⓜ *roz·*myar
skate *jeździć na łyżwach yezh·*jyech na *wizh·*vakh
skateboarding *jazda na deskorolce* ⓕ *yaz·*da na des·ko·*rol·*tse
skis *narty* pl *nar·*ti
ski *jeździć na nartach yezh·*jyech na *nar·*takh
skiing *narciarstwo* ⓝ nar·*chyarst·*fo
skin *skóra* ⓕ *skoo·*ra
skirt *spódnica* ⓕ *spood·nee·*tsa
sky *niebo* ⓝ *nye·*bo
sleep *sen* ⓜ sen
sleep *spać* spach
sleeping bag *śpiwór* ⓜ *shpee·*voor
sleeping berth *miejsce sypialne* ⓝ *myeys·*tse si·*pyal·*ne
sleeping car *wagon sypialny* ⓜ *va·*gon si·*pyal·*ni
sleeping pills *pigułki nasenne* pl pee·*goow·*kee na·*se·*ne

sleepy *śpiący shpyon·*tsi
slice *plasterek* ⓜ plas·*te·*rek
slide film *film do slajdów* ⓜ feelm do *slai·*doof
Slovakia *Słowacja* ⓕ swo·*va·*tsya
slow *wolny vol·*ni
slowly *powoli* po·*vo·*lee
small *mały ma·*wi
smaller *mniejszy* mnyey·*shi
smallest *najmniejszy* nai·*mnyey·*shi
smell *zapach* ⓜ *za·*pakh
smile *uśmiechać się* oosh·*mye·*khach shye
smoke *palić pa·*leech
snack *przekąska* ⓕ pshe·*kons·*ka
snail *ślimak* ⓜ *shlee·*mak
snake *wąż* ⓜ vonzh
snow *śnieg* ⓜ shnyeg
snowboarding *jazda na snowboardzie* ⓕ *yaz·*da na snow·*bor·*jye
snow pea *groszek zielony* ⓜ *gro·*shek zhye·*lo·*ni
soap *mydło* ⓝ *mid·*wo
soccer *piłka nożna* ⓕ *peew·*ka *nozh·*na
socialist *socjalista* ⓜ so·tsya·*lees·*ta
social welfare *opieka społeczna* ⓕ o·*pye·*ka spo·*wech·*na
socks *skarpetki* pl skar·*pet·*kee
soft drink *napój bezalkoholowy* ⓜ *na·*pooy bes·al·ko·kho·*lo·*vi
soldier *żołnierz* ⓜ *zhow·*nyezh
Solidarity (union) *Solidarność* ⓕ so·lee·*dar·*noshch
some *kilka keel·*ka
someone *ktoś* ktosh
something *coś* tsosh
sometimes *czasem cha·*sem
son *syn* ⓜ sin
song *piosenka* ⓕ pyo·*sen·*ka
soon *wkrótce* fkroot·*tse
sore *obolały* o·bo·*la·*vi
sour cream *śmietana* ⓕ shmye·*ta·*na
south *południe* ⓝ po·*wood·*nye
souvenir *pamiątka* ⓕ pa·*myont·*ka
soy milk *mleko sojowe* ⓝ *mle·*ko so·*yo·*ve
soy sauce *sos sojowy* ⓜ sos so·*yo·*vi
space (room) *przestrzeń* ⓕ *pshes·*tshen'
Spain *Hiszpania* ⓕ kheesh·*pa·*nya
sparkling wine *wino musujące* ⓝ *vee·*no moo·soo·*yon·*tse
speak *mówić* moo·*veech*
special *specjalny* spets·*yal·*ni
specialist *specjalista* ⓜ spets·ya·*lees·*ta
speed (drug) *speed* ⓜ speed

speed (travel) *prędkość* ① prend·koshch

speed limit *ograniczenie prędkości* ⑩ o·gra·nee·che·nye prend·kosh·chee

speedometer *szybkościomierz* ⑩ shib·kosh·chyo·myesh

spider *pająk* ⑩ pa·yonk

spoilt (food) *zepsuty* zep·soo·ti

spoke *szprycha* ① shpri·kha

spoon *łyżka* ① wish·ka

sport *sport* ⑩ sport

sportsperson *sportowiec* ⑩ spor·to·vyets

sprain *zwichnięcie* ⑩ zveekh·nyen·chye

spring (coil) *sprężyna* ① spren·zhi·na

spring (season) *wiosna* ① vyos·na

square (town) *rynek* ⑩ ri·nek

stadium *stadion* ⑩ sta·dyon

stairway *klatka schodowa* ① klat·ka skho·do·va

stale *stęchły* stenkh·wi

stamp (postage) *znaczek* ⑩ zna·chek

stand-by ticket *bilet z listy rezerwowej* ⑩ bee·let z lees·ti re·zer·vo·vey

star *gwiazda* ① gvyaz·da

(four-)star (cztero-)gwiazdkowy ⑩ (chte·ro·)gvyazt·ko·vi

start *start* ⑩ start

start *zaczynać* za·chi·nach

station *stacja* ① sta·tsya

statue *pomnik* ⑩ pom·neek

stay (at a hotel) *przenocować* pshe·no·tso·vach

stay (in one place) *pozostać* po·zo·stach

steak (beef) *stek* ⑩ stek

steal *kraść* krashch

steep *stromy* stro·mi

step *krok* ⑩ krok

stereo *stereo* ⑩ ste·re·o

Stockholm *Sztokholm* ⑩ shtok·kholm

stockings *pończochy* pl pon'·cho·khi

stolen *kradziony* kra·jyo·ni

stomach *żołądek* ⑩ zho·won·dek

stomachache *ból żołądka* ⑩ bool zho·wont·ka

stone *kamień* ⑩ ka·myen'

stoned (drugged) *urżnięty* oorzh·nyen·ti

stop (bus, tram) *przystanek* ⑩ pshis·ta·nek

stop (cease) *przestać* pshes·tach

stop (prevent) *zatrzymać* za·tshi·mach

storm *burza* ① boo·zha

story *opowiadanie* ⑩ o·po·vya·da·nye

stove *piec* ⑩ pyets

straight *prosty* pros·ti

strange *dziwny* jeev·ni

stranger *nieznajomy* ⑩ nye·zna·yo·mi

strawberry *truskawka* ① troos·kaf·ka

stream *strumień* ⑩ stroo·myen'

street *ulica* ① oo·lee·tsa

street market *handel uliczny* ⑩ han·del oo·leech·ni

strike *strajk* ⑩ straik

string *sznurek* ⑩ shnoo·rek

stroke (health) *wylew* ⑩ vi·lef

stroller *wózek spacerowy* ⑩ voo·zek spa·tse·ro·vi

strong *silny* sheel·ni

student *student* ⑩ stoo·dent

stupid *głupi* gwoo·pee

style *styl* ⑩ stil

subtitles *napisy* pl na·pee·si

suburb *dzielnica* ① jyel·nee·tsa

subway (train) *metro* ⑩ met·ro

Sudeten mountains *Sudety* pl soo·de·ti

sugar *cukier* ⑩ tsoo·kyer

suitcase *walizka* ① va·lees·ka

summer *lato* ⑩ la·to

sun *słońce* ⑩ swon'·tse

sunblock *krem przeciwsłoneczny* ⑩ krem pshe·cheef·swo·nech·ni

sunburn *oparzenie słoneczne* ⑩ o·pa·zhe·nye swo·nech·ne

Sunday *niedziela* ① nye·jye·la

sunglasses *okulary słoneczne* pl o·koo·la·ri swo·nech·ne

sunny *słoneczny* swo·nech·ni

sunrise *wschód słońca* ⑩ fskhood swon'·tsa

sunset *zachód słońca* ⑩ za·khood swon'·tsa

sunstroke *udar słoneczny* ⑩ oo·dar swo·nech·ni

supermarket *supermarket* ⑩ soo·per·mar·ket

superstition *zabobon* ⑩ za·bo·bon

surf *fale przybrzeżne* pl fa·le pshi·bzhezh·ne

surf *surfować* ser·fo·vach

surface mail (land) *poczta zwykła (lądowa)* ① poch·ta zvik·wa (lon·do·va)

surface mail (sea) *poczta zwykła (morska)* ① poch·ta zvik·wa (mor·ska)

surfboard *deska surfingowa* ① des·ka ser·feen·go·va

surfing *surfing* ⑩ ser·feeng

surname *nazwisko* ⑩ naz·vees·ko

surprise *niespodzianka* ① nye-spo-*jyan*-ka
sweater *sweter* ⓜ *sve*-ter
Sweden *Szwecja* ① *shve*-tsya
sweet *słodki* swod-kee
swelling *opuchlizna* ① o-pookh-*leez*-na
swim *pływać* pwi-vach
swimming *pływanie* ⓝ pwi-*va*-nye
swimming pool *basen* ⓜ *ba*-sen
swimsuit *kostium kąpielowy* ⓜ
  kos-tyoom kom-pye-*lo*-vi
Switzerland *Szwajcaria* ① shvai-*tsar*-ya
synagogue *synagoga* ① si-na-*go*-ga
syringe *strzykawka* ① stshi-*kaf*-ka

T

table *stół* ⓜ stoow
tablecloth *obrus* ⓜ o-broos
table tennis *tenis stołowy* ⓜ
  te-nees sto-*wo*-vi
tailor *krawiec* ⓜ *kra*-vyets
take *brać* brach
talk *rozmawiać* roz-*ma*-vyach
tall *wysoki* vi-*so*-kee
tampon *tampon* ⓜ *tam*-pon
tanning lotion *olejek do opalnia* ⓝ
  o-*le*-yek do o-pa-*la*-nya
tap *kran* ⓜ kran
tasty *smaczny* smach-ni
Taurus *Byk* ⓜ bik
tax *podatek* ⓜ po-*da*-tek
taxi *taksówka* ① tak-*soof*-ka
taxi stand *postój taksówek* ⓜ
  pos-tooy tak-*soo*-vek
tea *herbata* ① her-*ba*-ta
teacher *nauczyciel* ⓜ na-oo-*chi*-chyel
team *drużyna* ① droo-*zhi*-na
teaspoon *łyżeczka* ① wi-*zhech*-ka
teeth *zęby* pl zem-bi
telegram *telegram* ⓜ te-*le*-gram
telephone *telefon* ⓜ te-*le*-fon
telephone *telefonować* te-le-fo-*no*-vach
telescope *teleskop* ⓜ te-*les*-kop
television *telewizja* ① te-le-*veez*-ya
tell *powiedzieć* po-*vye*-jyech
temperature (fever) *gorączka* ①
  go-*ronch*-ka
temperature (weather) *temperatura* ①
  tem-pe-ra-*too*-ra
temple (body) *skroń* ① skron'
tennis *tenis* ⓜ *te*-nees
tennis court *kort tenisowy* ⓜ
  kort te-nee-*so*-vi

tent *namiot* ⓝ *na*-myot
tent peg *śledź namiotowy* ⓜ
  shlej na-myo-*to*-vi
terrorism *terroryzm* ⓜ te-ro-*rizm*
test *próba* ① *proo*-ba
thank *dziękować* jyen-*ko*-vach
that *który* ktoo-ri
theatre *teatr* ⓜ *te*-atr
their *ich* eekh
there *tam* tam
they *oni* o-nee
thick *gruby* groo-bi
thief *złodziej* ⓜ *zwo*-jyey
thin *cienki* chyen-kee
think *myśleć* mish-lech
thirsty *spragniony* sprag-*nyo*-ni
this *to* ⓝ to
this (one) *ten* ⓜ ten
throat *gardło* gard-wo
thrush (health) *pleśniawka* ①
  plesh-*nyaf*-ka
thunderstorm *burza z piorunami* ①
  boo-zha z pyo-roo-*na*-mee
Thursday *czwartek* ⓜ *chfar*-tek
ticket *bilet* ⓜ *bee*-let
ticket collector *kontroler biletowy* ⓜ
  kon-*tro*-ler bee-le-*to*-vi
ticket machine *automat biletowy* ⓜ
  ow-to-mat bee-le-*to*-vi
ticket office *kasa biletowa* ①
  ka-sa bee-le-*to*-va
tide *przypływ* ⓜ pshi-pwif
tight *ciasny* chyas-ni
time *czas* ⓜ chas
timetable *rozkład jazdy* ⓜ
  ros-kwad yaz-di
tin (can) *puszka* ① *poosh*-ka
tin opener *otwieracz do konserw* ⓜ
  ot-*fye*-rach do *kon*-serf
tiny *drobny* drob-ni
tip (gratuity) *napiwek* ⓜ na-*pee*-vek
tire *opona* ① o-*po*-na
tired *zmęczony* zmen-*cho*-ni
tissues *chusteczki* pl khoos-*tech*-kee
to *do* do
toast (food) *grzanka* ① *gzhan*-ka
toaster *opiekacz* ⓜ o-*pye*-kach
tobacco *tytoń* ⓜ *ti*-ton'
today *dzisiaj* jee-shyai
toe *palec u nogi* ⓜ *pa*-lets oo *no*-gee
tofu *tofu* ⓝ *to*-foo
together *razem* ra-zem
toilet *toaleta* ① to-a-*le*-ta

english–polish

229

toilet paper *papier toaletowy* ⓜ
pa·pyer to·a·*le*·to·vi
tomato *pomidor* ⓜ po·*mee*·dor
tomato sauce *keczup* ⓜ *ke*·choop
tomorrow *jutro* yoo·tro
tonight *dzisiaj wieczorem*
jee·shai vye·*cho*·rem
too (also) *też* tesh
too (much) *za* za
tooth *ząb* ⓜ zomb
toothache *ból zęba* ⓜ bool zem·ba
toothbrush *szczotka do zębów* ①
shchot·ka do zem·boof
toothpaste *pasta do zębów* ①
pas·ta do zem·boof
torch (flashlight) *latarka* ① la·*tar*·ka
touch *dotykać* do·ti·kach
tour *wycieczka* ① vi·*chyech*·ka
tourist *turysta* ① too·*ris*·ta
tourist office *biuro turystyczne* ⓝ
byoo·ro too·ris·*tich*·ne
towards *w kierunku* v kye·*roon*·koo
towel *ręcznik* ⓜ *rench*·neek
tower *wieża* ① *vye*·zha
track (path) *ścieżka* ① *shchyesh*·ka
track (sport) *bieżnia* ① *byezh*·nya
trade *handel* ⓜ *han*·del
traffic *ruch* ⓜ rookh
trail *szlak* ⓜ shlak
train *pociąg* ⓜ *po*·chyonk
train station *stacja kolejowa* ①
sta·tsya ko·le·*yo*·va
tram *tramwaj* ⓜ *tram*·vai
translate *przetłumaczyć*
pshe·twoo·*ma*·chich
translator *tłumacz* ⓜ *twoo*·mach
transport *transport* ⓜ *trans*·port
travel *podróżować* po·droo·zho·vach
travel agency *biuro podróży* ①
byoo·ro po·*droo*·zhi
travellers cheque *czeki podróżne* pl
che·kee po·*droozh*·ne
travel sickness *choroba lokomocyjna* ①
kho·ro·ba lo·ko·mo·*tsiy*·na
tree *drzewo* ⓝ *dzhe*·vo
trip (journey) *podróż* ① *po*·droozh
trolley-bus *trolejbus* ⓜ tro·*ley*·boos
trousers *spodnie* pl *spo*·dnye
truck *ciężarówka* ① chyen·zha·*roof*·ka
trust *ufać* oo·fach
try (attempt) *próbować* proo·bo·vach
T-shirt *koszulka* ① ko·*shool*·ka
tube (tyre) *dętka* ① *dent*·ka

Tuesday *wtorek* ⓜ *fto*·rek
tuna *tuńczyk* ⓜ *toon'*·chik
tune *melodia* ① me·*lo*·dya
turkey *indyk* ⓜ *een*·dik
turn *skręcić* skren·cheech
TV *telewizor* ⓜ te·le·*vee*·zor
tweezers *pinceta* ① peen·*tse*·ta
twin beds *dwa łóżka* pl dva *woosh*·ka
twins *bliźnięta* pl bleezh·*nyen*·ta
two *dwa* dva
type *typ* ⓜ tip
tyre *opona* ① o·*po*·na

U

Ukraine *Ukraina* ① oo·kra·*ee*·na
umbrella *parasol* ⓜ pa·*ra*·sol
uncomfortable *niewygodny* nye·vi·*go*·dni
understand *rozumieć* ro·zoo·myech
underwear *bielizna* ① bye·*leez*·na
unemployed *bezrobotny* bez·ro·*bot*·ni
uniform *mundur* ⓜ *moon*·door
universe *wszechświat* ⓜ *fshekh*·shfyat
university *uniwersytet* ⓜ oo·nee·ver·*si*·tet
unleaded petrol *benzyna bezołowiowa* ①
ben·zi·na bes·o·wo·*vyo*·va
unsafe *niebezpieczny* nye·bes·*pyech*·ni
until *do* do
unusual *niezwykły* nye·*zvi*·kwi
up *do góry* do *goo*·ri
urgent *pilny* peel·ni
USA *USA* pl oo·*es*·a
useful *użyteczny* oo·zhi·*tech*·ni

V

vacancy *wolne miejsca* pl *vol*·ne myes·tsa
vacant *wolny* *vol*·ni
vacation *wakacje* pl va·*ka*·tsye
vaccination *szczepienie* ⓝ shche·*pye*·nye
validate *uprawomocniać*
oo·pra·vo·*mots*·nyach
valley *dolina* ① do·*lee*·na
valuable *cenny* *tse*·ni
value (price) *wartość* ① *var*·toshch
van *furgonetka* ① foor·go·*net*·ka
veal *cielęcina* ① chye·len·*chee*·na
vegetable *warzywo* ⓝ va·*zhi*·vo
vegetarian *wegetarianin* ⓜ
ve·ge·tar·*ya*·neen
vegetarian *wegetariański*
ve·ge·tar·*yan'*·skee

venereal disease *choroba weneryczna* ①
kho·ro·ba ve·ne·*rich*·na

venue *miejsce* ⓝ *myes*·tse

very *bardzo* bar·dzo

video camera *kamera wideo* ①
ka·me·ra vee·*de*·o

video recorder *magnetowid* ⓜ
mag·ne·to·veed

video tape *taśma wideo* ① *tash*·ma
vee·*de*·o

view *widok* ⓜ *vee*·dok

village *wieś* ① vyesh

Vilnius *Wilno* ⓝ *veel*·no

vine *winorośl* ① vee·no·roshl

vinegar *ocet* ⓜ *o*·tset

vineyard *winnica* ① vee·*nee*·tsa

violin *skrzypce* pl skship·tse

Virgo *Panna* ① *pa*·na

virus *wirus* ⓜ *vee*·roos

visa *wiza* ① *vee*·za

visit *odwiedzać* od·*vye*·dzach

vitamins *witaminy* pl vee·ta·*mee*·ni

vodka *wódka* ① *vood*·ka

voice *głos* ⓜ gwos

volleyball (sport) *siatkówka* ①
shyat·*koof*·ka

volume *księga* ① *kshyen*·ga

vote *głosować* gwo·*so*·vach

W

wage *zarobki* pl za·*rob*·kee

wait *czekać* che·kach

waiter *kelner* ⓜ *kel*·ner

waiting room *poczekalnia* ①
po·che·*kal*·nya

wake (someone) up *budzić* boo·jeech

walk *spacerować* spa·tse·*ro*·vach

want *chcieć* khchyech

war *wojna* ① *voy*·na

warm *ciepły* chyep·wi

Warsaw *Warszawa* ① var·*sha*·va

wash (oneself) *myć się* mich shye

wash (something) *prać* prach

washing machine *pralka* ① *pral*·ka

wasp *osa* ① *o*·sa

watch *zegarek* ⓜ ze·*ga*·rek

watch *oglądać* o·*glon*·dach

water *woda* ① *vo*·da

water bottle *manierka* ① ma·*nyer*·ka

(hot) water bottle *termofor* ⓜ ter·*mo*·for

waterfall *wodospad* ⓜ vo·do·spad

watermelon *arbuz* ⓜ *ar*·boos

waterproof *wodoodporny* vo·do·od·*por*·ni

water-skiing *narty wodne* pl *nar*·ti vod·ne

way *droga* ① *dro*·ga

we *my* mi

weak *słaby* swa·bi

wealthy *bogaty* bo·*ga*·ti

wear *nosić* no·sheech

weather *pogoda* ① po·*go*·da

wedding *ślub* ⓜ shloob

Wednesday *środa* ① *shro*·da

week *tydzień* ⓜ *ti*·jyen'

weekend *weekend* ⓜ *wee*·kend

weigh *ważyć* va·zhich

weight *waga* ① *va*·ga

welcome *witać* *vee*·tach

well adv *dobrze* dob·zhe

west *zachód* ⓜ *za*·khood

wet *mokry* mo·kri

what *co* tso

wheel *koło* ⓝ *ko*·wo

wheelchair *wózek inwalidzki* ⓜ
voo·zek een·va·*leets*·kee

when *kiedy* kye·di

where *gdzie* gjye

which *który* ktoo·ri

whisky *whisky* ⓝ *wis*·kee

white *biały* bya·wi

white wine *białe wino* ⓝ bya·we *vee*·no

who *kto* kto

why *dlaczego* dla·*che*·go

wide *szeroki* she·ro·kee

wife *żona* ① *zho*·na

win *wygrać* vi·grach

wind *wiatr* ⓜ vyatr

window *okno* ⓝ *ok*·no

windscreen *przednia szyba* ①
pshed·nya *shi*·ba

wine *wino* ⓝ *vee*·no

winner *zwycięzca* ⓜ zvi·*chyens*·tsa

winter *zima* ① *zhee*·ma

wire *drut* ⓜ droot

wish *życzyć* zhi·chich

with *z* z

within (time) *w* v

without *bez* bes

woman *kobieta* ① ko·*bye*·ta

wood *drewno* ⓝ *drev*·no

wool *wełna* ① *vew*·na

work *praca* ① *pra*·tsa

work *pracować* pra·*tso*·vach

workout *trening* ⓜ *tre*·neeng

work permit *zezwolenie na pracę* ⓝ
zez·vo·*le*·nye na *pra*·tse

Y

world *świat* ⓜ shfyat
World Cup *Puchar Świata* ⓜ
  poo·khar shfya·ta
World War I/II *pierwsza/druga wojna*
  światowa ① pyerf·sha/droo·ga voy·na
  shfya·to·va
worms (intestinal) *robaki* pl ro·ba·kee
worried *zmartwiony* zmart·fyo·ni
wrist *nadgarstek* ⓜ nad·gars·tek
write *pisać* pee·sach
writer *pisarz* ⓜ pee·sash
wrong *zły* zwi

Y

year *rok* ⓜ rok
yellow *żółty* zhoow·ti
yes *tak* tak
yesterday *wczoraj* fcho·rai
yet *już* yoosh
yoga *joga* ① yo·ga
yogurt *jogurt* ⓜ yo·goort

you inf sg *ty* ti
you pol sg *pan/pani* ⓜ/① pan/pa·nee
you inf pl *wy* vi
you pol pl *panowie* ⓜ pa·no·vye
you pol pl *panie* ① pa·nye
you pol pl *państwo* ⓜ&① pan'·stfo
young *młody* mwo·di
your inf sg *twój* tfooy
your pol sg *pana/pani* ⓜ/①
  pa·na/pa·nee
your inf pl *wasz* vash
your pol pl *państwa* ⓜ&① pl pan'·stfa
youth hostel *schronisko młodzieżowe* ⓝ
  skhro·nees·ko mwo·jye·zho·ve

Z

zip/zipper *zamek błyskawiczny* ⓜ
  za·mek bwis·ka·veech·ni
zodiac *zodiak* ⓜ zo·dyak
zoo *zoo* ⓝ zoo
zoom lens *teleobiektyw* ⓜ te·le·o·byek·tif

This dictionary is arranged according to Polish alphabetical order (shown below). Polish nouns in the **dictionary** have their gender indicated by ⓜ (masculine), ⓕ (feminine) or ⓝ (neuter). If it's a plural noun, you'll also see pl, but you won't see a gender marker as all plural nouns in this dictionary belong to the general (genderless) plural category (refer to the **a–z phrasebuilder** for more on this). When a word that could be either a noun or a verb has no gender indicated, it's a verb. For added clarity, certain words are marked as adjectives a or verbs v. Adjectives, however, are given in the masculine form only. Both nouns and adjectives are provided in the nominative case only. For information on case and gender, refer to the **a–z phrasebuilder**. For any food terms, refer to the **culinary reader**.

A a	Ą ą	B b	C c	Ć ć	D d	E e	Ę ę
F f	G g	H h	I i	J j	K k	L l	Ł ł
M m	N n	Ń ń	O o	Ó ó	P p	R r	S s
Ś ś	T t	U u	W w	Y y	Z z	Ź ź	Ż ż

A

adres ⓜ *a-*dres *address*
aleja ⓕ *a-le-*ya *avenue*
alergia ⓕ *a-ler-*gya *allergy*
alkohol ⓜ *al-ko-*khol *alcohol*
ambasada ⓕ am·ba·*sa*·da *embassy*
angielski ⓜ an·*gyel*·skee
  English (language/nationality)
Anglia ⓕ *an*·glya *England*
antyk ⓜ *an*·tik *antique*
aparat ⓜ *a·pa·*rat *camera*
apteka ⓕ ap·*te*·ka *chemist • pharmacy*
aptekarz ⓜ ap·*te*·kash *pharmacist*
autobus ⓜ ow·*to·*boos *bus (city)*
autokar ⓜ ow·*to·*kar *bus (intercity)*
automat biletowy ⓜ
  ow·*to·*mat bee·le·*to·*vi *ticket machine*
autostop ⓜ ow·*to·*stop *hitchhike*
autostrada ⓕ ow·to·*stra*·da *motorway*

B

babcia ⓕ *bab*·chya *grandmother*
bagaż ⓜ *ba·*gash *luggage*
balet ⓜ *ba·*let *ballet*

balkon ⓜ *bal·*kon *balcony*
bandaż ⓜ *ban·*dash *bandage*
bank ⓜ bank *bank*
bankomat ⓜ ban·*ko·*mat
  automated teller machine (ATM)
bar ⓜ bar *bar*
  — mleczny *mlech·*ni
  self-service cafeteria
bardzo *bar·*dzo *very*
basen ⓜ *ba·*sen *swimming pool*
benzyna ⓕ ben·*zi·*na *gas • petrol*
bez bes *without*
bezpieczny bes·*pyech·*ni *safe* a
bezpłatny ⓜ bes·*pwat·*ni *free (gratis)*
bezpośredni bes·po·*shred·*nee *direct*
bęben ⓜ *bem·*ben *drum*
Białoruś ⓕ bya·*wo·*roosh *Belarus*
biały *bya·*wi *white*
biblioteka ⓕ beeb·lyo·*te·*ka *library*
biedny *byed·*ni *poor (not wealthy)*
biegać *bye·*gach *run*
bilet ⓜ *bee·*let *ticket*
  — powrotny po·*vro·*tni *return ticket*
  — w jedną stronę v *yed·*nom *stro·*ne
  one-way ticket
  — z listy rezerwowej
  z *lees·*ti re·zer·*vo·*vey *stand-by ticket*

biuro ⓝ *byoo*·ro office
— podróży po·*droo*·zhi travel agency
— turystyczne too·ris·*tich*·ne tourist office
biżuteria ⓕ bee·zhoo·*ter*·ya jewellery
bliski *blees*·kee close a
bocian (biały) ⓜ *bo*·chyan (*bya*·wi) (white) stork
boczek ⓜ *bo*·chek bacon
bogaty bo·*ga*·ti wealthy
bolesny bo·*les*·ni painful
ból ⓜ bool pain
— głowy *gwo*·vi headache
— okresowy o·kre·*so*·vi period pain
— zęba *zem*·ba toothache
— żołądka zho·*wont*·ka stomachache
Boże Narodzenie ⓝ *bo*·zhe na·ro·*dze*·nye Christmas
brać brach take
brat ⓜ brat brother
Bratysława ⓕ bra·ti·*swa*·va Bratislava
brązowy bron·*zo*·vi brown
brzytwa ⓕ *bzhit*·fa razor
budynek ⓜ boo·*di*·nek building
budzić boo·jeech wake (someone) up
budzik ⓜ *boo*·jeek alarm clock
bursztyn ⓜ *boorsh*·tin amber
burza ⓕ *boo*·zha storm
butelka ⓕ boo·*tel*·ka bottle
buty pl *boo*·ti boots · shoes
być bich be

C

całować tsa·*wo*·vach kiss
cały *tsa*·wi all
cena ⓕ *tse*·na price
centrum ⓝ *tsen*·troom city centre
— zakupowe za·koo·*po*·ve shopping centre
chcieć khchyech want
chleb ⓜ khlep bread
chłodny *khwo*·dni cool (temperature)
chłopak ⓜ *khwo*·pak boyfriend
chłopiec ⓜ *khwo*·pyets boy
chmura ⓕ *khmoo*·ra cloud
chodzić *kho*·jeech go
choroba ⓕ kho·*ro*·ba disease · illness
— lokomocyjna lo·ko·mo·*tsiy*·na travel sickness
chory *kho*·ri sick

chrześcijanin ⓜ khshesh·chee·*ya*·neen Christian
chusteczki pl khoos·*tech*·kee tissues
ciało ⓝ *chya*·wo body
ciasta pl *chyas*·ta pastry
ciasto ⓝ *chyas*·to cake
ciąć chyonch cut
ciągnąć *chyong*·nonch pull
cichy *chee*·khi quiet
ciemny *chyem*·ni dark
cienki *chyen*·kee thin
ciepły *chyep*·wi warm
ciężki *chyensh*·kee heavy (weight)
ciotka ⓕ *chyot*·ka aunt
ciśnienie ⓝ cheesh·*nye*·nye pressure (tyre)
co tso what
codzienny tso·*jye*·ni daily
coś tsosh something
córka ⓕ *tsoor*·ka daughter
cukier ⓜ *tsoo*·kyer sugar
cukiernia ⓕ tsoo·*kyer*·nya cake shop
cukrzyca ⓕ tsook·*shi*·tsa diabetes
cyfrowy tsi·*fro*·vi digital
cyrk ⓜ tsirk circus
czarny *char*·ni black
czas ⓜ chas time
Czechy pl *che*·khi Czech Republic
czek ⓜ chek check (banking) · cheque (banking)
czekać *che*·kach wait
czeki podróżne pl *che*·kee po·*droozh*·ne travellers cheque
czekolada ⓕ che·ko·*la*·da chocolate
czerwiec ⓜ *cher*·vyets June
czerwony cher·*vo*·ni red
często *chen*·sto often
czuć chooch feel (touch)
czwartek ⓜ *chfar*·tek Thursday
czynsz ⓜ chinsh rent
czysty *chi*·sti clean · pure
czytać *chi*·tach read

D

dać dach give
daktyl ⓜ *dak*·til date (fruit)
daleki da·*le*·kee far
Dania ⓕ *da*·nya Denmark
data ⓕ *da*·ta date (day)
— urodzenia oo·ro·*dze*·nya date of birth

dąb ⓜ domb oak (tree)
delikatesy pl de·lee·ka·te·si delicatessen
dentysta ⓜ den·tis·ta dentist
depozyt ⓜ de·po·zit deposit
deser ⓜ de·ser dessert
deszcz ⓜ deshch rain
dętka ① dent·ka tube (tyre)
dieta ① dye·ta diet
dlaczego dla·che·go why
długi dwoo·gee long
dno ⓝ dno bottom (position)
do do to • until
dobry do·bri good
dobrze dob·zhe well
dolar ⓜ do·lar dollar
dolina ① do·lee·na valley
dom ⓜ dom home • house
  — towarowy to·va·ro·vi
  department store
dorosły ⓜ do·ro·swi adult n
dostać dos·tach get
dowód tożsamości ⓜ
  do·vood tozh·sa·mosh·chee
  identification card (ID)
drewno ⓝ drev·no wood n
drobny drob·ni tiny
droga ① dro·ga road • way
drogi dro·gee expensive
druga klasa ① droo·ga kla·sa
  second class
drugi droo·gee second a
drukarka ① droo·kar·ka printer (computer)
drużyna ① droo·zhi·na team
drzewo ⓝ dzhe·vo tree
drzwi dzhvee door
dużo doo·zho (a) lot • many
duży doo·zhi big
dwa dva two
dworzec autobusowy ⓜ
  dvo·zhets ow·to·boo·so·vi bus station
dyplom ⓜ dip·lom certificate (education)
dyskietka ① dis·kyet·ka disk (floppy)
dziadek ⓜ jya·dek grandfather
dzieci pl jye·chee children
dziecko ⓝ jye·tsko child
dzielić się jye·leech shye share (with)
dzielnica ① jyel·nee·tsa suburb
dzień ⓜ jyen' day
Dzień Bożego Narodzenia ⓜ
  jyen' bo·zhe·go na·ro·dze·nya
  Christmas Day

dziennikarz ⓜ jye·nee·kash journalist
dziewczyna ① jyev·chi·na girl • girlfriend
dzisiaj jee·shyai today
dziwny jeev·ni strange
dzwonić dzvo·neech call (phone)
dżin ⓜ jeen gin
dżinsy pl jeen·si jeans
dżip ⓜ jeep jeep

E

egzema ① eg·ze·ma eczema
ekspresowy eks·pre·so·vi express a
elektryczność ① e·lek·trich·noshch
  electricity
email ⓜ e·mail email
emeryt/emerytka ⓜ/①
  e·me·rit/e·me·rit·ka pensioner

F

fabryka ① fa·bri·ka factory
faks ⓜ faks fax machine
fala ① fa·la wave (beach)
farmaceuta ⓜ far·ma·tsew·ta
  chemist (pharmacist)
filiżanka ① fee·lee·zhan·ka cup
film ⓜ feelm film (camera/cinema)
Finlandia ① feen·lan·dya Finland
fioletowy fyo·le·to·vi purple
firma ① feer·ma business
flesz ⓜ flesh flash (camera)
flet ⓜ flet flute
fotograf ⓜ fo·to·graf photographer
fotografika ① fo·to·gra·fee·ka
  photography
fotografować fo·to·gra·fo·vach
  photograph
Francja ① fran·tsya France
fryzjer ⓜ fri·zyer hairdresser
funt ⓜ foont pound (money/weight)

G

galeria sztuki ① ga·ler·ya shtoo·kee
  art gallery
garaż ⓜ ga·razh garage
gaz ⓜ gaz gas (for cooking)
gazeta ① ga·ze·ta newspaper
gdzie gjye where

gej Ⓜ gey *gay (homosexual)*
gimnastyka Ⓕ geem·nas·ti·ka *gymnastics*
gimnazjum Ⓝ geem·na·zyoom
   high school
głęboki gwem·bo·kee *deep*
głodny gwo·dni *hungry*
głowa Ⓕ gwo·va *head*
główny gwoov·ni *main*
głuchy gwoo·khi *deaf*
godzina Ⓕ go·jee·na *hour*
godziny otwarcia pl go·jee·ni ot·far·chya
   opening hours
gol Ⓜ gol *goal (sport)*
gorący go·ron·tsi *hot*
gorączka Ⓕ go·ronch·ka *fever*
gospodarstwo agroturystyczne Ⓝ
   gos·po·darst·fo a·gro·too·ris·tich·ne
   agritourist farm
gospodarstwo rolne Ⓝ
   gos·po·darst·fo rol·ne *farm*
gościnność Ⓕ gosh·chee·noshch
   hospitality
gotować go·to·vach *cook*
gotowanie Ⓝ go·to·va·nye *cooking*
gotowy go·to·vi *ready*
gotówka Ⓕ go·toof·ka *cash*
góra Ⓕ goo·ra *mountain*
granat Ⓜ gra·nat *garnet*
granica Ⓕ gra·nee·tsa *border*
grób Ⓜ groob *grave*
grudzień Ⓜ groo·jyen' *December*
grypa Ⓕ gri·pa *influenza*
grzejnik Ⓜ gzhey·neek *heater*
guma Ⓕ goo·ma *gum*
   — do żucia do zhoo·chya *chewing gum*
gwałt Ⓜ gvowt *rape*
gwarancja Ⓕ gva·ran·tsya *guarantee*

H

hałaśliwy kha·wash·lee·vi *noisy*
herbata Ⓕ kher·ba·ta *tea*
heroina Ⓕ khe·ro·ee·na *heroin*
historia Ⓕ khees·to·rya *history*
historyczny khees·to·rich·ni *historical*
Hiszpania Ⓕ kheesh·pa·nya *Spain*
Holandia Ⓕ kho·lan·dya *Netherlands*
homoseksualista Ⓜ
   kho·mo·sek·soo·a·lees·ta *homosexual*

I

i ee *and*
ich eekh *their*
identyfikacja Ⓕ ee·den·ti·fee·ka·tsya
   identification
ile ee·le *how much*
imię Ⓝ ee·mye *given name*
imigracja Ⓕ ee·mee·gra·tsya
   immigration
infekcja Ⓕ een·fek·tsya *infection*
informacja Ⓕ een·for·mats·ya *information*
informatyka Ⓕ een·for·ma·ti·ka *IT*
inny ee·ni *another (a different one)*
interesujący Ⓜ een·te·re·soo·yon·tsi
   interesting
internet Ⓜ een·ter·net *Internet*
inżynier Ⓜ een·zhi·nyer *engineer*
Irlandia Ⓕ eer·lan·dya *Ireland*
iść eeshch *go (on foot)*

J

Ja ya *I*
jadłospis Ⓜ ya·dwo·spees *menu*
jak yak *how*
jakiś ya·keesh *any (some)*
jakość Ⓕ ya·koshch *quality*
Japonia Ⓕ ya·po·nya *Japan*
jaskinia Ⓕ yas·kee·nya *cave*
jasny yas·ni *light (colour)*
jaszczurka Ⓕ yash·choor·ka *lizard*
jazda Ⓕ yaz·da *ride* n
jechać ye·khach *go (by mechanised means)*
jeden ye·den *one*
jesień Ⓕ ye·shyen' *autumn • fall*
jeszcze (nie) yesh·che (nye) *(not) yet*
jeść yeshch *eat* v
jeśli yesh·lee *if*
jetlag Ⓜ jet·lag *jet lag*
jezioro Ⓝ ye·zhyo·ro *lake*
jeździć yezh·jeech *ride (bike, horse)*
język Ⓜ yen·zik *language*
jutro yoo·tro *tomorrow*
już yoosh *already • yet*

K

kamień Ⓜ ka·myen' *stone*
kamping Ⓜ kam·peeng *camping ground*

kanapka ① ka·*nap*·ka *sandwich*
kantor ⑩ *kan*·tor *currency exchange*
kapelusz ⑩ ka·pe·*loosh* *hat*
kapłan ⑩ *kap*·wan *priest*
kara ① *ka*·ra *fine* n
karetka pogotowia ①
  ka·*ret*·ka po·go·*to*·vya *ambulance*
Karpaty kar·*pa*·ti *Carpathian mountains*
karton ⑩ *kar*·ton *carton*
karty *kar*·ti *cards (playing)*
kasa biletowa ① *ka*·sa bee·le·*to*·va
  ticket office
kasjer/kasjerka ⑩/① *kas*·yer/kas·*yer*·ka
  cashier
kask *kask* *helmet*
kaszel ⑩ *ka*·shel *cough*
katar ⑩ *ka*·tar *cold (illness)*
katedra ① ka·*te*·dra *cathedral*
katolik ⑩ ka·*to*·leek *Catholic* n
kawa ① *ka*·va *coffee*
kawałek ⑩ ka·*va*·wek *piece*
kawiarnia ① ka·*vyar*·nya *café*
każdy *kazh*·di *each • everyone • every*
kąpiel ① *kom*·pyel *bath*
kelner ⑩ *kel*·ner *waiter*
kibic ⑩ *kee*·beets *fan (sport, politics)*
kiedy *kye*·di *when*
kierować kye·*ro*·vach *drive*
kierownik ⑩ kye·*rov*·neek
  manager (of a business)
kierunek ⑩ kye·*roo*·nek *direction*
Kijów ⑩ *kee*·yoof *Kiyev*
kilka *keel*·ka *few • several • some*
kino ⑩ *kee*·no *cinema*
kiosk ⑩ *kyosk* *kiosk*
klasyczny kla·*sich*·ni *classical*
klasztor ⑩ *klash*·tor *convent • monastery*
klej ⑩ *kley* *glue*
klient ⑩ *klee*·yent *client*
klimatyzacja ① klee·ma·ti·*za*·tsya
  air conditioning
klimatyzowany ⑩ klee·ma·ti·zo·*va*·ni
  air-conditioned
klucz ⑩ *klooch* *key (door etc)*
kłaść *kwashch* *put*
kłódka ① *kwood*·ka *padlock*
kobieta ① ko·*bye*·ta *woman*
koc ⑩ *kots* *blanket*
kochać *ko*·khach *love*
kolacja ① ko·*la*·tsya *dinner • supper*
kolano ⑩ ko·*la*·no *knee*

kolczyki kol·*chi*·kee *earrings*
kolejka ① ko·*ley*·ka *queue • round (drinks)*
kolor ⑩ *ko*·lor *colour*
kołdry i pościel ① *kow*·dri ee *posh*·chyel
  bedding
koło ⑩ *ko*·wo *wheel* n
komar ⑩ *ko*·mar *mosquito*
komis ⑩ *ko*·mees *secondhand shop*
komisariat policji ⑩
  ko·mee·*sar*·yat po·*leets*·yee
  police station
komunia ① ko·*moo*·nya *communion*
komunista ⑩ ko·moo·*nees*·ta *communist*
koncert ⑩ *kon*·tsert *concert*
konferencja ① kon·fe·*ren*·tsya
  conference (big)
koniec ⑩ *ko*·nyets *end*
konsulat ⑩ kon·*soo*·lat *consulate*
konto ⑩ *kon*·to *account (bill)*
  — bankowe ban·*ko*·ve *bank account*
kontrakt ⑩ *kon*·trakt *contract*
koń ⑩ *kon'* *horse*
kończyć *kon'*·chich *finish*
kopać *ko*·pach *kick*
korek ⑩ *ko*·rek *plug (bath)*
koronka ① ko·*ron*·ka *lace (fabric)*
kort ⑩ *kort* *court (tennis)*
  — tenisowy te·nee·*so*·vi *tennis court*
korupcja ① ko·*roop*·tsya *corruption*
kościół ⑩ *kosh*·chyoow *church*
  — prawosławny pra·vo·*swav*·ni
  Orthodox Church
kość ① *koshch* *bone*
kosmetyczka ① kos·me·*tich*·ka
  beautician
kostium kąpielowy ⑩
  kos·tyoom kom·pye·*lo*·vi *swimsuit*
kostka ① *kost*·ka *ankle*
koszt ⑩ *kosht* *cost*
koszula ① ko·*shoo*·la *shirt*
koszykówka ① ko·shi·*koof*·ka *basketball*
kot ⑩ *kot* *cat*
koza ① *ko*·za *goat*
kradziony kra·*jyo*·ni *stolen*
kraj ⑩ *krai* *country*
kran ⑩ *kran* *faucet • tap*
kraść *krashch* *steal*
krawiec ⑩ *kra*·vyets *tailor*
kredyt ⑩ *kre*·dit *credit*
krem ⑩ *krem* *cream (lotion)*
krew ① *kref* *blood*

krewetka ⓕ kre-*vet*-ka *prawn*
krok ⓜ krok *step*
krople do oczu *kro*-ple do o-*choo*
  eye drops
krowa ⓕ *kro*-va *cow*
król ⓜ krool *king*
królowa ⓕ kroo-*lo*-va *queen*
krótki *kroot*-kee *short (length)*
kryształ ⓜ *krish*-tow *crystal*
książka ⓕ *ksyonsh*-ka *book* n
  — telefoniczna te-le-fo-*neech*-na
  phone book
księgarnia ⓕ kshyen-*gar*-nya *book shop*
kto kto *who*
ktoś ktosh *someone*
który *ktoo*-ri *that • which*
kucharz ⓜ koo-khash *cook*
kuchnia ⓕ *kookh*-nya *kitchen*
kupować koo-*po*-vach *buy*
kurs wymiany ⓜ koors vi-*mya*-ni
  exchange rate
kurtka ⓕ *koort*-ka *jacket*
kuszetka ⓕ koo-*shet*-ka *couchette*
kwiaciarnia ⓕ kvya-*chyar*-nya *florist*
kwiat ⓜ kvyat *flower*
kwiecień ⓜ *kfye*-chen' *April*

las ⓜ las *forest*
latać *la*-tach *fly* v
latarka ⓕ la-*tar*-ka *flashlight • torch*
lato ⓝ *la*-to *summer*
lek ⓜ lek *drug (medicinal)*
lekarstwo ⓝ le-*karst*-fo
  medicine (medication)
  — na kaszel na *ka*-shel *cough medicine*
lekarz ⓜ *le*-kash *doctor*
lekki *le*-kee *light (weight)*
len ⓜ len *linen (material)*
lepszy *lep*-shi *better*
lesbijka ⓕ les-*beey*-ka *lesbian*
lewy *le*-vi *left (direction)*
leżeć *le*-zhech *lie (not stand)* v
licencja ⓕ lee-*tsen*-tsya *licence*
lipiec ⓜ *lee*-pyets *July*
list ⓜ leest *letter (mail)*
listopad ⓜ lees-*to*-pat *November*
Litwa ⓕ *lee*-tfa *Lithuania*
lodówka ⓕ lo-*doof*-ka *refrigerator*
lody pl *lo*-di *ice cream*

lodziarnia ⓕ lo-*jyar*-nya *ice-cream parlour*
lot ⓜ lot *flight*
lotnisko ⓝ lot-*nees*-ko *airport*
lubić *loo*-beech *like* v
ludzie pl *loo*-jye *people*
luksusowy ⓜ look-soo-*so*-vi *luxury*
luty ⓜ *loo*-ti *February*
luźny *loozh*-ni *loose*

ładny *wad*-ni *fine • pretty*
łapówka ⓕ wa-*poof*-ka *bribe*
łatwy ⓜ *wa*-tfi *easy*
łazienka ⓕ wa-*zhyen*-ka *bathroom*
lód ⓜ lood *ice*
łódź ⓕ wooj *boat*
łóżko ⓝ *woozh*-ko *bed*
  — małżeńskie mow-*zhen'*-skye
  double bed
łyżeczka ⓕ wi-*zhech*-ka *teaspoon*
łyżka ⓕ *wish*-ka *spoon*

magnetowid ⓜ mag-ne-*to*-veed
  video recorder
maj ⓜ mai *May*
makijaż ⓜ ma-*kee*-yash *make-up*
malarstwo ⓝ ma-*lars*-tfo
  painting (a work)
mały *ma*-wi *small*
małżeństwo ⓝ mow-*zhen'*-sto *marriage*
manierka ⓕ ma-*nyer*-ka *water bottle*
mapa ⓕ *ma*-pa *map (of country)*
  — drogowa dro-*go*-va *road map*
marihuana ⓕ ma-ree-khoo-*a*-na
  marijuana
marionetka ⓕ ma-ryo-*net*-ka *puppet*
martwy ⓜ *mart*-fi *dead*
marzec ⓜ *ma*-zhets *March*
masaż ⓜ *ma*-sash *massage*
masło ⓝ *mas*-wo *butter*
maszyna ⓕ ma-*shi*-na *machine*
materac ⓜ ma-*te*-rats *mattress*
materiał ⓜ ma-*ter*-yow *fabric*
matka ⓕ *mat*-ka *mother*
mąż ⓜ monzh *husband*
mdłości pl *mdwosh*-chee *nausea*
meble pl *me*-ble *furniture*

mecz ⓜ mech *match (sports)*
meczet ⓜ *me·*chet *mosque*
medycyna ⓕ me·di·*tsi·*na *medicine (study/profession)*
menedżer ⓜ me·ne·jer *manager (sport)*
metro ⓝ *me·*tro *metro • subway*
mężczyzna ⓜ menzh·*chiz·*na *man*
mi mee *me*
miasto ⓝ *myas·*to *city*
mieć myech *have*
miejsce ⓝ *myeys·*tse *place • seat*
— **urodzenia** oo·ro·*dze·*nya *place of birth*
miejscowy ⓜ *myeys·*tso·vi *local*
miesiąc ⓜ *mye·*shonts *month*
— **miodowy** myo·*do·*vi *honeymoon*
mieszać *mye·*shach *mix*
mieszkać *myesh·*kach *live (somewhere)*
mieszkanie ⓝ myesh·*ka·*nye *apartment • flat*
między *myen·*dzi *between*
międzynarodowy myen·dzi·na·ro·*do·*vi *international*
mięso ⓝ *myen·*so *meat*
mijać *mee·*yach *pass (go by)*
miłość ⓕ *mee·*woshch *love*
miły *mee·*wi *kind • nice*
minuta ⓕ mee·*noo·*ta *minute*
Mińsk ⓜ *meen·*sk *Minsk*
miska ⓕ *mee·*ska *bowl (plate)* n
mleko ⓝ *mle·*ko *milk*
młody *mwo·*di *young* a
mnich ⓜ mneekh *monk*
mniej mnyey *less*
mniejszy *mnyey·*shi *smaller*
moda ⓕ *mo·*da *fashion* n
mokry *mo·*kri *wet* a
monety pl mo·*ne·*ti *coins*
morze ⓝ *mo·*zhe *sea*
Morze Bałtyckie ⓝ *mo·*zhe bow·*tits·*kye *Baltic Sea*
Moskwa ⓕ mosk·fa *Moscow*
most ⓜ most *bridge (structure)*
motel ⓜ *mo·*tel *motel*
motor ⓜ *mo·*tor *motorbike*
motorówka ⓕ mo·to·*roof·*ka *motorboat*
możliwy ⓜ mozh·*lee·*vi *possible*
mówić moo·veech *say • speak*
mrożony mro·*zho·*ni *frozen*
mróz ⓜ mrooz *frost*
msza ⓕ msha *mass (Catholic)*
mucha ⓕ *moo·*kha *fly*

muzeum ⓝ moo·*ze·*oom *museum*
muzyka ⓕ moo·*zi·*ka *music*
my mi *we*
mydło ⓝ *mid·*wo *soap*

N

na na *on*
nad nad *above*
nagły przypadek ⓜ *na·*gwi pshi·*pa·*dek *emergency*
najbliższy nai·*bleezh·*shi *nearest*
najlepszy nai·*lep·*shi *best*
najmniejszy nai·*mnyey·*shi *smallest*
największy nai·*vyenk·*shi *biggest*
namiot ⓜ *na·*myot *tent*
napiwek ⓜ na·*pee·*vek *tip (gratuity)*
napój ⓜ *na·*pooy *drink* n
naprawić na·*pra·*veech *repair*
naprzeciwko na·pshe·*cheef·*ko *opposite*
naprzód na·*pshoot *ahead*
narciarstwo ⓝ nar·*chyarst·*fo *skiing*
narkotyki nar·ko·*ti·*kee *drugs (illicit)*
narodowość ⓕ na·ro·*do·*voshch *nationality*
narty pl *nar·*ti *skis*
następny nas·*temp·*ni *next (following)*
nasz nash *our*
nauczyciel ⓜ na·oo·*chi·*chyel *teacher*
nauka ⓕ na·*oo·*ka *science*
nauki humanistyczne pl na·*oo·*kee khoo·ma·nees·*tich·*ne *humanities*
nazwisko ⓝ naz·*vees·*ko *surname*
negatyw ⓜ ne·*ga·*tif *negatives (photos)*
nic neets *nothing*
nić ⓕ neech *thread*
nie nye *no • not*
niebieski ⓜ nye·*byes·*kee *blue*
niebo ⓝ *nye·*bo *sky*
niedziela ⓕ nye·*jye·*la *Sunday*
Niemcy pl *nyem·*tsi *Germany*
niemowlę ⓝ nye·*mov·*le *baby*
niemożliwy ⓜ nye·mozh·*lee·*vi *impossible*
niemy ⓜ *nye·*mi *mute*
niepalący ⓜ nye·pa·*lon·*tsi *nonsmoking*
niepełnosprawny ⓜ nye·pew·no·*sprav·*ni *disabled*
niestrawność ⓕ nye·*strav·*noshch *indigestion*
niewygodny ⓜ nye·vi·*go·*dni *uncomfortable*

nieznajomy @ nye·zna·yo·mi *stranger*
nigdy *neeg·di never*
niski *nees·kee low · short (height)*
noc ① *nots night*
nocleg @ *nots·leg accommodation*
nocny *nots·ni overnight*
noga ① *no·ga leg (body)*
nosić *no·sheech carry · wear*
notatnik @ *no·tat·neek diary*
notes @ *no·tes notebook*
Nowa Zelandia ① *no·va ze·lan·dya New Zealand*
nowoczesny m *no·vo·ches·ni modern*
nowy *no·vi new*
Nowy Rok @ *no·vi rok New Year's Day*
nożyczki pl *no·zhich·kee scissors*
nóż @ *noosh knife*
nudny *noo·dni boring*
numer @ *noo·mer number*

O

obaj/obie/oboje @/①/① *o·bai/o·bye/o·bo·ye both*
obiektyw @ *o·byek·tif lens (camera)*
obok *o·bok beside*
obsługa ① *ob·swoo·ga service n*
obywatelstwo @ *o·bi·va·telst·fo citizenship*
od *od from · per (day) · since (time)*
oddychać *o·di·khach breathe*
odjazd @ *od·yazd departure (by land)*
odjeżdżać *od·yezh·jach depart*
odlot @ *od·lot departure (by air)*
odpoczywać *od·po·chi·vach relax · rest*
odpowiedź ① *od·po·vyej answer*
odwiedzać *od·vye·dzach visit*
oglądać *o·glon·dach watch*
ogród @ *o·grood garden*
ogrzewanie @ *o·gzhe·va·nye heating*
ojciec @ *oy·chyets father*
okno @ *ok·no window*
oko @ *o·ko eye*
okolica ① *o·ko·lee·tsa countryside*
okraść *o·krashch rob*
okulary pl *o·koo·la·ri glasses (spectacles)*
— słoneczne *swo·nech·ne sunglasses*
okulista *o·koo·lees·ta optometrist*
ołówek @ *o·woo·vek pencil*
ołtarz @ *ow·tazh altar*
on *on he*

ona *o·na she*
oni *o·nee they*
operacja ① *o·pe·ra·tsya operation (medical)*
opona ① *o·po·na tyre*
opóźnienie @ *o·poozh·nye·nye delay*
orzech @ *o·zhekh nut (food)*
orzeszek ziemny *o·zhe·shek zhyem·ni groundnut · peanut*
osoba ① *o·so·ba person*
osobny *o·so·bni separate*
ostatni *os·tat·nee last (final)*
ostatnio *os·tat·nyo recently*
otwarty *ot·far·ti open (business)*
owoc @ *o·vots fruit*

P

paczka ① *pach·ka package · packet · parcel*
palec @ *pa·lets finger*
— u nogi *oo no·gee toe*
pamiątka ① *pa·myont·ka souvenir*
pan m *pan Mr*
pan/pani @/① *pan/pa·nee you pol sg*
pana/pani @/① *pa·na/pa·nee your pol sg*
pani *pa·nee Mrs · Ms*
panie *pa·nye you pol ① pl*
panna ① *pa·na Miss*
panowie *pa·no·vye you pol @ pl*
państwa *pan'stfa your pol @&① pl*
państwo *pan'stfo you pol @&① pl*
papieros @ *pa·pye·ros cigarette*
para ① *pa·ra pair (couple)*
parasol @ *pa·ra·sol umbrella*
park @ *park park*
— narodowy *na·ro·do·vi national park*
pasażer @ *pa·sa·zher passenger*
pastylka ① *pas·til·ka pill*
patrzeć *pat·shech look*
październik @ *pazh·jyer·neek October*
pchli targ @ *pkhlee tark fleamarket*
pełny *pew·ni full*
pensja ① *pen·sya salary*
pensjonat @ *pen·syo·nat guesthouse*
perkusja ① *per·koo·sya drums (kit)*
peron @ *pe·ron platform*
piątek @ *pyon·tek Friday*
pić *peech drink*
piekarnia ① *pye·kar·nya bakery*
pieniądze pl *pye·nyon·dze money*

pierwsza klasa ① pyerf·sha kla·sa first class
pierwszy pyerf·shi first a
pies Ⓜ pyes dog
pieszy pye·shi pedestrian n
piękny pyen·kni beautiful
piętro Ⓝ pyen·tro floor (storey)
pijany pee·ya·ni drunk
pilny peel·ni urgent
piłka ① peew·ka ball (sport)
— nożna nozh·na football (soccer)
— ręczna rench·na handball
piosenka ① pyo·sen·ka song
pisać pee·sach write
piwo Ⓝ pee·vo beer
plakat Ⓜ pla·kat poster
plan Ⓜ plan map (of town)
plastykowy plas·ti·ko·vi plastic a
plaża ① pla·zha beach
plecak Ⓜ ple·tsak backpack
płacić pwa·cheech pay
płaski pwas·kee flat a
płaskowyż Ⓜ pwas·ko·vish plateau
płaszcz Ⓜ pwashch coat
— nieprzemakalny nye·pshe·ma·kal·ni
raincoat
pływać pwi·vach swim
pływanie Ⓝ pwi·va·nye swimming
po po · za after
pochmurny pokh·moor·ni cloudy
pociąg Ⓜ po·chyonk train
poczekalnia ① po·che·kal·nya
waiting room
poczta ① poch·ta mail (postal system)
pod pod below
podatek Ⓜ po·da·tek tax
podgrzewany pod·gzhe·va·ni heated
podłoga ① pod·wo·ga floor
podobny po·do·bni similar
podpis Ⓜ pod·pees signature
podpisać się pod·pee·sach shye sign
podróż ① po·droozh trip (journey)
— służbowa swoozh·bo·va
business trip
podróżować po·droo·zho·vach travel
poduszka ① po·doosh·ka pillow
podwójny pod·vooy·ni double
pogoda ① po·go·da weather
pokaz Ⓜ po·kas demonstration · show
pokój Ⓜ po·kooy peace · room
— dwuosobowy dvoo·o·so·bo·vi
double room
— jednoosobowy ye·dno·o·so·bo·vi
single room

polecać po·le·tsach recommend
policja ① po·lee·tsya police
policjant Ⓜ po·lee·tsyant
police officer (in city)
Polska ① pol·ska Poland
połamany po·wa·ma·ni broken
połączenie Ⓝ po·won·che·nye
connection (transport)
połówka ① po·woof·ka half
południe Ⓝ po·wood·nye midday · south
pomagać po·ma·gach help v
pomnik Ⓜ pom·neek monument
pomoc ① po·mots help
pomyłka ① po·miw·ka mistake
poniedziałek Ⓜ po·nye·jya·wek Monday
poparzenie Ⓝ po·pa·zhe·nye burn
popołudnie Ⓝ po·po·wood·nye
afternoon
poprzedni po·pshed·nee last (previous)
poprzez po·phes across
popularny po·poo·lar·ni popular
portmonetka ① port·mo·net·ka purse
posiłek Ⓜ po·shee·wek meal
posterunkowy Ⓜ pos·te·roon·ko·vi
police officer (in country)
posyłać po·si·wach post
poszewka ① po·shef·ka pillowcase
pościel ① posh·chyel bed linen
potrawa ① po·tra·va dish (food)
potwierdzać pot·fyer·dzach
confirm (a booking)
poważny po·vazh·ni serious
powódź ① po·vooj flood
pozwolenie Ⓝ poz·vo·le·nye permission
pożar Ⓜ po·zhar fire (inferno)
pożyczać po·zhi·chach borrow
pójść pooyshch go (on foot)
półka ① poow·ka shelf
północ ① poow·nots midnight · north
później poozh·nyey later
późno poozh·no late
praca ① pra·tsa job · work
pracodawca Ⓜ pra·tso·daf·tsa employer
pracować pra·tso·vach work
pracownik Ⓜ pra·tsov·neek employee
Praga ① pra·ga Prague
pralka ① pral·ka washing machine
pralnia ① pral·nya laundry (place)
prawie pra·vye almost
prawnik Ⓜ prav·neek lawyer

prawo ⓝ *pra·vo law*
— **jazdy** *yaz·di drivers licence*
prędkość ⓕ *prend·koshch speed (travel)*
przez *pshes per (day)*
prom ⓜ *prom ferry*
prosić *pro·sheech ask (for something)*
prosty *pros·ti simple · straight*
prowizja ⓕ *pro·vee·zya commission*
prysznic ⓜ *prish·neets shower*
prywatny *pri·vat·ni private*
przed *pshet before · in front of*
przedstawienie ⓝ *pshet·sta·vye·nye performance*
przedszkole ⓝ *pshet·shko·le crèche · kindergarten*
przedwczoraj ⓜ *pshet·fcho·rai day before yesterday*
przekąska ⓕ *pshe·kons·ka snack*
przenocować *pshe·no·tso·vach stay (at a hotel)*
przestać *pshes·tach stop (cease)*
przetłumaczyć *pshe·twoo·ma·chich translate*
przetwarzać *pshet·fa·zhach recycle*
przewodnik ⓜ *pshe·vod·neek guide (person) · guidebook*
przez *pshes across*
przy *pshi at*
przydomek ⓜ *pshi·do·mek nickname*
przygotować *pshi·go·to·vach prepare*
przyjaciel/przyjaciółka ⓜ/ⓕ *pshi·ya·chyel/pshi·ya·choow·ka friend*
przyjazdy ⓜ *pshi·yaz·di arrivals (general)*
przyjechać *pshi·ye·khach arrive*
przyjść *pshiyshch come (by mechanised means)*
przyloty ⓜ *pshi·lo·ti arrivals (plane)*
przynosić *pshi·no·sheech bring*
przystanek ⓜ *pshis·ta·nek stop (bus, tram)*
ptak ⓜ *ptak bird*
pusty *poos·ti empty a*

rachunek ⓜ *ra·khoo·nek bill (restaurant) · receipt*
rak ⓜ *rak cancer*
randka ⓕ *rand·ka date (appointment)*
rano ⓝ *ra·no morning*
raz *ras once*

recepta ⓕ *re·tse·pta prescription*
religia ⓕ *re·lee·gya religion*
relikt ⓜ *re·leekt relic*
restauracja ⓕ *res·tow·ra·tsya restaurant*
rezerwacja ⓕ *re·zer·va·tsya reservation (booking)*
rezerwować *re·zer·vo·vach book (make a booking)*
ręka ⓕ *ren·ka arm (body) · hand*
rękodzieła pl *ren·ko·jye·wa crafts*
rękodzielnictwo ⓝ *ren·ko·jyel·neetst·fo handicraft*
robić *ro·beech do · make*
rodzice pl *ro·jee·tse parents*
rodzina ⓕ *ro·jee·na family*
rok ⓜ *rok year*
rolnik ⓜ *rol·neek farmer*
Rosja ⓕ *ro·sya Russia*
rower ⓜ *ro·ver bicycle*
rozkład jazdy ⓜ *ros·kwad yaz·di timetable*
rozmieniać *roz·mye·nyach change (money)*
rozumieć *ro·zoo·myech understand*
rozwiedziony ⓜ *roz·vye·dzo·ni divorced*
różny *roozh·ni different*
ruchliwy *rookh·lee·vi busy (street, etc)*
ryba ⓕ *ri·ba fish*
rybołówstwo ⓝ *ri·bo·woos·tfo fishing*
rynek ⓜ *ri·nek market · square (town)*
rzeka ⓕ *zhe·ka river*
rzeźba ⓕ *zhezh·ba sculpture*

S

samochód ⓜ *sa·mo·khoot car*
samolot ⓜ *sa·mo·lot airplane*
samoobsługowy *sa·mo·ob·swoo·go·vi self-service*
schronisko górskie ⓝ *skhro·nees·ko goor·skye mountain lodge*
schronisko młodzieżowe ⓝ *skhro·nees·ko mwo·jye·zho·ve youth hostel*
seks ⓜ *seks sex*
sekunda ⓕ *se·koon·da second*
ser ⓜ *ser cheese*
sezon ⓜ *se·zon season n*
siatkówka ⓕ *shyat·koof·ka volleyball*
— **plażowa** *pla·zho·va beach volleyball*
sierpień ⓜ *shyer·pyen´ August*

silnik ⓜ *sheel*·neek *engine*
silny *sheel*·ni *strong*
siostra ⓕ *shyos*·tra *sister*
skarga ⓕ *skar*·ga *complaint*
sklep ⓜ sklep *shop*
skóra ⓕ *skoo*·ra *leather • skin*
skręcić *skren*·cheech *turn*
skrzypce pl *skship*·tse *violin*
słaby *swa*·bi *weak*
słodki *swod*·kee *sweet* a
słoneczny swo·*nech*·ni *sunny*
słońce ⓝ *swon'*·tse *sun*
Słowacja ⓕ swo·*va*·tsya *Slovakia*
słownik ⓜ *swov*·neek *dictionary*
słowo ⓝ *swo*·vo *word*
słuchać *swoo*·khach *listen*
słyszeć *swi*·shech *hear*
smaczny *smach*·ni *tasty*
smutny *smoo*·tni *sad*
sobota ⓕ so·*bo*·ta *Saturday*
soczewki kontaktowe pl
    so·*chef*·kee kon·tak·*to*·ve *contact lenses*
sok ⓜ sok *juice*
sos ⓜ sos *sauce*
sosna ⓕ *sos*·na *pine (tree)*
sól ⓕ sool *salt*
spacerować spa·tse·*ro*·vach *walk*
spać spach *sleep*
spotkać *spot*·kach *meet (get together)*
spotkanie ⓝ spot·*ka*·nye *appointment*
spragniony sprag·*nyo*·ni *thirsty*
sprawdzenie ⓝ sprav·*dze*·nye *bill (check)*
sprzątanie ⓝ spshon·*ta*·nye *cleaning*
sprzedawać spshe·*da*·vach *sell*
sprzedawca/sprzedawczyni ⓜ/ⓕ
    spshe·*daf*·tsa/spshe·daf·*chi*·nee *sales assistant*
sprzedaż ⓕ *spshe*·dash *sale*
srebro ⓝ *sre*·bro *silver*
stacja ⓕ *sta*·tsya *station*
    — benzynowa ben·zi·*no*·va
    gas station • petrol station
    — kolejowa ko·le·*yo*·va *railway station*
stary *sta*·ri *old*
statek ⓜ *sta*·tek *ship*
stołówka ⓕ sto·*woof*·ka *cafeteria*
stopnie pl *sto*·pnye *degrees (temperature)*
stół ⓜ stoow *table*
strona ⓕ *stro*·na *page • side*
strumień ⓜ *stroo*·myen' *stream* n
styczeń ⓜ *sti*·chen' *January*

suchy *soo*·khi *dry* a
Sudety pl soo·*de*·ti *Sudeten mountains*
surowy soo·*ro*·vi *raw*
suszony soo·*sho*·ni *dried*
suszyć *soo*·shich *dry (clothes)*
Sylwester ⓜ sil·*ves*·ter *New Year's Eve*
syn ⓜ sin *son*
sypialnia ⓕ si·*pyal*·nya *bedroom*
szachy pl *sha*·khi *chess*
szampan ⓜ *sham*·pan *champagne*
szampon ⓜ *sham*·pon *shampoo*
szary *sha*·ri *grey*
szatnia ⓕ *shat*·nya
    changing room • cloakroom
szczepienie ⓝ shche·*pye*·nye *vaccination*
szczęśliwy shchen·*shlee*·vi *happy • lucky*
szczotka ⓕ *shchot*·ka *brush (general)*
szczyt ⓜ shchit *peak (mountain)*
szeroki she·*ro*·kee *wide*
szklanka ⓕ *shklan*·ka *glass (drinking)*
Szkocja ⓕ *shko*·tsya *Scotland*
szkoła ⓕ *shko*·wa *school*
szosa ⓕ *sho*·sa *highway*
szpital ⓜ *shpee*·tal *hospital*
szprycha ⓕ *shpri*·kha *spoke*
Sztokholm ⓜ *shtok*·kholm *Stockholm*
sztuka ⓕ *shtoo*·ka *art • play (theatre)*
szukać *shoo*·kach *look for*
Szwajcaria ⓕ shvai·*tsar*·ya *Switzerland*
Szwecja ⓕ *shve*·tsya *Sweden*
szybki *shib*·kee *fast*
szynka ⓕ *shin*·ka *ham*

Ś

ścieżka ⓕ *shchyesh*·ka *footpath • path*
ślub ⓜ shloob *wedding*
śmieci pl *shmye*·chee *garbage*
śniadanie ⓝ shnya·*da*·nye *breakfast*
śnieg ⓜ shnyeg *snow*
śpiwór ⓜ *shpee*·voor *sleeping bag*
środa ⓕ *shro*·da *Wednesday*
środek ⓜ *shro*·dek *centre*
środowisko ⓝ shro·do·*vees*·ko
    environment
świat ⓜ shfyat *world*
światło ⓝ *shvyat*·wo *light*
świeca ⓕ *shvye*·tsa *candle*
świekra ⓕ *shfyek*·ra
    mother-in-law (husband's mother)
świeży *shfye*·zhi *fresh*

święto ⓝ *shvyen·to* holiday
świętowanie ⓝ *shvyen·to·va·nye* celebration
święty *shvyen·ti* saint
świt ⓜ *shveet* dawn

T

tak *tak* yes
taksówka ⓕ *tak·soof·ka* taxi
także *tak·zhe* also
tam *tam* there
tani *ta·nee* cheap
taryfa ⓕ *ta·ri·fa* fare n
teatr ⓜ *te·atr* theatre
telefon ⓜ *te·le·fon* telephone
— **komórkowy** *ko·moor·ko·vi* cell phone · mobile phone
— **publiczny** *poob·leech·ni* public phone
telefonować *te·le·fo·no·vach* telephone
telegram ⓜ *te·le·gram* telegram
teleobiektyw ⓜ *te·le·o·byek·tif* zoom lens
telewizor ⓜ *te·le·vee·zor* TV
ten ⓜ *ten* this (one) pron
tenis ⓜ *te·nees* tennis
teraz *te·ras* now
teściowa ⓕ *tesh·chyo·va* mother-in-law (wife's mother)
teść ⓜ *teshch* father-in-law
też *tesh* too (also)
tlen ⓜ *tlen* oxygen
tłumacz/tłumaczka ⓜ/ⓕ *twoo·mach/twoo·mach·ka* interpreter · translator
tłusty ⓜ *twoos·ti* fat a
to ⓝ *to* this
toaleta ⓕ *to·a·le·ta* toilet
torba ⓕ *tor·ba* bag
torebka ⓕ *to·rep·ka* handbag
towarzysz ⓜ *to·va·zhish* companion
tramwaj ⓜ *tram·vai* tram
trasa ⓕ *tra·sa* route
— **podróży** *po·droo·zhi* itinerary
troche *tro·khe* little (quantity)
trolejbus ⓜ *tro·ley·boos* trolley-bus
trudny *trood·ni* difficult
turysta ⓜ *too·ris·ta* tourist
tutaj *too·tai* here
twardy *tfar·di* hard (not soft)
twój *tfooy* your inf sg
ty *ti* you inf sg

tydzień ⓜ *ti·jyen'* week
tylko *til·ko* only
tylny *til·ni* rear (location) a
tył ⓜ *tiw* back (position)
typ ⓜ *tip* type
typowy *ti·po·vi* typical

U

ubezpieczenie ⓝ *oo·bes·pye·che·nye* insurance
ubranie ⓝ *oo·bra·nye* clothing
ucho ⓝ *oo·kho* ear
uchodźca ⓜ *oo·khoj·tsa* refugee
uczucia *oo·choo·chya* feelings
uczucie ⓝ *oo·choo·chye* feeling (physical)
Ukraina ⓕ *oo·kra·ee·na* Ukraine
ulica ⓕ *oo·lee·tsa* street
umieć *oo·myech* can (know how to)
Unia Europejska ⓕ *oo·nya ew·ro·pey·ska* European Union
uniwersytet ⓜ *oo·nee·ver·si·tet* college · university
upadać *oo·pa·dach* fall (down)
upał ⓜ *oo·pow* heat
uprawomocniać *oo·pra·vo·mots·nyach* validate
urodziny pl *oo·ro·jee·ni* birthday
urwisko ⓝ *oor·vee·sko* cliff
usta pl *oos·ta* mouth
użyteczny *oo·zhi·tech·ni* useful
używany *oo·zhi·va·ni* secondhand

W

w *v* in · within (time)
wadliwy *vad·lee·vi* faulty
waga ⓕ *va·ga* weight
wagon restauracyjny ⓜ *va·gon res·tow·rat·siy·ni* dining car
wagon sypialny ⓜ *va·gon si·pyal·ni* sleeping car
wakacje pl *va·ka·tsye* holidays · vacation
walizka ⓕ *va·lees·ka* suitcase
Warszawa ⓕ *var·sha·va* Warsaw
wartość ⓕ *var·toshch* value (price)
warzywo ⓝ *va·zhi·vo* vegetable
wasz *vash* your inf pl
ważny *vazh·ni* important
wąż ⓜ *vonzh* snake

wcześnie vchesh-nye *early*

wczoraj fcho-rai *yesterday*

wegetarianin ⓜ ve-ge-tar-ya-neen *vegetarian*

wegetariański ve-ge-tar-yan-skee *vegetarian*

wejście ⓝ veysh-chye *entry • gate (airport, etc)*

wejść veyshch *enter*

wentylator ⓜ ven-ti-la-tor *fan (machine)*

wewnątrz vev-nontsh *inside* adv

wędrować ven-dro-vach *hike*

wędrówka ⓕ ven-droof-ka *hiking*

wiadomości pl vya-do-mosh-chee *news*

wiadomość ⓕ vya-do-moshch *message*

wiatr ⓜ vyatr *wind*

widok ⓜ vee-dok *view*

wieczór ⓜ vye-choor *evening*

wiedzieć vye-jyech *know (be aware of)*

wiek ⓜ vyek *age*

Wielkanoc ⓕ vyel-ka-nots *Easter*

wieś ⓕ vyesh *village*

wieża ⓕ vye-zha *tower*

więcej vyen-tsey *more*

większy ⓜ vyenk-shi *bigger*

Wigilia ⓕ vee-gee-lya *Christmas Eve*

Wilno ⓝ veel-no *Vilnius*

wina ⓕ vee-na *fault (someone's)*

winda ⓕ veen-da *elevator • lift*

winnica ⓕ vee-nee-tsa *vineyard*

wino ⓝ vee-no *wine*

wiosna ⓕ vyos-na *spring (season)*

wirus ⓜ vee-roos *virus*

wiza ⓕ vee-za *visa*

wkrótce fkroot-tse *soon*

wliczony ⓜ vlee-cho-ni *included*

właściciel/właścicielka ⓜ/ⓕ vwash-chee-chyel/vwash-chee-chyel-ka *landlord/lady • owner*

Włochy pl vwo-khi *Italy*

włosy pl vwo-si *hair*

wnuk/wnuczka ⓜ/ⓕ vnook/vnooch-ka *grandchild*

woda ⓕ vo-da *water*

  — **mineralna** mee-ne-ral-na *mineral water*

  — **po goleniu** po go-le-nyoo *aftershave*

  — **z kranu** z kra-noo *tap water*

wodoodporny vo-do-od-por-ni *waterproof*

wodospad ⓜ vo-do-spad *waterfall*

wojna ⓕ voy-na *war*

wojsko ⓝ voy-sko *military*

woleć vo-lech *prefer*

wolny vol-ni *free (available) • free (not bound) • slow*

wódka ⓕ vood-ka *vodka*

wózek ⓜ voo-zek *trolley*

  — **inwalidzki** een-va-leets-kee *wheelchair*

  — **spacerowy** spa-tse-ro-vi *stroller*

wpuszczać fpoosh-chach *admit (let in)*

wracać vra-tsach *return*

wrzesień ⓜ vzhe-shyen' *September*

wschód ⓜ vskhood *east* n

  — **słońca** swon'-tsa *sunrise*

wspaniały ⓜ vspa-nya-wi *great (fantastic)*

współpracownik/współpracowniczka ⓜ/ⓕ fspoow-pra-tsov-neek/fspoow-pra-tsov-neech-ka *colleague*

wstęp ⓜ fstemp *admission (price)*

wszy pl vshi *lice*

wszystko ⓝ fshist-ko *everything*

wścieklizna ⓕ fshchyek-leez-na *rabies*

wtorek ⓜ vto-rek *Tuesday*

wtyczka ⓕ ftich-ka *plug (electricity)*

wy vi *you* inf pl

wybierać vi-bye-rach *choose*

wybrzeże ⓝ vi-bzhe-zhe *coast*

wychodzić vi-kho-jeech *go out*

wycieczka ⓕ vi-chyech-ka *tour*

wycierać vi-chye-rach *dry (oneself)*

wygodny vi-go-dni *comfortable*

wygrać vi-grach *win*

wyjście ⓝ viysh-chye *exit*

wyłączony vi-won-cho-ni *excluded*

wymiana ⓕ vi-mya-na *exchange*

wymieniać vi-mye-nyach *exchange*

wynająć vi-na-yonch *rent*

wynajmować vi-nai-mo-vach *hire*

wypadek ⓜ vi-pa-dek *accident*

wyprzedany vi-pshe-da-ni *booked out*

wysiadać vi-shya-dach *get off (bus, train)*

wysoki vi-so-kee *high • tall*

wyspa ⓕ vis-pa *island*

wystawa ⓕ vis-ta-va *exhibition*

wysyłać vi-si-wach *send*

wzgórze ⓝ vzgoo-zhe *hill*

W

polish–english

245

Z

z z *from • with*

za za *after • behind • too (much)*
— **granicą** gra·*nee*·tsom *abroad*

zabawa za·*ba*·va *fun*

zabawny za·*bav*·ni *funny*

zachód ⓜ za·khood *west*
— **słońca** swon'·tsa *sunset*

zaczynać za·*chi*·nach *start*

zagranica ⓕ za·gra·*nee*·tsa *overseas*

zagraniczny za·gra·*nee*·chni *foreign*

zajęty za·*yen*·ti *busy • engaged*

zakład ⓜ *za*·kwad *bet*

zakładać się za·*kwa*·dach shye *bet*

zakonnica ⓕ za·ko·*nee*·tsa *nun*

zakupy pl za·*koo*·pi *shopping*

zamawiać za·*ma*·vyach *order* v

zamek ⓜ *za*·mek *castle • lock*

zamężna ⓕ za·*men*·zhna
married (of woman)

zamknięty zam·*knyen*·ti
closed • locked • shut

zamykać za·*mi*·kach *close*
— **na klucz** na klooch *lock*

zapałki pl za·*pow*·kee
matches (for lighting)

zapłata ⓕ za·*pwa*·ta *payment*

zapomnieć za·*pom*·nyech *forget*

zapoznać za·*poz*·nach *meet (first time)*

zapraszać za·*pra*·shach *invite*

zarabiać za·*ra*·byach *earn*

zaręczony za·ren·*cho*·ni
engaged (to be married)

zaręczyny pl za·ren·*chi*·ni
engagement (to marry)

zastrzyk ⓜ *zast*·shik *injection*

zatłoczony za·two·*cho*·ni *crowded*

zatrzymać za·*tshi*·mach *stop (prevent)*

zawrotny za·*vrot*·ni *dizzy*

zawsze *zaf*·she *always*

ząb ⓜ zomb *tooth*

zdjęcie ⓝ *zdyen*·chye *photo*

zdrowie ⓝ *zdro*·vye *health*

zegar ⓜ *ze*·gar *clock*

zegarek ⓜ ze·*ga*·rek *watch*

zepsuty zep·*soo*·ti
broken down • corrupt • spoiled (food)

zespół ⓜ *zes*·poow *band (music)*

zezwolenie ⓝ ze·zvo·*le*·nye *permit*

zęby pl *zem*·bi *teeth*

zgodzić się *zgo*·jeech shye *agree*

zgubiony zgoo·*byo*·ni *lost*

zielony zhye·*lo*·ni *green*

Ziemia ⓕ *zhye*·mya *Earth*

ziemia ⓕ *zhye*·mya *land*

zima ⓕ *zhee*·ma *winter*

zimno ⓝ *zhee*·mno *cold (temperature)* n

zimny *zheem*·ni *cold* a

zjazd ⓜ zyazd *downhill*

złoto ⓝ *zwo*·to *gold*

zły ⓜ zwi *angry • bad • wrong*

zmęczony zmen·*cho*·ni *tired*

zmiana ⓕ *zmya*·na *change*

znać znach *know (be acquainted with)*

zniżka ⓕ *zneesh*·ka *discount*

zwierzę ⓝ *zvye*·zhe *animal*

zwolennik ⓜ zvo·*le*·neek
supporter (politics)

zwrot pieniędzy ⓜ zvrot pye·*nyen*·dzi
refund

zwyczaj ⓜ *zvi*·chai *custom*

zwyczajny zvi·*chai*·ni *ordinary*

Ż

żaden *zha*·den *neither • none*

żart ⓜ zhart *joke*

żeński *zhen'*·skee *female*

żołądek ⓜ zho·*won*·dek *stomach*

żołnierz ⓜ *zhow*·nyezh *soldier*

żółty *zhoow*·ti *yellow*

żona ⓕ *zho*·na *wife*

żonaty zho·*na*·ti *married (of man)*

żubr ⓜ zhoobr *bison*

żubrówka ⓕ zhoo·*broof*·ka *bison vodka*

życie ⓝ *zhi*·chye *life*

życzyć *zhi*·chich *wish*

żyć zhich *live (life)*

żydowski zhi·*dof*·skee *Jewish*

The topics covered in this book are listed below in Polish. Show this page to your Polish friends if you're having trouble understanding them.

don't just stand there, say something!

o see the full range of our language products, go to:

lonelyplanet.com

What kind of traveller are you?

A. You're eating chicken for dinner *again* because it's the only word you know.

B. When no one understands what you say, you step closer and shout louder.

C. When the barman doesn't understand your order, you point frantically at the beer.

D. You're surrounded by locals, swapping jokes, email addresses and experiences
– other travellers want to borrow your phrasebook or audio guide.

If you answered A, B, or C, you NEED Lonely Planet's language products ...

- **Lonely Planet Phrasebooks** – for every phrase you need in every language you want

- **Lonely Planet Language & Culture** – get behind the scenes of English as it's spoken around the world – learn and laugh

- **Lonely Planet Fast Talk & Fast Talk Audio** – essential phrases for short trips and weekends away – read, listen and talk like a local

- **Lonely Planet Small Talk** – 10 essential languages for city breaks

- **Lonely Planet Real Talk** – downloadable language audio guides from lonelyplanet.com to your MP3 player

... and this is why

- **Talk to everyone everywhere**
  Over 120 languages, more than any other publisher

- **The right words at the right time**
  Quick-reference colour sections, two-way dictionary, easy pronunciation, every possible subject – and audio to support it

Lonely Planet Offices

Australia
90 Maribyrnong St, Footscray,
Victoria 3011
☎ 03 8379 8000
fax 03 8379 8111
✉ talk2us@lonelyplanet.com.au

USA
150 Linden St, Oakland,
CA 94607
☎ 510 893 8555
fax 510 893 8572
✉ info@lonelyplanet.com

UK
72-82 Rosebery Ave,
London EC1R 4RW
☎ 020 7841 9000
fax 020 7841 9001
✉ go@lonelyplanet.co.uk

lonelyplanet.com